Living for Shalom

Living for Shalom

The Story of Ross Langmead

JEANETTE WOODS

Foreword by Alison Langmead

WIPF & STOCK · Eugene, Oregon

LIVING FOR SHALOM
The Story of Ross Langmead

Copyright © 2021 Jeanette Woods. All rights reserved. Except for brief quotations in critical publications or reviews, no part of this book may be reproduced in any manner without prior written permission from the publisher. Write: Permissions, Wipf and Stock Publishers, 199 W. 8th Ave., Suite 3, Eugene, OR 97401.

Wipf & Stock
An Imprint of Wipf and Stock Publishers
199 W. 8th Ave., Suite 3
Eugene, OR 97401

www.wipfandstock.com

PAPERBACK ISBN: 978-1-6667-1538-5
HARDCOVER ISBN: 978-1-6667-1539-2
EBOOK ISBN: 978-1-6667-1540-8

Unless otherwise indicated, all Scripture quotations are taken from THE MESSAGE, copyright © 1993, 2002, 2018 by Eugene H. Peterson. Used by permission of NavPress. All rights reserved. Represented by Tyndale House Publishers, Inc.

Some Scripture taken from the Holy Bible, NEW INTERNATIONAL VERSION®, NIV® Copyright © 1973, 1978, 1984, 2011 by Biblica, Inc.® Used by permission. All rights reserved worldwide.

08/24/21

This book is dedicated to:
Alison
Benjamin
Kia
And all who loved and miss Ross.

Contents

Ross Langmead's Family   ix
Foreword by Alison Langmead   xi
Acknowledgments   xv
Abbreviations   xvii
Introduction   xix

Chapter 1	Childhood: 1949 to 1966	1
Chapter 2	Study: 1967 to 1970	23
Chapter 3	Teaching: 1971 to 1973	37
Chapter 4	Music: 1972 to 1974	46
Chapter 5	Marriage: 1973 to 1975	56
Chapter 6	Travel: 1975 to 1976	74
Chapter 7	Commission: 1977 to 1978	85
Chapter 8	Parenting: 1977 to 1978	95
Chapter 9	Community Work: 1979 to 1980	101
Chapter 10	Pastoring: 1981 to 1985	113
Chapter 11	Diabetes: 1986	132
Chapter 12	Lecturing: 1986 to 1989	137
Chapter 13	Adventure: 1990	150
Chapter 14	Advocacy: 1991 to 1992	163
Chapter 15	Missiology: 1993 to 1997	176
Chapter 16	Ecomissiology: 1998 to 2002	199
Chapter 17	Mentoring: 2003 to 2007	223

Chapter 18	Leadership: 2008 to 2012	239
Chapter 19	Love: 2013	256
Chapter 20	Endnote: 2013	262
Chapter 21	Inspiration	275
Contributors		285
Bibliography		287

Ross Langmead's Family

Ross Oliver Langmead, Born 13 August 1949 in Albury, NSW, Australia

Paternal grandparents:

Leslie Roy Langmead, 1892–1965
Elizabeth Violet Potts, 1884–1960

Maternal grandparents:

George Henry Walker, 1892–1952
Jessie Louise Butler-Nixon, 1892–1982

Parents:

Oliver Leslie Langmead, 1921–94
Jean Mary Walker, 1922–2012

Siblings:

Jeanette Dawn Woods, b. 1947
Leslie George Langmead, b. 1950
Howard Langmead, b. 1953
Peter Charles Langmead, b. 1955
Grace Elizabeth Langmead, b. 1958

Spouse:

Alison Joy Wright, Born 6 November 1948 in Richmond, Victoria, Australia
Married 1 December 1973

Paternal grandparents:

Fred Claypole Wright, 1878–1950
Sabina Maud Gamble, 1880–1960

Maternal grandparents:

Lawrence Henry Jaggers, 1880–1956
Violet Caroline Harvey, 1883–1938

Parents:

Alan Fred Wright, 1922–2018
Joyce Elizabeth Jaggers, 1922–97

Siblings:

Peter Harvey Wright, b. 1946
Murray Alan Wright, b. 1951

Children and grandchildren:

Benjamin Ross Langmead, b. 1978, m. Pauline Emmanuelle Agius, 2006–21; Sage Aleena (step-granddaughter) b. 2000; Zara Joy, b. 2010
Kia Marinna Langmead, b. 1980, m. Thierry Réné Brusa, b. 2013; Marlo Georges, b. 2016; Lila Magali, b. 2018

Foreword

The unfolding of a life is always unique. Ross Langmead's was no exception.

If you are reading this book, it is likely that you either met, knew, or have heard of Ross and would like to enter into an account of his life to gain a fuller insight into who he was, what motivated him, challenged him, enabled, and inspired him.

I am one such person, despite being his partner for almost forty years. You could be forgiven for thinking that I would hardly need to read his biography. But, in fact, it has been a very warm and deeply absorbing journey for me to receive this carefully researched, sensitive, yet honestly portrayed manuscript. It has offered me the gift of fuller knowledge, insight, and love of the man I lived and journeyed with. I will be forever grateful.

Each reader will come to the reading of this book with their own lens—their own feelings, memories, opinions, questions, and needs. I could not have written Ross's biography. I would have found the task of writing for the wide range of people who considered Ross their friend, father, brother, relative, teacher, colleague, mate, mentor, pastor, helper, encourager, musical hero, and so on, far too daunting.

I am glad, for the sake of Jeanette's research, that besides living in the same family household for her first twenty-one years, she had an amazing store of Ross's own trail of recorded writings to delve into and work from. They took the form of diaries, journals, detailed family letters, notebooks, articles, lectures, theses, songs, books both written and edited, as well as his own website which he had enjoyed learning how to create and expand. However, to be able to read, absorb, discern, and decide the most poignant and relevant material to present, and in what form, is Jeanette Woods's great gift to us. Gratitude!

Living for Shalom aptly describes how Ross combined his many gifts with a deep and grounded faith in Jesus who inspired his desire to live and work towards the good of all, including the whole creation. His greatest challenge was always around how to keep the kind of balance that was needed when also grappling with the vagaries of Type 1 diabetes from his mid-thirties, despite his consistent attempts to do so. This struggle no doubt contributed to an earlier death than any of us would have liked.

During our courtship, this man who could be so beautifully ordinary and yet rise to the heights of life's demands and leadership capabilities, could also occasionally sing us to tears. He wrote in the second verse of his love song to me:

> Well you went and stole my mind, I just stood aside and stared,
> And I liked you but I felt a mile away, a mile below,
> And I often let you in, and I was glad you were my friend,
> And the stealing had begun and I love you.

As Ross sang that song to me, sitting cross-legged with his guitar on my loungeroom floor, I was moved by its poetic beauty and somewhat mystified by its claim. I guess I was beginning to register the mystery of love. Love can lead to a changed way of seeing and feeling. Love sees the gold in another, or in something, when everyday human seeing may not. As I tried to make sense of this experience, I realized that this was the perspective Jesus was living and revealing when he was walking this earth. He is a window into the great and mysterious upside-down priorities of the love of God, the heart of life, that Ross and I and so many others are drawn to live in. Jesus saw the society he was born into with "different eyes"—with the great love, the love that can see the effects of inequality, poverty, sickness, greed, piety, power play, and enmity—and offered, when it was seemingly destroyed by those he offended, the letting go of his life in forgiving love to restore both individuals and society.

This book's account of Ross's life reveals an authentic journey into how learning to trust and to participate in that great love, can play out in a single lifetime: how his early childhood in Hong Kong prepared him for an expanded worldview; how he looked at and worked with the questions of life through study, practical exploration, writing, friendship, teaching, singing, and research; how he encouraged others to grapple together with the many challenges of life, taking time out to consider, to learn, to pray, and to act with courage; how working with unemployed youth and exploring the multicultural needs of a municipality could shape his theology of being the church in the world and ground his future work as a missiologist; how he consulted professionals as he tried to face the truths of his own issues; how songwriting could open the windows of the soul when other things could not; and how others have felt the benefit of having known him.

One of the ongoing struggles of Ross's journey was the mystery of the nature of prayer, even though it was part of his whole life in various forms.

As I read this account, I came to realize—through tears as I read the words and recalled the music of some of the songs Jeanette has cited—that Ross's songs were indeed his prayer flowing from the depths of his being for our lives together, and for the life of the world. Thank you, Ross.

I assure readers that this is a very real account of a man who humbly and consistently gave life his best. He was in the midst of exploring the graces afforded by a more contemplative approach to life (inspired by Richard Rohr) along with the creative possibilities that looming retirement would allow, when suddenly, Ross's life among us, though revived to breathe for one further week in intensive care, ended and opened into eternity. That week afforded some of us precious time to simply be with him. The final lovely gift was our friend Fay White facilitating our extended family in surrounding him with familiar songs and harmony as his life support was removed.

My prayer for this biography is that each reader will draw from it something that informs and inspires their own authentic life and living, not only for themselves but also for a better, kinder world—the essence of *Living for Shalom*. I suspect that that would have been the only grounds on which Ross may have granted permission for his story to be written, if that!

God be with us, each one.

ALISON LANGMEAD

Acknowledgments

Ross's story has been told in this book by combining his own writings with the contributions of many friends and family members. I could not have completed this daunting task on my own, and my heartfelt thanks go to all those who responded to my survey, wrote their stories and memories of Ross, answered many questions, suggested other people to contact, and communicated with me by letter, email, phone, and Zoom. In some way, you have all been included in the book.

For those who have taken the time to read and comment as the project progressed, to share helpful advice, and to urge me to keep going, I am full of gratitude. Jason Goroncy, Ross's friend and colleague, was my mentor and encourager, and always believed in this project. He contributed many hours of reading and invaluable assistance, and saved me from too many mistakes. My husband, Peter, has supported this venture all the way, and gave much practical assistance as well as loving words. His special contribution has been to collect and digitize the photos, and to collate Ross's music so that we can enjoy it today.

David Wong, designer/artist, as the graphic artist for the Western Suburbs Conference Report, kindly allowed me to reproduce some of his images. Photographs in the book were generously contributed by family and friends to enhance the many written words in this tome.

I am grateful to Wipf and Stock, my publisher, who invested in the book and helped me to bring it to completion. They are responsible for the American spelling and thousands of Oxford commas, but any mistakes or inaccuracies are mine.

I am especially indebted to Alison, Benjamin, and Kia for facing up to what must have been a difficult journey of remembrance for Ross's family. Your generosity in giving me freedom to include your loving but raw memories has given integrity and authenticity to this book. The result is my gift to you, your families, and generations unborn.

JEANETTE WOODS

Abbreviations

AAMS	Australian Association for Mission Studies
ACER	Australian Council for Educational Research
AJMS	*Australian Journal of Missiologial Studies*
ANZATS	Australia and New Zealand Association of Theological Schools
ASM	American Society of Missiology
BA	Bachelor of Arts
BCV	Bible College of Victoria
BD	Bachelor of Divinity
BSJG	Baptist Social Justice Group
BUV	Baptist Union of Victoria
CCT	Christian College of Theology
CSSM	Children's Special Service Mission
DipEd	Diploma of Education
DTheol	Doctor of Theology
EPUY	Education Program for Unemployed Youth
ETC	Eastern Theological College
GIA	Global Interaction Australia
IAMS	International Association for Mission Studies
ICU	Intensive Care Unit
KJV	King James Version
MCD	Melbourne College of Divinity
MA(Theol)	Master of Arts (Theology)

MS	Mission Studies
MTh	Master of Theology
NIV	New International Version
PhD	Doctor of Philosophy
SPJMS	*South Pacific Journal of Mission Studies*
SU	Scripture Union
SWM	School of World Mission
UNOH	Urban Neighbours of Hope
VCC	Victorian Council of Churches
WCIG	Westgate Community Initiatives Group
WBC	Westgate Baptist Community
WV	World Vision

Introduction

On what would have been Ross Langmead's seventieth birthday, I hesitantly sent an email to my sister-in-love, Alison, offering to explore the idea of writing his life story. I always believed that someone should write it, but did not expect that it would be me. Although we grew up in the same household, and Ross was the next sibling after me, our lives had taken different directions when I left home; we did not even live in the same city until we were middle-aged.

Some months later, after discussions, questions, and consultation with the family, I committed to start the project. My expectation was that it would take a couple of years to work my way through the many boxes of his diaries and records, and then to write the story. It also became clear that I would need the perspectives and memories of others to help me find the themes and insights that would shape this book. When I sent out questions to a growing list of contacts, I did not anticipate the volume or quality of responses, and it soon became apparent that the project would be a collaboration. With over sixty-five people sending me reflections, memories, and wonderful stories, the congruence was amazing, and directions began to emerge.

Then the virus hit us, and suddenly, life changed. Being at home with an empty diary, and not even visits from our family, was a dramatic change of lifestyle. Instead of researching and writing in the spaces, I had uninterrupted days, weeks, and then months through our extended lockdowns in Melbourne. Ross's book became my main focus, and before long, I was immersed in his writings. I began to know my brother in a way I never had before, and the book was written by the end of the year—a silver lining from COVID-19.

One of the challenges of writing a biography is that the author cannot change the plot or the characters, and I wondered how I would make the story interesting. Would it have drama and climaxes, ups and downs? Would threads emerge to draw the reader in, and a real narrative arise out of the thousands of mundane events that make up daily life? Can the thought life of a philosopher/theologian/musician/activist become a gripping story? I discovered that I was in good company with these wonderings:

> What a wee little part of a person's life are his acts and his words. His real life is led in his head and is known to none but himself. All day long, the mill of his brain is grinding, and his thoughts, not those of other things, are his history. These are his life, and they are not written. Every day would make a whole book of 80,000 words—365 books a year. Biographies are but the clothes and buttons of the man—the biography of the man himself cannot be written.[1]

What distinguishes Ross from many other people, apart from his outstanding academic achievements, justice activism, and legacy of music, is that we do indeed have insights into "the mill of his brain." His discipline and perseverance in self-reflection in not only his journaling, but also in his public writings, tell us something of the inside story of this man; some of it will be revelatory to even his closest friends. At times it felt as though I was entering a sacred place without permission, and I felt the weight of having to discern what was appropriate to share. In these decisions I am extremely grateful to Alison for the negotiated journey and her generous permission for what has been included.

> Read no history, nothing but biography, for that is life without theory.[2]

Ross's life was never just based on theory, and if there is any conflict portrayed in this book, it is the ongoing struggle he had to balance theory with practice, words with action. His other challenge was to budget his energy. We all know that he was never able to leave much time for himself.

This story is also an account of a man exploring his personality, gifts, and family heritage. In some ways I, as Ross's sister, have unique insights into the complexities of the unique family into which we were both born. I relate to many of the struggles Ross experienced to shed his "inner custodian," and other aspects of our family of origin. On the other hand, I am probably the least impartial person to comment on the family dynamics. Ross would be happy to know that this project has caused me to engage in further reflection on our family background. I am grateful to the other siblings for their insights and memories, and along the way we have hopefully learned more about each other.

---

1. Twain, *Autobiography*, xviii.
2. Disraeli, *Contarini Fleming*, pt 1, ch 23.

No life is lived alone, and Ross's network was very wide. At every point in this story, it would have been possible to expand the narrative to include more people, and more detail about family, friends, and colleagues. The book would simply have been too long, and I can only note how much is missing and hope that, in reading the story, you will be inspired to recall your own reflections and interactions with Ross.

The most important outcome for me as the writer is that my faith has been challenged in several ways as I worked on the project, and tried to do justice to Ross's life and legacy. I am less ready to apply labels to people, or to their belief systems; Ross himself does not fit easily into any of the traditional theological streams. I have been stimulated by reading works in my research that raise thoughtful questions about God, and have been encouraged by Ross's dogged commitment to truth and integrity of process.

Most of all, I have a renewed commitment to living as a Jesus-follower in my neighborhood, which was the central and driving force in Ross's life. I am grateful to have joined the many who have been inspired and encouraged by Ross's life, and pray that this book will reach many more, including those who did not have the privilege of knowing him.

"Shalom" was Ross's signature in his correspondence, but it was more than that. The love, peace, and justice included in the meaning of this rich Hebrew word together sum up the themes of his life here on earth, even with its imperfections and disappointments. Shalom is also the destination of a pilgrim who has been on the road: the place of rest, joy, wholeness, and completion. Ross's death was not just the end of life, but the fulfillment of his exploration of reconciliation through Jesus with God, himself, and others.

May we all, like Ross, live for shalom,
JEANETTE WOODS (LANGMEAD)

Chapter 1

Childhood: 1949 to 1966

The childhood shows the man, as morning shows the day.
JOHN MILTON

The blond, curly haired two-year-old sat in his high chair with his family at the table.

"Ross, do you want to go to Hong Kong to live?" asked his dad, who had just received news that his new job would be in the British colony attached to the Chinese mainland.

"Eat my custard first," the toddler replied, with a thoughtful look on his face. Ross apparently started when he was young to think about priorities and attention to the important things in life. Many of his adult friends note that intentionality was a strength when they knew him, and this family anecdote indicates that it began early.

Ross Oliver Langmead was born on 13 August 1949, in the Albury Base Hospital in New South Wales, Australia. His parents were living at that time just over the state border in Wodonga, Victoria, where they were serving as the local Salvation Army officers. His mum always maintained that the doctor who delivered Ross was drunk. There are eight congratulatory telegrams from family and friends, including one from his uncle and aunt that read: "Delighted to hear of Lois Oliver's safe arrival." Communications were not always totally reliable in those days.

Jeanette was two when her baby brother became the center of attention. She remembers trying to get help from their mum when she wanted to do the actions to a song on the wireless, but realized that her mother was distracted with a baby in her arms. The complex patterns of sibling relationships had begun to be woven in a family that would grow to include six children.

Ross was the first son born to Jean Mary Walker and Oliver Leslie Langmead; he was given his father's name as a middle name, and the name "Ross" came from his mother's side and her Scottish heritage. His siblings later sometimes called him "Ross the boss." Of the six siblings in the Langmead family, Ross was the only child who had the fair-haired Walker looks in a family of dark hair and eyes.

After his birth, Ross was in hospital for several weeks, failing to thrive. As an infant, he was said to be sickly and was lactose-intolerant. He was often unwell, and in his early months once became so ill that Jean feared he may not recover in the cold, damp house that never seemed to feel warm in winter. She sent a message for Oliver to come home from the youth camp that he was leading, and he asked everyone at the camp to pray. Within hours, Ross made a dramatic recovery and grew to be a strong, healthy child.

Oliver and Jean both came from Salvationist families, having met each other through Jean's older brother, Wilbur. Oliver was the middle son of Roy Langmead and Elizabeth Violet Potts, who married in 1915; three weeks later, Roy enlisted and went out with the Australian 29th Battalion to serve on the Western Front in France. Somehow surviving the worst twenty-four hours in Australian military history in Fromelles, he was taken prisoner for the next three years before he and Violet were reunited. Three boys were born in rapid succession, but Grandad was never the same after privation, gassing, and trauma. Like many returned servicemen, he rarely spoke to the family about his experiences.

(Elizabeth) Violet was the eldest of nine children, including seven brothers, of whom four enlisted and who also returned safely from war. She was thirty-eight when Oliver was born, and she raised their sons with discipline and high expectations. Oliver was an outstanding student who was dux of Balwyn Central School but was forced to decline the scholarship he was awarded to continue, and instead started work as an estimator to help the family survive the Great Depression.

Jean was born to missionary parents in Beijing in June 1922. The second child and elder daughter of George and Jessie Walker, she lived her entire childhood in China, with a short stint in India when conditions were too dangerous in China. Her parents spent all their married lives as Salvation Army officers, and Jean was very influenced by the years spent in China (many at boarding school), her separation from her parents when they were interned by the Japanese for three years, and their lifelong Christian service.

When Jean returned to Australia on her own at the age of eighteen, she trained as a nurse and midwife, and was actively involved at the Dulwich Hill Corps in Sydney, which had been founded by her father.

As Oliver's parents also had a strong Salvationist background, originally in Healesville in the mountains and later at the Canterbury Corps in Melbourne, there was a strong alignment of purpose and values for Ross's parents when they met. They were engaged at the end of the war and married in May 1946. As they emerged from the Depression and World War II, the young couple had their hopes and lives ahead of them and were committed to serving God and other people. Entering the Salvation Army Training College in Melbourne brought a challenging test for them as there was no provision for children to live in the college. So, Oliver and Jean were forced to farm out their beloved one-year-old daughter to friends and relatives for the year of training, and only saw Jeanette on weekends.

Thus, the two years spent at the Wodonga Corps after graduating from college were happy ones for the Langmead family. They were reunited with Jeanette, and then the births of Ross and of Leslie soon after in 1950 made them a family unit at last. Jean, however, suffered a miscarriage between Ross's and Leslie's births, so one can only surmise that it wasn't all easy for her. Their conditions were poor, to say the least. Army officers at that time lived on an extremely low stipend and both husband and wife were expected to work without much recognition of the need for days off or down time. With three children under five, there was no time for relaxing.

Just after Leslie was born, in January 1950, the Langmeads were appointed to move to another country corps, this time in Yea, Victoria. With a preschooler, a toddler, and a newborn baby, family life and work was demanding. Adding to that, the living accommodation was in the back half of the Army hall, meaning that there was no escape from the job. The weather in Yea is notoriously damp and foggy, and Jean told stories of a tiny home festooned with wet diapers that never dried, three children under five, and a job that she was expected to share with Oliver. The noise from the brass band playing on the other side of the wall would sometimes wake the babies. Only sixteen months apart, Ross and Les began to grow and play together, and the diapers just kept coming.

Oliver and Jean had always been interested in working overseas, especially because of Jean's Chinese upbringing. The Chinese Communist Party, however, had emerged and driven the Nationalist Party off the mainland to Taiwan in 1949, and China was effectively closed to missionary endeavors. Knowing of their interest in working in Asia, the Army had asked Captain and Mrs. Langmead, while they were in Wodonga, if they would be open to going to Indonesia instead. They agreed to that idea but had heard nothing more until the letter arrived one morning in Yea. In typical Salvo style, it was not a request: "Re: your work in Hong Kong," began the official letter. They had their marching orders, and as soon as Ross finished his custard, they began the big move that would shape their family life for the next five years. At least Hong Kong was attached to China's mainland and was as close as they could be.

As they prepared for the sea voyage that would take them to a distant continent for the next five years, all Oliver and Jean knew was that they would oversee a children's home. Barely thirty years old, they had no specific qualifications for what turned out to be an enormous task, and they did not speak a word of Cantonese. Jean spoke Mandarin fluently from her childhood but would have to start afresh to master the dialect of southern China. They ordered white summer Salvationist uniforms and began to pack up their minimal belongings into steamer trunks. Oliver painted all the trunks green, added padlocks, and numbered them; some of them are still in use today. While these were being freighted to Sydney, the family began its farewell tour, beginning with Oliver's family in Melbourne.

Those were the days before air travel, and overseas missionary appointments were generally for at least five years. Sea voyages were lengthy, although they provided a welcome buffer between leaving home and arriving in a new location, job, and culture. All communication for these years apart would be by sea-mail or telegram—no emails, no phone calls, no Zoom or Skype—and this separation from family in Australia was sacrificial for everybody. Adults parted with elderly parents and children would grow up without their grandparents. Roy and Violet hugged the family tightly at Spencer Street and Oliver's brother came specially from Western Australia to see them off; Jeanette, Ross, and Leslie had no idea how emotionally fraught the occasion was. They were excited about a night train trip on the Spirit of Progress to Sydney for the next and final farewells with Jean's family.

When the wide-gauge, luxurious, air-conditioned train crossed the state border and arrived in Albury in the middle of the night, all passengers had to transfer to a new train, as New South Wales had a narrower, standard gauge. Salvo friends from the Wodonga Corps were waiting at midnight in the dark on the station with an Army flag and thermos flasks of hot drinks to share in the brief changeover. As the faithful friends sang and waved the flag, the children were carried half asleep to their seats on the next train that would take them to Sydney.

From Sydney, the family traveled on north to Newcastle where Jean's parents were the Divisional Commanders for the Salvation Army in that region. This stay with the family was documented with some lovely family photos; they were to be the last taken with Pa Walker. Jean would not see her father again on this earth and Ross would grow up without memory of the amazing, courageous George Walker.[1]

The Walker family all gathered at the wharf for the departure of the family on the ship. The adults were quiet, subdued at the thought of the imminent separation. The three children raced up the gangway, around the decks, and in and out of their adjoining cabins. Before the days of air travel, departures took hours, yet nothing seemed important enough to talk about in the waiting. Eventually the boarding signal sounded, and the last embraces began. When the loving family stopped hugging him, Ross was the one who led the charge up the swinging gangway and the family of five secured their place on the deck where they could see their farewell group on the wharf.

Then it was time to throw down the colored streamers for the people gazing up from the wharf below to catch. The pastel colours unfurled from along the deck of the ship, and the family groups below held on tightly as though the flimsy paper strings could delay the departure. Ross saw his mum's tears but was impatient for the ship to move. Down below on the wharf, the family and Salvationist friends began singing in harmony: "God be with you till we meet again." Many decades later, Jean would still feel emotional when she heard that haunting song.

As the ship began to pull almost imperceptibly away from the wharf, the streamers snapped one by one like a literal breaking of ties. Soon the little family could no longer hear the singing as the group on the wharf appeared smaller and finally faded out of sight. The ship sailed out through the Sydney Heads and the adventure had begun.

The *MS Changsha* was one of four steamships owned by the China Navigation Company that combined cargo services with cruising. Although they were essentially freight ships, they were beautifully crafted with wood fittings, and the limited number of passengers on each voyage enjoyed wonderful service and comfort. For a family tired from packing and traveling, the three weeks on board with only eighteen passengers were to be a real holiday. For Jean, it meant high-class cuisine served up every meal, a break from most domestic responsibilities and, best of all, a program to occupy the children. Ross and his sister soon found friends their own age and were either cared for by a steward or played deck quoits and swam. This trip, unlike the return five years later, was calm and enjoyable for all.

---

1. See Hilton, *George Walker of China*.

Oliver, always keen on a project, commenced his systematic study of Cantonese and spent many hours studying. Jean knew that her native-level Mandarin gave her a huge advantage, so she enjoyed relaxing with the children and meeting the other passengers. She organized an onboard fifth birthday party for Jeanette for which the ship's bursar arranged a celebratory spread for all the children in the dining room.

Three weeks later, the *Changsha* sailed into Hong Kong harbor. The Union Jack flying at the wharf was at half-mast to show respect in the British colony for the death of King George VI. Queen Elizabeth II commenced her reign that day and is still on the British throne almost seventy years later, although she is no longer the monarch of Hong Kong. The family's new life was also about to begin, and they were greeted by a brass band from the children's home playing enthusiastically on Hong Kong's international wharf. The other passengers on the boat thought it was a special welcome to everyone as they disembarked, but the Langmead family knew it was for them. They had arrived.

Hong Kong in the fifties was a British colony leased from China, struggling to emerge after the war. It had become a destination for hundreds of thousands of refugees from over the border in Chairman Mao Zedong's

CHILDHOOD: 1949 TO 1966   7

China. With a population of about two million, Hong Kong was crowded and bustling, with its streets a congested and disparate mix of shiny black British cars, bicycles, rickshaws and pedestrians. Although rickshaws looked like a fun ride, the children picked up very soon on their parents' reluctance to be pulled around by another human.

Hong Kong means "Fragrant Harbor," and Victoria Harbor is still one of the busiest ports in the world, whether measured by shipping, cargo, or passengers. Life in the colony revolved around the water, large ships berthing, ferries scurrying across the bay and out to the islands, stately junks gliding across the water, and fleets of sampans which doubled as both couriers and people's homes. At night they transformed into cities, complete with the pungent aromas of families cooking, and the sounds of dogs barking.

For many, life was tough. Refugees had nowhere to live and could find no work. Squatter towns grew and public services were minimal. Only those with money could live well and hire servants, and the wealth gap was enormous. A shocking fire on Christmas Day 1953 left 50,000 homeless; the Salvation Army was heavily involved in caring for these people. Ross's parents were part of the relief team and they continued to work in the high-rise public housing that first began to appear in that period.

The Langmeads lived on mainland Kowloon on the site of what is now the Queen Mary Hospital. The main commercial and banking sector was on Hong Kong Island, a short ferry ride away, and other smaller islands were easily reached by water. There was the British Navy base at Stonecutters' Island, the leper colony at Hei Ling Chau, and the holiday island of Cheung Chau. One of the family outings was to watch the teams of coolies removing a mountain, basket by basket, dumping the earth in the harbor to build the old Kai Tak airport runway that stretched out into the sea. There was something mesmerizing about watching the landforms change shape and defer to massive infrastructure development and reclamation of the sea.

The colony was leased by China to the British for ninety-nine years, but nobody was concerned about the timeframe back in the fifties as there was still half a century to go. Today, we see the news footage of the student protests against the new regime with the People's Republic of China peering over the border at the tiny, but heavily populated area. Since the return handover at the end of the lease in 1998, Hong Kong has been known as a Special Administrative Region, operating like a country except for defense and foreign affairs. Today its future as a democracy is under threat.

The Salvation Army King's Park Children's Home was established during the Japanese occupation in the war, and was originally built for orphaned children in the colony. In later years, many of the children actually had families but were abandoned, and it was not unusual to find a baby in a cardboard box deposited at the gate overnight. The buildings were repurposed Nissen huts, long wooden structures with black pitch and gravel roofs, tethered with steel cables against the seasonal typhoons. Ross's family home was the front half of one of the dozen huts, with the orphanage kitchen with its heat and noise in the back half. The front door opened onto the concrete roundabout and grassed area where any number of the three hundred children would be playing at any one time. Oliver and Jean were on duty all the time, day and night, and staff came directly to the front door of their living room. There was no boundary between home and work.

The other huts were used as long dormitories, staff quarters, a chapel, schoolrooms, workshops and offices, and the task of running this orphanage and its daily needs must have been immense, especially in a language that they had yet to master. Oliver led the staff team in the day-to-day administration of the home and care of the orphans, while Jean took care of medical needs. And they both studied Cantonese every morning for five years. Learning another language as an adult is demanding and slow, and Jean and Oliver slogged away at the nine-toned, complex Cantonese language. They simply could not believe how quickly Ross and his siblings began to speak it apparently without effort.

For Ross, the orphanage was a huge family of kids who were always available to play right outside the door, and in order to play he needed to communicate. So from the first day Ross mimicked what he heard, combined it with sign language and some guesswork, and never looked back as he rode his scooter around the roundabout with the crowds of Chinese children. In a short time, Ross and Jeanette became fluent speakers with perfect pronunciation and tones, and Les followed not far behind. The children were called upon often to interpret for their parents and were taken by the amahs to show off at the market so that people could hear the little foreigners who spoke good Cantonese. Eventually, Oliver and Jean found that they elicited quicker responses if they spoke in Cantonese at home, and that helped everyone's fluency. The Sunday night Bible stories, however, were always in English with much explanation in Cantonese.

It was an unusual life for an Australian family, but the children knew nothing else. Three hundred extra Chinese siblings simply meant more kids to play with and Ross's parents never had to worry about entertaining him. He stood out from the black-haired crowd with his blond hair, but was accepted in every way and had a very carefree life.

The Chinese staff wanted to confer Cantonese names on the family to welcome them with respect, so after some consideration they were bestowed a surname—Leung—which was taken from Oliver's name, Leung Mei Duk, a transliteration of Langmead. Then each child had a name added that sounded something like their English name and had a meaning: Ross became Leung Lok Si, or "happy scholar." Some might say it was prophetic.

The family adapted quickly to eating Chinese food daily. Jean took promising girls into her home and trained them to go out to domestic servant roles in expatriate homes, which meant that the family was always in the hands of learners. That was a sought-after job at the time, but in later years Oliver upgraded the school and workshops so that the orphans were able to continue to secondary and tertiary education that led to better qualifications and more varied career options.

Apart from an occasional meal with other Western families, the main treat for the family was a walk down to the main street in the tropical evening, usually in pajamas, for a snack and an icy bottle of 7-Up soda in a café. Hong Kong streets were full of life, day and night, and there was plenty to see. Another favorite walk for Ross was the climb up the hill behind the home to watch the sunset over Hong Kong harbor. Ferries and sampans traversed the busy bay and the lights on the Hong Kong island side would begin to twinkle across the water. These were rare quiet moments for the family caught up in a demanding life.

Eventually Ross was old enough to follow his sister to Kowloon Junior School, an English Foundation School attached to the King George V High School in Ho Man Tin district. It is still there today, complete with the same buildings and brown uniforms. His early days, however, did not go as smoothly as hoped, as he began complaining of tummy aches and refusing to go to school. Nurse Jean had her suspicions and asked him one night if he liked his new school. Ross replied that it was OK, but that there were too many "foreigners" there and he didn't like everyone speaking English. Jean had a chat with his teacher, who came up with the idea that Ross could be the class monitor who would communicate with the school workers in Chinese when there was a need. Most of the other expatriate children did not speak Cantonese, so he felt special and could chat away to the cleaners or maintenance staff when his teacher needed an interpreter. This seemed to work, and saved Ross's stellar academic career from being derailed in kindergarten.

Ross's school reports from his two years at Kowloon Junior School already capture some of the traits that characterized him as an adult:

> He still shows shyness but joins in well. Kindergarten 1954
>
> Ross was very nervous but is now happily settled in. Ross is a kind-hearted, friendly little boy. He has done well in music. Transition. 1955
>
> His oral number work and reading are of a high standard. Quiet and good mannered in school yet full of boyish fun and good humour in the playground. Transition 1955
>
> His arithmetic is very satisfactory and accurate, but spoilt at times by careless forming of figures. (2A, 1956)

The school was an innovative school for its time (and today offers the International Baccalaureate), moving children up through the stages according to ability, not age. So Ross started school at five years and two months, spending only one term in kindergarten, two terms in transition, moving directly to Year 2 at six years and four months. His academic career was launched.

Ross made friends with some expatriate children at the British school but was glad to get home to ride bikes and play with his Chinese mates in the orphanage. He could not wait to revert to Cantonese after trying to speak English all day at school.

Like most expat families, he was driven to and from school by a trusted driver chosen and trained by his parents. With Jeanette and later Les, he joined in the fun with the other kids after school while waiting to be picked up, sliding down the long gutter beside the steps to the high school on handfuls of pine needles, and swapping trinkets for the much-prized plastic icy-pole sticks that he was forbidden to buy from hawkers. He developed a distinctly British accent because he learnt his English at school, only to drop it immediately when he later returned to Australia in exchange for a broad Aussie pronunciation in an attempt to fit in.

Photos from the time show the Langmead children wearing the distinctive uniform with its brown and yellow badge, along with bespoke leather sandals and woven rattan school cases that were both handmade at the orphanage. Those items signaled a crossover from one kind of life to another. He was attending an excellent school for wealthy expatriates who lived in huge houses, who did not speak much Cantonese, and who were attended by whole teams of servants. He then came home to the world of poor, abandoned children from conditions of abject poverty who slept in dormitories and were dependent on generous sponsors to continue their education. With unerring instincts, Ross knew which world he preferred when he was still young. His shyness at school was not just his personality; it was his response to some dissonance and his resulting discomfort in that world. He felt much more at ease chattering in perfect Cantonese to the school cleaner and playing games with the orphans at home. They were, after all, his family.

In 1953, Ross's brother, Howard, was born. His next brother, Peter, arrived in 1955, and the hut-style house was becoming crowded. Howard joined the older three when he was old enough to sleep in a bed, and the four of them were in two double-decker bunks. Peter was still in his cot when the family left Hong Kong in 1956. Oliver and Jean were strict parents and talking after lights out was forbidden. Ross and his siblings created a whole secret language of sounds that included tongue clicks, quiet whistles, and finger taps on the table between the two beds so that they could communicate in bed. There was also the challenge of bed-swapping without being caught, and of throwing and exchanging soft toys across the room.

It may surprise his friends who knew him in later years, but Ross was often the ringleader in any mischief. He was physically strong and active, a natural leader—always Ross the boss—and by nature prepared to take risks. If their parents needed to leave the house, the Chinese amahs would look after the children. Ross soon discovered that the polite Chinese helpers would not stand up to him and the fun began.

Each week on a Wednesday night, Jean and Oliver attended the prayer meeting with the staff, leaving the house after the children were in bed. Ignoring the amah's protests, Ross would lead the way with his older sister following cautiously. Shimmying up the steel cables that tethered the hut against typhoons, the two children would climb up the gravel-covered pitch roof until they could sit on the top and survey the world below. It was incredibly slippery and quite miraculous that this epic adventure occurred so often without disaster. One suspects that the amahs were praying as hard as the attenders at the prayer meeting.

As Les grew up, he and Ross became partners in crime, usually with Ross leading the way. There were all sorts of misadventures, perhaps partly because the children were left to their own devices with the entire orphanage as their playground. One day Oliver went to the garage and found the boys with paint brushes: they were painting the company Volkswagen microbus with bright green paint they had found in the garage.

Perhaps because of Ross's escapades, he suffered more childhood injuries than the other siblings combined. He broke his arm several times, poured hot water on himself, fell off his bike frequently, and tore around at top speed, unfazed by the possible consequences. He was a risk-taker through his childhood years, and it is interesting to speculate how that characteristic developed in his adult life. His most dramatic injury occurred back in Australia when he fell through a window and nearly sliced his arm off. But more of that later.

Life in the orphanage had a predictability that suited Ross. There was structure to the confined family life, combined with plenty of space on the large property to explore and interact with friends. Oliver and Jean worked extremely hard and were on call around the clock to their large, adopted family; the tribe of five children living in a culture away from their extended family at times needed more intimacy and cohesion than was possible. There were plenty of willing friends and child-minders onsite and the children blended in easily with the life and events of the orphanage. Howard and, later, Peter, were much loved babies who were cuddled and carried around the property by all and sundry.

The times when the children had their parents to themselves were precious, and one of those was the annual expedition to the island of Cheung Chau. Each year in August, the family packed up and traveled to the island for a holiday; it was about an hour's ferry trip outside the harbor. A double-story house was rented from a missionary organization for a couple of weeks and the family moved in with some amahs to help—the house was basic.

For Ross, it was the highlight of the year because he always celebrated his birthday on 13 August on the island. It was always fun and well-documented in the family albums. Best of all, Dad and Mum were fully there for him and his siblings and they enjoyed board games, walks, cold drinks at the kiosk, and stories at night. The best memories. Both Howard and Jeanette have returned to Cheung Chau in recent years to ride the ferry and walk the tracks that still have no cars, to reconnect with those warm memories.

One year, there was a sudden emergency during the holiday when the family realized that Ross was missing. A casual hunt around the house and yard suddenly turned into a serious search. The children saw their parents looking anxious, calling out Ross's name and going further out along the tracks. One track led to cliffs that dropped away to rocks and pounding surf way below. Oliver stood at the top a long time, scanning the rocks, but hoping to find nothing. How could Ross just disappear? Eventually one of the amahs came up the road from the fishing village, holding Ross's hand. They had no idea of the drama caused by their absence, but the amah had given in to Ross's pleading to go for an outing and now they were back. There were hugs and tears all round, much to Ross's surprise. His big sister was amazed to see her dad crying; it was only Ross, after all.

The five years in Hong Kong went by, creating family memories and thousands of slide photos that were viewed over the years that became inseparable from real memories. There were many important visitors to the home, sports days at the school and annual concerts, trips to the beach house in the New Territories where the kids swam happily between the Lion's Mane jellyfish, ferry rides to Hong Kong Island, cable car trips to Victoria Peak, Chinese meals with friends and visitors, Easter and Christmas celebrations, and occasional high force typhoons that shook the whole colony. They were very formative years for Ross, shaping him through his multi-cultural childhood. Many family conversations in later years were prefaced with "When we were in Hong Kong."

In December 1956, the Langmeads boarded ship once again for the return voyage to Australia, this time on the *MS Changte*. In contrast to the first journey, this sea trip was horrendous and the roughest in memory. The small ship was buffeted by storms and typhoons, and was forced to divert and shelter in Manila Harbor in the Philippines. All passengers were confined to cabins for much of the journey and all the Langmeads were seasick except for Peter, who was the only child who turned up for meals at one stage. Jeanette was terrified and has been phobic about sea travel ever since; Ross and Les were frustrated not to be able to play on the deck; Howard and Peter were content to be entertained in the cabin except when Peter escaped and crawled up onto the heaving deck and had to be rescued from being washed overboard. Ross's little onboard playmate was rather mean and after one run-in he threw Ross's only toy car over the rail and into the ocean, where Ross watched it sink and disappear forever.

The ship finally sailed through the Heads of Sydney Harbor on Christmas Eve 1956, and the family were welcomed home by the Walker clan to enjoy a memorable Christmas with the family the next day. All the joys of Australian life were theirs to enjoy, all the things they had missed, and with his rediscovered tribe of Sydney cousins, Ross watched television for the first time.

The family traveled on to Melbourne to settle in their temporary accommodation with their Langmead cousins in a large old house in semi-rural Heathmont. Four adults, nine children, a dog, and one outdoor dunny made for crowded conditions. The cousins were true Aussie kids, roaming the surrounding orchards and bush, only coming home for dinner at night. Ross's family had come from an urban environment and were used to servants doing the cooking, cleaning, and picking up after the children. Somehow, the Langmeads became a united family and a force to be reckoned with at the local primary school as they defended one another. Ross, desperate to fit into his new world, adjusted his British accent within weeks, and set about to master the local football obsession. He was academically well-ahead of his cohort in the casual little school, and he enjoyed having some older male cousins.

The family with grandparents, Roy and Vi Langmead.

A favorite game with the cousins was sardines: one child hid somewhere like the tiny outdoor toilet, eating stolen apples from next door, while the rest roamed the property looking for the hiding place until one person was left outside. There was lots of running amongst the scrub and blackberries, and on one occasion cousin Roy, who had suffered from polio and had a lame leg, fell or was pushed into the blackberry bushes and could not get out. Jean came running to help and landed on top of Roy when she tried to pull him out; the other eight cousins were in big trouble for laughing at their plight. Ross's childhood in Hong Kong soon faded to a collection of well-rehearsed family anecdotes and slide nights. Local kids at school had almost no interest in his childhood abroad, and even less idea where Hong Kong was. He just wanted to be an Aussie.

Ross's school history is a patchwork of the schools he attended, totaling six by the time he graduated. The family moved to a rented place in eastern Ringwood where he was enrolled at the local primary school, then to West Heidelberg where he went to the Olympic Village primary school, and then Rosanna High School in the north of Melbourne.

Another move took the family to inner western Kensington, where Jeanette and then Ross gained entrance to University High School (UHS), which was a short tram ride away. With varying degrees of success, he and all his siblings negotiated these varied educational experiences but were all fortunate to end up at the selective entry UHS. It delivered top-level education, and was across the road from Melbourne University, to which many of its students graduated.

Well above the class average all the way in high school, he gained honors in all his senior subjects, including subjects as diverse as French, math, history, and physics. This was an indication of his wide range of ability, from which he found it difficult to decide on a direction. The intelligence cluster of math, languages, and music was already evident and would launch him on his tertiary study. His final school reference read:

> Ross has been a conscientious and able form captain, a talented musician (band) and a keen hockey player. His contribution to the school as leader of the Inter-school Christian Fellowship has been greatly appreciated. An exemplary young man, the school proudly recommends him. (Final report and school reference, 1966)

In the sixties, students paid fees for university, making matriculation and tertiary entry too daunting for ordinary families. The Langmeads were living below the poverty line financially with a family of eight, but the children had educational aspirations. Oliver, however, couldn't imagine how his children would go to university as they wanted to. The only path to tertiary education was to win a scholarship, and Ross was certainly in the running. His sister was already finishing her degree on a teaching scholarship, and Ross followed suit. They were the first Langmeads ever to enter university and now there would be another teacher in the family.

In 1958, Ross's youngest sibling was born, and the family was complete. Grace was a long-awaited sister, especially for Jeanette, who longed for a female sibling to balance off four brothers. The six children spanned nearly twelve years and were a tight-knit family. Their parents referred to them as the "big ones" and the "little ones" in their growing-up years, no doubt as a convenient way of dividing and conquering. The privileges and burdens of each place in the birth order, however, combined with gender, personality, and a patriarchal family model, meant that there was a complex psychological jostling that lasted well into the adult years. All the siblings have their own perspectives on how this played out and the discussions have continued to this day. Ross is not with us to defend his assumption of the "eldest son" role, which was probably a combination of parental expectations and his own sense of duty over the years.

The gender mix meant that the two girls shared a room and Ross slept in a room in bunks with his three brothers until his mid-teens when a move to a larger home provided more bedrooms. Being bundled together as "the boys" led to both camaraderie and competitiveness over the years and was the other way of sorting the siblings.

Discipline was always strict, and arguments, especially with Oliver, were not tolerated. Most topics were not up for questioning or debate. Ross's father determined what was right and fair, and his punishment, by today's standards, was harsh at times. Family routines ran like clockwork and everyone had jobs. Meals were served on the dot of six every night; no one was ever late, and no one left the table until family prayers were finished. This continued until the children were young adults. The family meals were simple but adequate, and treats were rare. It was before takeaway food became common, but the Langmeads could not have afforded to buy for eight people anyway. Very occasionally they would buy chips (no fish) to eat on a car trip, and the children would count them out to make sure everyone had a fair share.

There was no television in the home, except an occasional rental in the long summer holidays, and that would be returned the night before school started. Combined with zero tolerance for pop culture and music, and complete lack of cultural exposure to classical music or the arts, it meant that they grew up with a narrow worldview. Although Jean was expected to play her part in their joint Salvationist ministry, she carried the bulk of the load in the home. With a family of eight, that was substantial. The twin-tub washing machine went through its paces a couple of times every day. Jean only had the energy to do what had to be done to keep the family going, and over the years she suffered from frequent bouts of ill-health.

That's not to say there was no happy side to family life. Without television, there was lively conversation, board games (but not card games, which were associated with gambling), learning to play musical instruments, and road trips to stay with cousins. These trips were planned down to the minute, RACV strip maps furnished to follow the route, picnic meals labeled for each stop, and loo breaks scheduled in. The drive to Sydney would commence in the early hours and the family was renowned for arriving on the dot of the estimated arrival time thirteen hours later. These holiday stays were fun times because the adults wanted to relax and catch up, and Ross and his siblings could run free with the cousins in ways they were not permitted to at home.

The Langmeads were no ordinary family, as Ross noted in his eulogy for Oliver in 1994. Being a Salvationist officer family determined not only where the family lived, constant moves, and changes of schools and friends, but also meant that they led an extraordinary life which revolved around being Salvationists. Some years later, all six siblings had moved out of the Army, some into other churches, and some choosing a non-religious life. Although their reasons for leaving varied, all, however, would agree that the Army played a huge role in their younger years, leaving them with a mixed legacy. For Ross, this was all part of his journey to break free from his family, his parents, and a church that demanded deep commitment.

By the time Ross was a young teen, the routines were set. Sundays began with "Knee drill" or prayer, followed by the open-air meeting involving the band and adults. Meanwhile, the children met for Directory, which was a teaching session. Then the morning "Holiness meeting" or church service took place, which was obligatory for band and songsters. The whole family attended this, and as they grew up, participated in the service. Ross played in the band, and once he reached his teens, joined the open-air event.

Sunday lunch at the Langmeads was always a roast meal and sweets, with a dozen places set at the table ready for the family plus four people who would be invited home. This generosity meant there was rarely an empty place, and the family welcomed all sorts of friends or needy people to their table. After lunch was Young People's meeting, or Sunday School, mostly supervised by Oliver and attended by all the children. The boys played in the youth band and the girls played their timbrels for this event while the older children assisted with the kinder age kids.

There would be a short break before soup and scones for dinner, and then it would be time for the evening open-air meeting, which finished just in time for the night "salvation" meeting. The whole family attended again, including the younger siblings, who were cuddled until they slept and then carried home. If they hadn't had enough events for the Lord's Day, quite often the young people would gather at the Langmeads' for Youth Squash, which involved singing, chatting, and supper. The Army was Ross's entire social scene, and he was popular in his friendship circle.

Study was forbidden on Sundays, and there literally was no time to do anything but spend the day at the Army events. Nothing was ever bought at the shops on the day that was deemed to be the Sabbath, and if the family ran out of fresh milk, powdered milk was used. Not only did the family not work or study on Sundays, but they were not permitted to cause anyone else to labor.

During the week there was a night out for band and songster practice, and another night for Corps Cadets (a Christian faith study course with practical training for teenagers), as well as youth group and other social events, musical programs, regional youth rallies, and outreach trips. Once a soldier was committed to membership and to being in the musical groups, these events were not optional, and sickness was the only reason a member would not attend. One of Oliver's favorite choruses was, "By the pathway of duty, lies the river of God's grace."

For Ross, it was hard to see past the duty part. The combination of the Army lifestyle, the strictness and expectations of his father, a narrow view of the church and the world, and a life full of obligations and pressure to conform meant inevitable clashes. Ross would experience conflict in his relationship with his dad and his church, which were often the same thing from his point of view.

Ross would be the first to acknowledge the immense heritage of his Salvo years. There was discipline and loyalty and great male bonding in the band, and the teenagers never lacked friends, mentors, and encouragement. Systematic teaching of the faith was a strength, and something that Ross continued for the whole of his life. A culture of service and living for others was a strong influence, and the Salvo way of caring for the poor and marginalized was part of the shaping of his life and beliefs. In contrast to a conservative theology and practice, the Salvos were early acceptors of the equality of female ministers; Ross was always a strong supporter of women in ministry.

Perhaps the greatest legacy would be the music. Salvationists all have opportunities to play instruments and sing. They are taught for no cost from when they are children, have endless opportunities to play in groups and perform, and absorb an ethos of spiritual music and worship as a way of life.

Ross's musical ear was apparent very early. As small children, the kids had a windup gramophone to play with, along with yellow 45 RPM records of children's songs. They sang along until they knew every song well, and Ross, who was about eight, began to sing harmonies without any help. His favorite song was:

> *There is a happy land far, far away*
> *Where saints in glory stand,*
> *Bright, bright as day.*[2]

Oliver, self-taught, trained the large children's group at the Army for anniversary concerts to sing in parts and to play percussion instruments. Ross's clear voice was always true. As the family grew up, the instruments were introduced one by one. Oliver played a concertina that he bought as a cadet in training, and as a bandsman played euphonium with its arpeggios and embellishing parts in the score.

Ross's commencement on a brass instrument came about dramatically after a serious accident that nearly claimed the use of his right arm. When he was eight, the family was enjoying a summer holiday in Sydney at Jean's brother Wilbur's home. There were nine children playing together outside,

---

2. Lyrics by Andrew Young (1807–89).

Oliver and Jean had gone out, and Ross's Auntie Glad had popped next door to borrow something. The boys' ball went over the fence, so Ross decided they would climb over, using a ladder. With a couple of children on it, the ladder overbalanced, and Ross fell backwards, smashing through the bathroom window. He landed inside with a huge gash on his right forearm that was spurting blood amidst splintered glass, much to the horror of Jeanette and her cousin who were in the bathroom.

Suddenly all nine cousins were screaming, and Auntie Glad was racing back from next door. Jeanette had the presence of mind to grab a clean towel and tie it over the awful wound until the ambulance arrived. The children were in various states of hysteria—one ran around the block, one fainted, and one peppered the paramedics with questions about whether Ross would die. Ross was taken to the local hospital where, miraculously, there happened to be a visiting surgeon who specialized in restoring the nerves and tendons that had been severed. Ross wore a splint for nearly two years and had no feeling or movement for a long time. Fortunately, he was left-handed.

As the therapy began to restore his arm's function, his parents offered him a brass cornet if he would do his exercises and learn to play it with his damaged right hand. Ross did just that and it became his first musical instrument that he played all his years as a Salvo. The effects of the wound did, however, compromise his movement in later life.

Times were changing in the world and stringed instruments became popular. Ross received a small ukulele as a birthday present and taught himself to play. He loved the simplicity and flexibility of it, and before long graduated to a small guitar and then a full-sized one. Somewhere along the way, Ross began fiddling on the piano, and his mathematical mind tuned in quickly to the patterns and sequences so that he could accompany himself and compose songs.

Between brass instruments, strings, and percussion, everyone in the family could play something, and that prompted Oliver to try some family music. The older ones had doubts about this plan from the beginning, but compliance was a given for the Langmeads and Oliver was not easily disobeyed. The novelty of a family musical troupe—sort of the Von Trapp Langmeads—was irresistible in the Army world, and invitations began to roll in for Christmas events, old folks' homes, and other opportunities. They had a repertoire for all these occasions, with Grace adding the cute factor as the youngest when she sang by herself. Oliver played a homemade tea chest bass or his euphonium, Jeanette the piano or her accordion, Ross and Les on brass (cornet, tenor, and later a concert pitch ballad horn) or guitars, Howard on a cornet or banjo ukulele, Peter on brass or drums, Grace on triangle and then ukulele, and Jean on percussion. As well as Christmas songs, they sang well-known Army songs in four-part harmony to great acclaim.

As they reached their teen years, there was an inevitable rumbling from the kids, mostly led by Ross. "Do we have to practice now when I have study to do?" he would ask, in as reasonable a tone of voice as he could muster. He was always the quickest to pick up the songs, which led to impatience; he also argued with Oliver about musical issues. "Should that be a repeat from the beginning?" and "Dad, try a G there instead of a C," and "That was way too slow," were his attempts to move things along; they generally did not go well.

The other siblings would sigh inwardly, knowing that the only way to finish the practice was to keep going without interruptions that might lead to arguments. Deep down, the older ones especially felt that they were too old to be corralled into a musical group that was not of their choice, and for which the time involved was not negotiable. As they performed to rave reviews and were enjoyed by all, Ross struggled along with the others and wondered how to bring it to an end.

By his mid-teens Ross was a proficient, self-taught musician who enjoyed exploring the world of music. Folk music was reaching its revival peak in the mid-sixties. The Seekers were formed in Melbourne in 1962, around the same time as Peter, Paul, and Mary in New York. Ross was greatly influenced by this style of music, especially Bob Dylan's message songs and later those by James Taylor. Ross experimented with playing a mouth organ at the same time as his guitar, like Dylan, and that became a signature style as his songs developed.

> *Like everyone I've got something I want to say,*
> *I'll sing it like Bobby, yeah, he found a way,*
> *It comes from the heart, a thousand lines,*
> *I'll sing and I'll blow the things that I know*
> *I hope nobody minds,*
> *I'll sing a song about Jesus, I feel, I feel Him like Paul,*
> *I found out He loves me, it makes me feel small,*
> *I'll trust this Jesus man.*
> *I'll sing it like Bobby, I'll feel it like Paul,*
> *I'll sing it like Jesus is Lord over all.*

(RL, "Influence Song," 1972)

For many people, Ross will be remembered by his music, and there is no doubt that the heritage of his childhood and youth gave him a gift amidst all the struggles. Despite his considerable academic prowess and cerebral style, music was his medium.

Chapter 2

Study: 1967 to 1970

Study without reflection is a waste of time; reflection without study is dangerous.

CHINESE PROVERB

With school days finished, excellent results and an Education Department studentship which covered tuition fees, a living allowance, and a place at Melbourne University, it was time to celebrate.

A plan emerged to drive north in January 1967. Ross would travel by train from Melbourne to Brisbane with his cousin John to meet up with another cousin, Roy, who wanted to visit his brother in northern Queensland. These three eldest sons of the three Langmead brothers planned to travel together to stay on the station with Ernie, who was working in Tarragona, 1,330 km northwest of Brisbane, and be joined by a friend, Don, for part of the trip. Ross and John were only seventeen and did not have driving licenses so Roy would drive his car and keep an eye on his younger relatives. They departed from Brisbane on Friday 13 January.

Ross's written log of this trip is the earliest journal of his that we have. Neatly recorded in an exercise book in his already distinctive left-handed upright writing style, it recounts an epic boys' coming-of-age road trip to the outback, as far away from home as he could go. Searing heat and with no air-conditioning, jokes and music, girls and chess interspersed with skinning kangaroos, lots of cold drinks, and run-ins with the police.

The car was a white Armstrong-Siddeley crew cab, ex-government fleet vehicle belonging to Roy; all four could fit inside the cabin and their gear was packed in the tray at the back. They may have appeared to be a bunch of larrikins out for a good time, but the boys were quite disciplined—well, most of the time, as both Ross and John may or may not have driven illegally in the outback. They were organized and won their way in the places they stayed by being courteous and helpful. Ross recorded that they had devotions together around picnic tables and attended church on Sunday, which is not your usual "schoolies" adventure. Being good Baptists and a Salvo, there was no alcohol involved, and no swearing. John does remember, however, some kissing with a good-looking jilleroo at a station party.

In Rockhampton they camped on a friend's property with permission, then moved under the house when it rained. Ross wrote:

> 8.30 p.m. Sat around to play guitar and mouth organ. Were singing "It's True" wildly when Roy spotted cop car cruising down the street. The tune changing to "My Jesus, I love thee," we saw two police pull up and come round to underneath the house. We stood up respectfully and greeted them. They had been sent around to check our accommodation (after an encounter earlier in the day involving a broken headlight and missing license). Seeing as "Our auntie's friend knows

this reverend, uh, er, Charles," was pretty weak, it must have been our sincerity and our religious parental standing which convinced the two police who were courteous yet not gullible.
(RL, Trip diary, January, 1967)

When they finally arrived at the station in Tarragona, Roy saw a lean, dark-skinned young man coming to greet them, and said he didn't know there were indigenous stockmen employed there. It turned out to be his own brother. Ernie was thinner and very tanned from eighteen months of outside work. The time the young men spent there was an eye-opener for the city dwellers during which they camped on a verandah, ate with shearers, mustered sheep, killed and ate a pig, shot a kangaroo, tanned the skin, and socialized with the station hands from all over. Ross was popular with his guitar, and John was the resident comedian. John recalls Ross's sense of humor as the flipside to his serious nature and that, though intelligent, he was not bookish. They both found music cathartic and continued to connect musically for many years. The diary records the purchase of many milkshakes and juices and their loss of appetite in the record heat as they traveled. At one stage it was 119 degrees Fahrenheit in the car cabin.

On the way back to Brisbane, Sid the car "did two big ends" and was going to cost too much to fix. Packing up their gear in the remote town of Augathella, they sold Sid off for scrap to a roo shooter and stayed the night in the local hotel; Ross and John sang in the bar, Roy fixed the jukebox, and their mate, Don, washed dishes in exchange for their rooms. The boys then set off to hitchhike back.

Those were the days when people commonly hitched rides around the outback, especially with truckies. The boys had, however, pooled and divided their money and it was every man for himself to make it easier to get rides. Oliver and Jean were not impressed that the younger two boys had to find their way home on their own. Ross later told a story of spending the night beside the road, and dancing around in their sheets like dervish ghosts when trucks drove past.

After a bumpy ride in the back of a tray truck and a couple of car rides, they all made it back somehow to Ross's uncle's house in Brisbane. Meanwhile, Ross and John caused consternation at the telegram office when they sent a telegram to their parents saying "Sid kicked the bucket. Hitchhiking back." The lady who was to read it out over the phone was worried that it was sad news of a death being reported disrespectfully.

This rite-of-passage expedition for Ross illustrated traits that were to become lifelong. He was a confident adventurer, a lover of travel, and was willing to take some risks within the parameters of his detailed planning and organization.

Ross arrived home from Queensland at the end of January 1967. A few days later, on 7 February, unprecedented heat in the southern areas caused 110 separate damaging bushfires in southern Tasmania. On Black Tuesday, as it became known, huge areas south of Hobart were burnt and sixty-three people lost their lives. Thirteen hundred homes were lost, and seven thousand people were made homeless. The Salvation Army wanted to send a team of volunteers from Melbourne to assist in the relief work. It was the perfect time for university students who were still on summer break, so Ross and Jeanette volunteered to go.

It was the first time either of them had flown on a plane, and the burnt areas and lines of flames glowed and curled below them as the plane descended into Hobart, the capital city of Tasmania. They were billeted separately in the suburbs and only saw each other briefly at the relief center each day. For a seventeen-year-old, it was demanding and confronting work. People who had suffered fire damage to their property lined up to register, and the volunteers listened to their stories, recorded their losses, and advised them concerning relief available. Others visited the fire areas to gather information and to contact people. For Ross, the contrast could not have been greater after his carefree trip north, but he threw himself into the experience and it was a jolting transition into a tragic situation. Again, he recorded his experiences:

> That afternoon I went to Colebrook, a badly burnt town, with the purpose of assessing its needs. The stench of dying sheep still lingered. 30 or so families had lost their homes. One farmer told me with tears in his eyes of the 3,000 sheep he had lost, his feeding area, outbuildings and machinery. This was the first year he has not insured his farm.
>
> The five visiting teams found tremendous gratefulness as we told them where to get cash grants, relief goods, medical attention, rehousing and legal advice, temporary accommodation and even school-books and uniforms. At times one felt inadequate as people poured out their troubles; besides physical rehabilitation, many people have suffered mental stress, particularly the aged and those at home when the fires struck.
>
> Some cannot understand why this tragedy should happen, like the woman who said to me, "Why should my house go when I prayed hard for its safety and others were lucky and did not trust God?" It was hard to explain God's ways as we cannot

fully understand either, but a Bible was left with the lady, who
was glad of a source of comfort. (RL, Report on trip, 1967)

This question about how prayer works was to stay with Ross, and eventually be wrestled with in his master's thesis ten years later. The trip was a different kind of growing up for the teenage Ross, but his voluntary work and sympathetic response were an early example of what would become a characteristic empathy with those in need.

School and holiday events over, it was time to launch his university life—and it would be a long one; his formal tertiary study would span over thirty years from 1967 to 1998. Ross enrolled in a Bachelor of Arts in 1967, majoring in math, Chinese, and geography in his first year. The family was living in historic bluestone Royal Terrace in Fitzroy, just a short bus ride or walking distance from the University of Melbourne, creating a convenient inner-city lifestyle for all the students in the family.

Study at the University of Melbourne in the sixties was centered around the Baillieu Library and the Student Union building. It was rare for students to work in jobs during the term as they do these days, and very few owned a car. Ross would have arrived at uni every morning in time to claim a study spot in the library, from where he would depart to attend lectures and tutorials, interspersed with coffee and meal breaks in the cafeteria in the Student Union with friends, or relaxing on the manicured lawns on sunny days. Attending university was a lifestyle, and a very pleasant one at that.

Lectures in the Arts faculty were exceptionally large, although Ross did not study any traditional humanities subjects. Chinese (Mandarin) was one of the smaller language subjects on offer, and the lecturer was a friend of Jean's from her China days. Both Jeanette and Ross chose the challenging subject with over six hundred graphical characters to memorize over the year, a set of tones to master, and an extremely complicated dictionary. Ross was probably hoping that his childhood memories of the Cantonese dialect would help him, but the national dialect of Mandarin proved to be almost like a new language. Nevertheless, his organization and liking for systems served him well, and at the end of the year Ross was awarded the Australian-Asian Association Prize. The Education Department had to approve subject choices with a view to teaching methods, and they gave Ross permission to continue, even though Chinese was not taught in schools at that time. With honors results in his math subjects, Ross, to the dismay of his Mandarin lecturer, decided to specialize in math, studying only pure and applied math, and statistics for the remainder of his degree.

A copy of one of his pure math essays in first year commences like this:

> Topology is a fascinating branch of mathematics once said to be set aside for mathematicians who did not know the difference between a coffee mug and a doughnut. It is the "study of properties of geometrical figures that persist even when the figures are subjected to deformations so drastic that all their metric and projective properties are lost." (RL, Essay, 1967)

Math at its purest. He scored an A minus: "Excellent material but presented in a somewhat disjointed fashion." He still had a little way to go for his honors results.

It was an interesting choice for two reasons: many of his adult friends later probably had no idea that he was a mathematician of considerable standing, and also that he pursued this discipline in an arts degree. His later academic path, for which he is better remembered, was very philosophical and theological, which seems a long way from mathematical pursuits. He probably could have taken several paths in his academic life, but his math background clearly equipped him for statistical research and systematic study in any area he chose.

At seventeen, when he commenced, Ross was young for tertiary study, but held his own as both a capable student and friendly young man. Some of the friends he made in his university years would be lifelong friends.

Bill James first met Ross at an Inter School Christian Fellowship leadership conference in 1965 when they were both in Year 11 at high school, and Ross was already showing leadership ability. Bill caught up again at uni through the Evangelical Union and was on the same path as Ross—a BA with the goal of teaching. Bill became one of the good friends that Ross valued over the years, and Ross sang at Bill and Fran's wedding in 1970. Bill says:

> Like most people who knew him, I respected Ross's considerable intellect, his impressive efficiency and self-discipline, his sense of humour and his outstanding musical talents. In my opinion, however, his most impressive achievement was his integrity. At university we were both conventional evangelicals (despite having moved on from the pietistic and hermeneutical simplicities of our Salvation Army and Brethren backgrounds). While I may not have always agreed with the developments in his thinking, I respected them, because I had no doubt that they were prompted by genuine convictions which had been attained through careful thought, and not as a result of factors such as trendiness or susceptibility to peer pressure. (Bill James, 2020)

The siblings helped each other to find several vacation jobs over the years. Ross started working when school finished in the summer of 1966 at Buckley and Nunn's department store in the Melbourne CBD when Jeanette was able to get his name on the list. Their home in Nicholson Street, Fitzroy, was an easy walk from the Bourke Street shops, and neither of them wanted to waste their hard-earned money on tram fares. They chatted as they walked together morning and evening, swapping stories of difficult customers, demanding bosses, and funny events. Transactions were all made by cash, and the salesperson inserted the money and invoice in a pneumatic tube cylinder that was sucked up to the accounts department several floors up and then returned with a receipt. Jeanette told him one night about how one young employee had put a dead mouse in the cylinder, causing screams from the accounts girls upstairs.

Retail work was further complicated by the conversion to decimal currency, and the existence of two forms of cash at that stage. For two years after February 1966, customers could pay in either currency, but would receive change in dollars and cents. That led to frequent mathematical explanations to confused shoppers, who believed that they had been ripped off when they paid in twelves but received tens as change. Undoubtedly, Ross's mathematical ability, clear communication, and boyish charm set many a mind at rest.

In his first year at university, Ross heard about an essay-writing competition and decided to enter. The ANZ bank sponsored the competition in conjunction with national family and marriage week in May 1967. Ross won second prize, and his entry was reprinted in *The War Cry*, the Salvo weekly newspaper, with the heading, "Son's Ideal."

He started by describing the stereotype of a father from a century before:

> A formidable and severe personality. Seated at the head of the table, he kept the peace, believed that children should be seen and not heard, and reigned as the undisputed head of the family. His word was law and he issued many more than 10 commandments.

He went on to contrast this with the modern father:

> He has been unseated from his place of authority in our society, to the extent that generally speaking, the male parent is no longer ruler but "pretender." Our modern society has devalued the image of the father, who becomes a harassed breadwinner, henpecked by his wife. But the father has an important role to play in the family, and contrary to today's image he is not just a person for whom to buy shirts and socks on father's day. He

is not only a breadwinner, but he has great responsibility in all spheres of the life of the family. No-one wants the return of the heavy-handed, despotic male parent, but authority is needed to regain the father's position as head of the family.

Reading his descriptions of the two stereotypes now, one would have to say that Ross's father was more like the first strict one. Ross himself strongly resisted any attempt by his father to steer his life, and his university years were, in fact, the period when his values and principles began to take a different tack to his own father's.

In awarding the second prize to Ross, the judges said:

> Clear, confident, reasoned, literate. Technically speaking, it is the best essay, but it lacks warmth. As the coherent expression of a 17-year-old it deserves high praise and possibly one of the journals at the university might be encouraged to print it in full.

The life stories of the Langmead siblings, like those of a great many families, are essentially of journeys of growth and separation from their parents. Ross wrote a summary of his family characteristics in 2011 and described Oliver as "strong, close, fundamentalist, authoritarian, ISFP" and Jean as "emotionally absent, ill, organized, Pollyanna-ish, ESTJ."[1] Ross felt that the key message from his father was: "You are not acceptable as you are; you must be better, always better" noting that his Enneagram type identified negatively with father, avoided condemnation, and tried to be blameless.

While Jeanette had the burden of the elder daughter in trying to please her father as well as being expected to assist her mother in running the household, Ross, as the eldest son, was given the mantle of the responsibility and thus the demand to follow his father's patriarchal traditions, beliefs, principles, and behavior. This became a source of increasing conflict in his late teens, which Ross embraced despite disliking confrontation.

The late sixties was a period of busy activism on university campuses, featuring regular lunchtime talks and rallies, distribution of leaflets and a great deal of debate. Ross's years at university were the early days of anti-Vietnam War protests. There were sit-down actions that culminated in the Vietnam Moratorium marches in 1970 when 200,000 people marched the streets. For Ross, this cause would become a pivot in his growing move to the political and Christian left. His father stood strongly for the conservative right in both arenas and was disturbed as he saw his son begin to flex his democratic muscles against Australia's involvement in the war in Vietnam. For Oliver, with his experience of the Communist takeover in China,

---

1. ISFP and ESTJ are Myers-Briggs personality types.

it was tantamount to supporting the "reds," and he would not have that in his home. The son of a World War I veteran, he equated duty and citizenship and the right thing to do with compliance with the government call-up, and any resistance to that call of duty was aligned with labor politics, unions, Catholics, and communists.

For Ross, there was a growing conviction that war was wrong, especially someone else's war. He moved rapidly to a Christian pacifist stance, and declared that he would indeed conscientiously object if his number were drawn from the barrel. The National Service Scheme was introduced by Prime Minister Robert Menzies and was not, contrary to popular perception, specifically for the Vietnam War, although it is often remembered that way. Under this scheme, Australian men turning twenty years were part of a ballot of birth dates, drawn randomly from a barrel. If their date were drawn, they would then be advised whether they were required to take on two years of full-time service in the army, during which time they would possibly be sent on active service to Vietnam.

Although there had been minor skirmishes in the home as the children became young adults, this was the first serious falling out. The thought of a son of his being a conscientious objector was as abhorrent to Oliver as going to fight a destructive war was to the pacifist Ross. The twice-yearly ballot came around in July 1969 for those born in the second half of that year. Only four dates were drawn for August, and one of them was the thirteenth—Ross had been conscripted. There was, however, a deferral option for students and apprentices, enabling Ross to finish his degree. Medical examinations, three in all, followed registration, and Ross's wounded right arm was noted. A letter from the surgeon who repaired it said:

> I wish to certify that on the 6th January 1958, ROSS OLIVER LANGMEAD, then aged eight, came into my care at St George Hospital following an injury to his right arm, occasioned by the arm being lacerated with glass. As a result of that injury he had extensively divided the flexor muscles of the right forearm and had also divided both ulnar and median nerves. The muscles and nerves were united at operation but naturally the injury was followed by some diminished function of the fingers and diminished sensation due to nerve injury. I have no doubt that he will be left with some disabilities of the right arm. (NA Fowler, North Shore Medical Centre, 8 July 1970)

And so Ross was medically disqualified, and the National Service and the Vietnam War would not be personal issues as he feared. The events of the late sixties, however, caused him to embrace and develop a pacifist stance which would only strengthen over the years. Two of Ross's early songs reference war and raise the questions that were clearly troubling for him in this period:

> *I talked to a man the other day, he sat on a bench in the park.*
> *He asked me what I thought about the war we are fighting just now,*
> *I said, "I guess we will always have war with leaders like those we have now"*
> *My second thoughts came immediately, I said, "But no-one knows how*
> *To love his brother, help each other anymore."*

(RL, "Man in the Park," 1969)

> *If someone asked you, "Why is there war in this world?*
> *How can we stop men from fighting? Where has love gone?*
> *Can men live in peace? Oh tell me what can we do?*
> *Would you say, "I don't know"*
> *Or would you say, "Only go to Jesus, he's the answer"?*
> *Would you shrug your shoulders and say, "I don't care"?*
> *Would you close your eyes to wrong and hatred everywhere?*
> *Would you take into account that Jesus died for you?*

(RL, "What Would You Say?," 1968)

Ross had begun his song journey of reconciling his questions with his faith through music. In his lifelong exploration of theology, philosophy, missiology, community, and education, many would feel that music was his most powerful expression.

Like many Christian students, he made the choice to join the Evangelical Union (known as the Christian Union after 1973), a fellowship of students from many denominations with Christian faith who met on campus. It was an active group in that era, with an objective that it still holds today: "to uphold the fundamental truths of the Christian faith as contained in the Bible." It held regular prayer meetings and Bible studies on campus, and occasionally staged campus-wide missions.

There is slight irony in the fact that, while EU had been criticized in the thirties for being unwilling and unable to engage critically with intellectual ideas and criticism of their brand of Christianity, in the sixties, a cerebral approach to Christianity characterized EU, and was both its strength and its weakness. EUers were encouraged to engage their fellow students with the gospel, through friendships and EU-wide activities like EU missions and debates with other clubs.

Another feature of the EU that appealed to Ross was the high engagement with overseas students, mostly from Asia. Many Christian students came to study in Melbourne, and they made connections with others who found the Overseas Christian Fellowship was welcoming and a good way to make friends. With Ross's background in Hong Kong, he found it easy to relate to students from South East Asia and was involved in many cooperative events between EU and OCF. He particularly enjoyed being invited to student houses around Parkville to share a home-cooked Chinese meal. The Langmead home became a center for student gatherings in that era, and Asian students were often amazed to discover that Ross's parents spoke fluent Cantonese and Mandarin between them.

Already a natural leader, Ross was involved in the small groups that met on the campus mostly for Bible study, prayer and mutual encouragement.

A friend writes:

> I first met Ross as a fresher when I was just 17 in 1970, and he was on a tram during O-week, playing guitar on the Wattle Park tram line. I had decided to put my Christianity on hold while I was at uni but as soon as I met that group of people in O-week, I was hooked as to who they were, amazing.
>
> Ross holds a special place in my heart as part of very happy times. The guys of EU in that era used to climb out through the window onto the roof of the Arts building and it was all very funny. (Sue Garner, 2020)

Apparently, Ross had not grown out of escapades that involved climbing onto roofs. Philip Hughes, who would later have a long career in research and would teach with Ross, met him through EU. He writes:

> I would see Ross in the room the Christian Association used in the Union Building. He and I both attended an Australian Fellowship of Evangelical Students conference in Victor Harbor. Ross went there on his motorbike (750 km) while I travelled by car. Ross had a very ordered and logical mind. He worked things through systematically. Even more importantly he was highly intentional in living according to his principles. Ross treated everyone equally. He befriended everyone and anyone. He was a good listener. He respected everyone. And he gave his time and efforts most to the people who needed him most. (Philip Hughes, 2020)

The EU was conservative in its theology but was an important forum for students who belonged to churches where intellectual and academic critique of the faith was not encouraged. That included the Salvation Army at that time. The Langmead siblings were part of the new wave of Salvationist students involved in tertiary study, unlike their parents who had not had that opportunity. Their desire to examine faith and doctrine and to engage with students from many other churches did not sit comfortably with the top-down, authoritarian style of the Army, which implicitly discouraged questioning or enquiry. Soldiers in an army follow their orders without asking questions.

A new group emerged in the sixties called The Salvation Army Students' Fellowship. It drew together these university and college students, ostensibly to provide a forum for discussion, but in fact became more like a group of dissidents. The elders saw this as rebellion in the ranks and were probably right. Ross attended their meetings for a while and there was much debate about Army doctrine and practice, but Ross knew his own mind quite early in his tertiary years.

Salvationists called other denominations "the churches," giving an implied otherness to the church streams. There was no time or space for interdenominational interaction, so for many young Salvationists, university, and the EU in particular, was the first opportunity to meet more Christians with broader styles of faith.

For Ross, the EU and other interdenominational groups such as Scripture Union provided a context to develop a new apologetic for his faith. Teaching by respected Bible scholars, debate with other mature young Christians, and new books to read were all part of his new stage of growth, and partway into his arts degree, he decided to make his move out of the Army.

Ross later acknowledged that there were two sides to his Salvo legacy. On the positive side, he inherited a love for the poor, demonstrated in the Army and in his parents' ministry. This was to influence him for the rest of his life. The informal style of worship was something he enjoyed, and it was strongly connected to what he called the "musical saturation" of his childhood and teen years, including the camaraderie of being part of a male musical ensemble. There were no slow hymns or repetitive liturgies, ad-lib testimonies were often a highlight, and sermons were full of practical stories and application to everyday living. He valued the systematic teaching and leadership training built into the various internal organizations that make up the Army, and the missionary heart that has taken the movement into over a hundred countries today.

What he wanted to escape from was what he labeled "frenetic activism," which was even more the case in a large family with officer parents. The demand to support the family by being part of the drivenness was difficult to resist, as it was the fabric of a tightly knit unit. Clashes of programs became more frequent as he tried to join groups and attend events in other organizations. Ross and each of his siblings struggled with whether this clash of loyalty was with the Army, or his parents, or God, or all three.

He also had reservations about aspects of the theology, particularly the lack of sacraments. As he made friends outside the Salvos, he found it difficult to explain to them what seemed to him to be at odds with the teaching of the New Testament. As he developed in his own theological understanding, he judged what he been taught since he was a child to be simplistic, and later, too conservative. Some would say that in his later adult life, he moved to the other end of the spectrum; his theology would undergo constant evaluation and sifting.

The Army stands strongly in the "holiness" stream of teaching and members are encouraged to reflect on their failures and consecrate themselves again and again in the quest for holiness. Ross became more aware of this influence as he matured, although some of his colleagues feel that it was always a factor in his drive for perfection. Perhaps it was a particular trap for a perfectionist.

At the very heart of his struggle was a distaste for the militaristic and authoritarian structure of the organization which, in itself, made it difficult for members to leave. The wearing of the distinctive uniforms can be seen as both a strength and a liability: the uniform is respected and recognized, opening doors for members to serve in many areas. It is also a leveler and gives a disciplined feel to an "army on the march." On the other hand, Ross felt that it emphasized the difference between "soldiers" and those "in the world" and worked against inclusiveness and a welcoming atmosphere in the church. The uniform has not changed significantly over the years, and for him, it was like a costume that was unlike any of his other clothes.

He was not comfortable with the militaristic language, with leaders called by ranks such as Captains and Colonels who were appointed to "corps" with "marching orders," and even death referred to as "promotion to glory." Ross was fast developing his pacifist stance in these years and increasingly these terms did not sit well with him.

Most of all, he wanted to be able to bring his friends to share faith and church with him but felt that it was too difficult. He pondered the problems for some time, knowing that it would have to be a clean break. No one was privy to the discussions he had with his parents, but by the time he broached the subject he had already made up his mind. This soldier was going AWOL.

Ross completed his BA with honors in pure mathematics, following on with a diploma of education in 1970 to prepare for teaching. Although his results in educational systems, psychology, methods, and practice were very sound, it was philosophy of education that earned him first-class honors and was to foreshadow the pathway he chose for the rest of his academic career. The philosopher was born.

Chapter 3

Teaching: 1971 to 1973

Let's just go ahead and be what we were made to be, without enviously or pridefully comparing ourselves with each other, or trying to be something we aren't. If you preach, just preach God's Message, nothing else; if you help, just help, don't take over; if you teach, stick to your teaching;

Romans 12:6–7

Teaching might even be the greatest of the arts since the medium is the human mind and spirit.

John Steinbeck

The Education Department studentship that enabled Ross to study at university required that when he graduated, Ross would be appointed to a school by the department to teach for three years. By coincidence, Ross was appointed to the high school in the town where he was born, Wodonga in northern Victoria. At twenty-one years of age, Ross left home and launched his adult life.

In those days, twenty-one was the age when young people were presented with the key to the door, and Ross celebrated, in August 1970, with a party in the Fitzroy home that had been so conveniently located for his student years. Generations of Langmead friends trooped up the stairs at 60 Nicholson Street to the lounge room on the middle floor for many parties, meetings, and other celebrations. Nana Walker usually made a trip from

Sydney to help with the milestone events, and there were many with eight in the family; Ross's was no exception. Her fried rice, casseroles, cakes, and fruit punch were legendary, and no-one went home hungry.

Looking at Ross's guest list is a window into his wide circle of good friends. Gifts ranged from cash to clothes, camera equipment from his family, toiletries, music (Simon and Garfunkel, Bob Dylan, Peter, Paul and Mary, Beethoven), books, travel and camping gear, and novelty gifts.

Ross, like most of his peers, could not afford to buy and run a car. The siblings all learnt to drive in the family vehicle under Oliver's watchful eye, and there was a sign-up page for booking the station wagon for events that could not be reached by public transport. Fortunately, the family home in Nicholson Street opposite the Exhibition Buildings in Carlton was perfectly placed for travel on the intersection of two tramlines, and was within walking distance of the Melbourne city center. Driving the car meant backing out around the clothesline into narrow and busy Royal Lane at the back and was the first skill in Oliver's thorough training plan. There was keen competition when several siblings had parties to attend in the suburbs on a Saturday night. The solution for Ross and subsequently all his younger siblings was to ride a motorcycle. Oliver and Jean must have spent many anxious evenings waiting for Ross to arrive home safely.

A friend, Alan Austin, tells a story about Ross when he was teaching in Wodonga.

> Wodonga was a three-hour ride non-stop from his parents' home in Fitzroy on a nifty Yamaha 350 motorcycle. Ross knew his mother Jean would worry when he rode. So, on one occasion, at least, Ross advised his mother during the week to expect him around 8 p.m. She would then calculate Ross's departure time and her anxiety would begin around 5 p.m., then escalate. Ross then swung his motorbike into Nicholson Street at about quarter past five and all was well. (This story raises the intriguing issue of when mild deception might be a loving act.) (Alan Austin, 2020)

In March 1969, Ross bought a Yamaha 180 CS-2E. It was his pride and joy, and he hoped that spending the extra to buy a brand-new machine would protect him from breakdowns and other hassles. From early on, Ross was a researcher when it came to purchasing goods, and his decision to buy the Yamaha was based on recommendations and facts. Things did not, however, go according to plan.

His log shows a litany of problems from the first service: in a strong letter to the dealers in June of that year, he listed multiple problems with the bike. By November, he had escalated and wrote an even stronger letter of complaint to the Yamaha Motor Company. Worst of all, in Ross's eyes, was that he had been embarrassed in the University Motorcycle Club, of which he was a keen member, and the Yamaha brand had been trashed.

Whether it was out of frustration with having to bail Ross out, or his sense of fair play—probably both—Oliver decided to go with Ross to see the manager of Yamaha.

> Dad taught us a fierce sense of justice. I remember when I was about 20, I'd bought a new motorbike, just about the first of its model off the production line, and it was a dud. I had 20 months of breakdowns, and time after time Dad had to come and pick me up stranded halfway between Melbourne and Geelong. The distributors kept blaming me for the engine seizing.
>
> Eventually dad took over. He put on his Army uniform and came with me and demanded to see the manager. He said, "My son bought a lemon from you, and he's had nothing but trouble since he paid good money for it. I want you to swap it for a new bike of a different model, and you'd better give him a good deal. If you don't, I'm going to call the newspaper photographers, take this bike down to Station Pier, and throw it into Port Phillip Bay." I got a new bike, twice the size and no changeover costs. (Eulogy for Oliver Langmead by Ross, 1994)

The following year, Ross planned a motorbike trip around Tasmania. Oliver pressured him with lots of questions: whether he had enough cash, whether he intended to let people know where he was all the time, whether he was prepared for all sorts of mishaps, and on it went. Just as Ross was mounting his bike to take off on his adventure, feeling like an irresponsible larrikin, Oliver hugged him and said, "Have a great time. I did the same when I was your age." As the father who had driven his wife and baby around in a cycle with an open side car many years before, he could relate to Ross's adventures.

Over the years, motorbike and car dramas were to become a recurring theme in Ross's life. He was good at many things, but keeping his vehicle going seemed to be a challenge.

Brothers and their bikes

To start his teaching career, Ross rode his motorbike three hundred kilometers up the notoriously dangerous Hume Highway to Wodonga. He dodged trucks, endured rain, hail, and wind, but always enjoyed the trip. The independence and exhilaration of riding a motorcycle, as well as the economy, outweighed the dangers and discomforts for him.

One of Ross's early songs captures the thrill of his cycle era:

> This story's 'bout a country road, where I was goin' I never knowed.
> I was doin' 94 if it weren't a hundred more, when I saw a freight train with a heavy load.
> The engine was 50 trucks ahead and I said, "I'll leave that train for dead."
> Well I was goin' mighty fast and I'd almost got past when I saw the railway crossing just ahead.
> I didn't believe what I saw and I can't remember much more
> But it did occur to me that I sort of hoped there'd be
> A winner and we wouldn't come a draw.
> I lay my sickle on its side and when I woke up I thought I'd died.
> Now I know just how it feels to go between the wheels of a train through an opening two foot wide.
> My mum's a nervous wreck you know, she says, "there are better ways to go."

But as I always say, It's all in the way you drive the thing, she shouldn't worry so.

(RL, "The Motorcycle Song," 1969)

Although there are not many records from Ross's teaching years, a few give an indication of how he taught math. One such handout sheet was apparently written for a parents' information night. When Ross commenced his teaching career, the "new math" was beginning to be the modern landscape for mathematics. It was felt in that era that old-style math involving memorizing tables and drills had failed to show students how math connects to real-world problem-solving. New math had young kids involved in abstract algebra, modular arithmetic, matrices, symbolic logic, Boolean algebra, and how it all related to real life.

History has judged new math to have failed, especially in basic arithmetical skills. But it was what Ross was required to teach, and his handout for parents covered sets, finite and infinite and cardinal numbers, complete with examples for parents to try. It's not hard to imagine that the rookie teacher's information nights were much appreciated by parents who had no idea what their children were talking about. Here's one of his examples:

> Express the following as listed sets: 1. The set of seasons of the year. 5. The set of earthlings who have visited Mars. (RL, "New Mathematics for Parents," 1970)

In September 1972, while teaching at East Preston High School, he wrote a math exercise sheet for his Form 3 Math class, handwritten and printed in the characteristic purple of the old spirit duplicator. It was headed "An exciting Pythagoras sheet to celebrate Mr. RL's Engagement." Question 19 went like this:

> Mr. Langmead, for his morning run, goes 4 km east, then 5½ km south, then, tired out by his engagement party the night before, decides to cut back diagonally across the paddocks. How far is it home? (RL, Form 3 Math sheet, 1973)

Clearly, Ross's mind was outside the classroom that week. Meanwhile his Form 5 Math II class were given a test on quadratic equations which concluded with:

> Q8. What are you doing over Easter? (No more than three pages please). (RL, Form 5 test, 1973)

Although he was a natural teacher, there must have been moments when this first-class math honors graduate must have felt he was casting his pearls before swine. His preparation and worksheets were always thorough and useful, but the little jokes he inserted were probably intended to keep his own sanity as well as to make himself seem more human to the diverse groups of students in his classes.

Ross was faced with the effects of disadvantage in both the schools he taught in. One of the songs he wrote in this period was about a Year 10 student called Rocky (real name), who was "hopeless." Ross's involvement with him revealed the issues faced by "rejects," and Ross was happy to know later that Rocky got a store-man's job and was not as sad as when he was at school.

> *The day is over and everyone's going, and Rocky is standing with a pump in his hand.*
> *The teacher says sadly he thinks he'll do badly; nothing is going to plan.*
> *He's no longer keen to be part of the team, cos there's twenty boys better, and anyway*
> *The boy with the hair says he'd better beware, cos they don't want him hanging around.*
>
> *Ooh, Rocky go hide, Rocky go call it a day,*
> *Make it or break it but don't hang around.*
>
> *"The trouble with schools is they don't know the rules and with blockheads like Rocky,*
> *Well you're breaking hard ground,*
> *He's wasting his year, and he doesn't appear to be taking in anything sound,*
> *I caught him last night in the thick of a fight*
> *And he said there were reasons, but anyway*
> *I gave him a few, and I've taken the view that we can't have him hanging around."*
>
> *Ooh, Rocky go hide...*
>
> *The tea's on the table...and how is God able to stand having Rocky around?*
>
> (RL, "Rocky," 1972)

After a year at Wodonga, Ross returned to the city and taught at East Preston High School for two years. By this time, he had sold his bike and graduated to a new flame-orange Renault car. When he left Wodonga, the principal wrote him this reference:

> Dear Sir,
>
> I have known Ross Langmead for 1 year. He has been a member of the staff of Wodonga High School while I have been the principal.
>
> Mr. Langmead is a fully trained and qualified teacher of Mathematics. He is conscientious, well prepared and thorough in his teaching.
>
> Mr. Langmead has a very pleasant, friendly personality and is a very valuable member of staff. He is always neatly dressed. His courtesy, consideration, high moral standards and approach to living are a particularly fine example to all those associated with him.
>
> Yours faithfully,
> AM Cracknell. Principal

Part of the reason that Ross wanted to move back to Melbourne was to pursue his studies, especially philosophy. In 1972, his subject list demonstrated this new direction, but still included some math in the form of assessment:

- Theory of Knowledge and Education A and B
- Measurement and Evaluation
- Test Theory

His results were outstanding, achieving first-class honors and first place in the cohort in three out of his four subjects. Continuing to study while working full-time, he pressed on over the next three years or so, completing his Master of Education in February 1975, with a thesis entitled "The Epistemological Status of Religious Belief and its Implications for Education," for which he was awarded H2A honors. Ross had established his academic prowess and was well prepared for the path he would follow.

The reason he chose this thesis topic was to explore how trained teachers could play a part in religious education in schools; he believed that the Russell Report on religious education would bring that into being.

In the early 1970s, at the urging of the then-Council for Christian Education in Schools, the Victorian Education Department appointed the Russell Committee on Religious Education. The Committee handed down its report in 1974. The report was in favor of religious education; its summary states:

> The Committee believes that a person's education is incomplete unless he has some awareness and understanding of the religious dimension of human experience. It therefore considers that religious education should be available to all children in government schools.

In order to ensure that the education of children in Victorian schools was complete, the Russell Report recommended, among other things, that

> the programs of religious education in each school be conducted by Departmental teachers, including persons given a special registration to teach religious education only, with the assistance where desired and practicable of representatives of the Churches and other bodies in the community acting as resource personnel.[1]

There is no doubt that Ross was keen to be part of such a program and saw his thesis as a way of looking into this proposed direction for general religious education. When the report was not accepted, he must have felt discouraged. The evangelical churches at the time were concerned that the loss of faith-specific Special Religious Education would mean that the Christian faith would lose its foothold in schools and were part of the opposition to the report. Teacher unions opposed it for a different reason—they did not want to see religion embedded in the curriculum at all. With the benefit of hindsight, it would seem it could have been a positive move to have studies of spirituality and faith being mandated in the curriculum and taught by qualified teachers, reaching all students, rather than the few who opt in for a particular program.

Meanwhile, new songs were emerging. He was beginning to write songs that focused on poverty and those who didn't want to know about it. This one is a scathing representation of those who have a different definition of poverty:

> *Well his daughter's in Noumea and the plane fares were dear, and his youngest son has written off his second car,*
> *And it's just a little cool for the heated swimming pool and the shares have never been down this far,*
> *And the tax on twenty grand would send a man down to the sand but then the home down by the beach is falling down,*
> *And you wonder if it's worth it and you sometimes want to curse it,*
> *There's never quite enough to go around.*

---

1. Romsey, "Submission."

Well we haven't got enough and things are looking bad, and you wonder why they don't do something soon.

Coda:

Jesus said, "Truly I say to you, As you did it to one of these my brethren you did it unto me."

(RL, "Poverty," 1972)

Chapter 4

Music: 1972 to 1974

My theme song is God's love and justice, and I'm singing it right to you, God.
Psalm 101:1

Music is a language that allows us to feel and express our faith deeply and soulfully. Whether it is our experience of grace or our passion for sharing it with others in mission, it is a dimension of life that combines feeling and beauty, theology and experience.
Ross Langmead

Music dances its way through all of Ross's life stages. From family music, Salvo bands, and songsters, Ross began to broaden his interests, and the university years were important in his development. He was an accomplished guitarist by this time despite his arm injury, and enjoyed accompanying and playing along with others. He began singing at youth events with his sister, and nobody was more surprised than Ross when, in his teens, they won the Youth for Christ annual talent quest.

His involvement in Scripture Union events at the beach and with children gave him many opportunities to play and build up his repertoire. There were three parts to the SU movement: Inter School Christian fellowship (of which Ross had been a member and leader at school; it had a summer camping program), Scripture Union (a movement to assist people to read the Bible systematically) and Children's Special Service Mission[1] (involving teams of mainly students running child-oriented and fun Christian activities at beaches). Hundreds of university students became involved in the summer programs, volunteering, being trained, paying their own way, and giving up summer vacation time.

Ross was to have a long association with SU in Victoria. As Theo's coffee shops that catered to older teens became part of these activities, Ross joined up and contributed his music and communication skills over several years.

The Evangelical Union members who met in their dedicated room on the fourth floor of the University's Student Union would strum guitars together, and Ross found that this was a way to meet new members and to encourage those who enjoyed making music. Many of his friends remember those days.

Shirley Frost recalls Ross as "such a gentleman"; he taught her to play guitar and told her that she brought out the best in him. With piano skills and a singing voice, Shirley was part of the informal groups that sang, led worship, and performed from time to time, especially at the weddings of their friends. These musical groups were the precursor to Ross's group, Daddy's Friends, with varying combinations and experimentation with their music.

---

1. Known today as Scripture Union Family Mission.

> He seemed to have a guitar in his hands at every opportunity he could, and we would all gather around him to share in the experiences. We sang a lot of Peter, Paul and Mary, Bob Dylan and many of the protest songs and performers of that era. It was the beginning of Vietnam, conscription and feminism. He was a kind of troubadour leading us into the protests through music. He wrote his own as well and I enjoyed his songs and marvelled at his talent. He wrote and sang a lot about his and our journeys with God and the life of Jesus and we were inspired. (Jenny Marr, 2020)

Inevitably, groups formed from time to time, and Peter Francis remembers several casual combinations with friends in the late sixties. In 1970, Ross's DipEd year, he took Peter and Jill with him on a trip to Heywood in the Western District of Victoria where Ross's sister was teaching, and the ad hoc group did the rounds of schools, youth groups, and churches to great acclaim. The country kids in this small town had never heard anything like these lively, funny, musicians and responded with enthusiasm. Both Peter and Jill would later become members of Daddy's Friends.

> EU, as it was then called, would gather in our dedicated room on the 4th floor of the Student Union building. People would strum guitars and I joined in. Ross was already great at encouraging and making friends of newcomers. I admired his playing, and he offered to teach me a finger style called "double thumbing." He took the time to write out a beginner's guide for me. I still use it to this day. That sort of selfless act was typical of Ross. (Peter Francis 2020)

> I first met Ross in his uni years at a gathering of musicians and song-writers from the three universities in Melbourne. All of us were connected with the universities' Christian clubs at Monash, Melbourne, and the newly formed LaTrobe. We shared the songs we were writing and without a doubt, Ross's strong, straight-forward, classically clear songs sung with freshness and a firm but un-histrionic conviction were a stimulus for me to write my faith story as well. He sang with an authenticity that was like the authenticity of the rocks and the trees—dependably present, solidly real, beautiful in their "is-ness" and re-assuringly "there." (Fay White, 2021)

In January of 1971 and then again in 1972, a group of friends who had enjoyed making music together in the EU days (Ross, Peter, Jill, Shirley, and Greg), sang at the annual national Inter Varsity Fellowship conference, first in Canberra and then the following year in Perth. For the latter event, Ross was commissioned to write the conference theme song:

> *In love came movement in the earth, and waters falling, on the earth,*
> *And grass was growing, from the earth, creation.*
> *Never ending power and justice, and mercy*
> *And show us the way back again, show us the way back again.*
>
> *Leading the way back into your love, into the garden, into your love,*
> *He paid the way back, into your love, this Jesus.*
> *Man he was but God forever, and loved us*
> *And showed us the way back again, showed us the way back again.*
>
> *Oh, give us words now, tell the good news, we need the Spirit.*
> *The things we do now, tell the good news of Jesus.*
> *Take our empty voices, Father, and give us the power of your word on our lips,*
> *To show man the way back again.*

(RL, "The Way Back Again," 1971)

This was the first of his commissioned songs, of which there were to be many over the years. His own copies of songs like this are handwritten and some were never published. They are, however, complete with diagrams of the required chords for those who might want to play the song as well as sing it. Ross was always generous with his music and his website still offers free use of his music for worship purposes.[2] He also changed his language over the years, and later, he was always keen to use inclusive language for gender, which may be another reason that some earlier songs were never published.

From the beginning of the formation of his musical groups, Ross believed that music should draw people in, and be enjoyable; it was a message medium. In contrast to the rock movement, where it was more about instruments and beat than voices, he felt that people needed to hear the words that were being sung. So by musical preference and deliberate choice, his early songs were often folk-style ballads with a strong narrative laced with humor.

Towards the end of 1971, he wrote to some of his friends to tell them he was returning from Wodonga to teach in the city and wanted to start a more serious musical group. It would be a group of four: Ross (guitar), Peter Francis (guitar), Jill Francis (vocal), and Alan Austin (double bass), a

---

2. www.rosslangmead.com.

combination that reflected the enormously popular Seekers. They discussed names and eventually agreed on *Daddy's Friends*. This clever name refers to Paul's letter to the Galatians where the Spirit within enables us to call God "Father," or "Daddy." The name would take them into secular venues, while at the same time give a subtle clue about the center of their message. The group would continue for three fantastic, frenetic years. Peter says:

> Ross had a maturity and vision beyond what the other three of us had. He was already ultra-organized. We would always include prayer and Bible study in our weekly practices. Ross introduced virtually all the songs we learned. Our first gig was at Melbourne Town Hall, which was probably a Youth for Christ Rally with a full house. (Peter Francis, 2020)

Alan Austin writes some background to gospel music in Australia as the context to the emergence of *Daddy's Friends*.

> Prior to the 1970s, gospel singers almost invariably turned up for an event—church service, gospel meeting, Youth for Christ rally, conference or other event—and sang one song, then sat down until later when they might sing one more. That changed when Ross's group accepted invitations only where we could present a bracket for 15 or 20 minutes, incorporating songs and spoken input. This was revolutionary at the time, although it caught on and eventually became routine.
>
> *Daddy's Friends*' concerts were a blend of secular folk songs, reflective spiritual music, and full-on gospel proclamation. That was also radical at the time. Concerts mixed original compositions and covers, progressing from about 30 percent original in the early stages to nearer 60 percent later on, as Ross's opus expanded. One of Ross's most popular blues compositions, "The Motorcycle Song," was a ridiculous story told in fast rhythmic folk-rock style. No message. Just fun.
>
> Humour was interwoven throughout the performances, in the spoken components as well as in some lyrics. "Now I'd like to introduce the group. Alan, this is Jill. Jill, I'd like you to meet Peter. I'm Ross. How do you do?" We would all shake hands with each other. Sounds corny, but it was refreshing back then and a significant shift. (Alan Austin, 2020)

Ross's blues harp was a distinctive part of the folk sound that he loved. Dylan's style grew on him, and he confessed that when he bought his harmonica, he had never heard anyone else play it with a neck brace, except for Dylan, who was also pictured with the brace on a record cover. As he wrote in his "Influence Song," the combination of Bob Dylan, James Taylor, and Paul Stookey was the inspiration for not only his musical style, but also the message.

> After many years searching for life's meaning, Paul found it head on when someone told him about living with Jesus. He says he read the Bible for a year trying to do what it says, but then he accepted Jesus Christ as a living person and gained new power to be a Jesus person. I met him a year or so later after a concert. He is the most beautiful Jesus person you could meet. His musical brilliance, his sensitive humanity, his great intellect and his deep understanding about life—they're all full of action for Jesus. (RL, "Under the Influence," n.d.)

Jill remembers weekly practices with everyone wearing overcoats because it was so cold without heating, and a week's intensive work in a holiday house on Phillip Island where they made lots of progress. They sang four-part vocals and worked them out together as they tackled each song by singing *a capella* and listening to each other. They would be able to tell from each other's smiles of mutual recognition whenever a chord hit "a sweet resonance."

> Mostly I just remember Ross's humility in happily allowing us all credit for the songs and the group when he was the one who gave us the impetus, inspiration and leadership, both spiritually and musically. (Jill Francis, 2020)

Daddy's Friends took off and was in high demand in Christian as well as secular venues. They were promoted as "Victoria's most sought after evangelical musical group—young Baptist university graduates who will thrill you for two hours and keep you singing for two weeks later," stated a poster for a Sydney event. Designated "Gospel folk," they combined their vocal talent with two guitars, a double bass, and the piano, writing much of their own music. They believed that they needed to share as people on the stage, earn the right to be listened to, and not be regarded just as performers.

Each member of *Daddy's Friends* was highly accomplished and educated. Jill was a music teacher with degrees in arts, education, and music, and played percussion, blues harp, and piano, as well as singing. Peter was an articled clerk with distinguished results in his law degree and played twelve-stringed guitar along with singing bass vocals. Alan was an accountancy student with his own business enterprises who worked part-time in schools for Scripture Union. He played the signature bass and piano as well as singing. Ross was completing his MEd while teaching math; he played guitar and blues harp, and sang and composed. Quite a multitalented lineup! Mark Garner joined them sometimes and performed skits, and Alan was the cartoon artist who could illustrate talks and jokes.

From Peter's memory, some of the favorite songs from the heyday of *Daddy's Friends* were "I've Got That Feeling God Is Love" (1970), "Bobby Is the Pillar of the Church" (1970), and "Jesus Who Walks in My Mind" (1973).

> Ev'ry day I hear a new story, I guess you know the things I've been
> When they say believe in me, well I'd like to believe what I'm told.
> But when the truth is unfolded, I think, yes I know you will find
> That the story that lives is the man who died—
> That's Jesus, who walks in my mind.
>
> Everybody's talking about Jesus, I guess it makes him a little bit sad,

Often words, they sound so good, and the hearts, they're sounding so bad.
Oh Jesus, help those who are searching, in the valley of death help them find
That the story that lives is the man who died,
This Jesus, who walks in my mind.

(RL, "Walks," 1973)

Playing and performing stimulated Ross, and the *Daddy's Friends* years were creative and productive. Ross wrote a great number of songs—thirty-three of his hundred or more songs were written by 1973—and themes began to emerge.

It was early days for Theo's coffee shops with Scripture Union in the summer holidays. Theo's started at Anglesea and grew with *Daddy's Friends*' involvement; the group played a central role in the first Tidal River Theo's in 1973. Set up in a tent amongst the campers for about ten days, it was a popular drop-in center where there was little else for teenagers to do at night. The team of volunteers, mostly students who paid their own way, would serve coffee and raisin toast and sit at the tables to chat with whoever came. Hundreds did each night, and music was a big drawcard. Ross led the team, assisted by Alan, and *Daddy's Friends* performed sets through the evening, adding skits and impromptu art, becoming the entertainment that drew the crowds. It was a gently Christian venture, aimed mostly at building friendships and being a listening ear for young people relaxing on vacation. Their music fitted the bill perfectly as they merged folk and gospel music, eschewed Christian jargon, and injected some humor into the program each night.

Another song from 1973 illustrates Ross's efforts to write songs that told the good news in everyday language.

> Well I'm ever so glad the Lord of creation entered the world, it makes me humble.
> Born as a baby, the Lord of creation.
> It blows your mind to think of a perfect man,
> A new way to live, He pointed the way,
> He was killed by the mob, oh what did He say?
> "I will rise again on the very third day"
> Sure as eggs the tomb was empty without delay,
>
> Let's sing about Jesus, let's sing about Jesus
> Let's talk about, Jesus is the way, Oh Jesus is the truth, Jesus is the life,
> Oh, when you're living the true way, It's just like a new day,
> There's nothing I could really say to describe Him or how I feel.

(RL, "Sure as Eggs v. 2," 1973)

In 1974, Ross went to Rosebud to set up Theo's there. By this time, *Daddy's Friends* were a big hit wherever they went and deciding on their commitments was a challenge. All four members of the group were married and working, as well as being involved in their churches; even a weekly practice was hard to keep up. It became apparent that to maintain their quality of music and creativity with so many performances, something would have to give.

Ross began to be invited to lead music workshops, and he loved to teach. Based on their success as a Christian performing/message group, he shared his insights with various groups of musos. One of his programs was called "Practice and Professionalism." He deplored the fact that many saw musos as unreliable, no good at speaking, touchy about time limits, and obsessed with music. He then proceeded to explain the dynamics of a good group and how to form one.

Amidst the constant commitments and pressure to write and find suitable songs, the group wanted to record and keep their music. In partnership with Scripture Union, Ross and the group recorded several records: two under the Theo's banner, called *Ross Langmead Sings Big News*, then *Ross Langmead with Daddy's Friends*. *Daddy's Friends* produced two tapes in early 1974: *Expressing*, and *Daddy's Friends—A Tape We Knocked Up for Our Friends*, for their fans who were keen to get hold of some of their songs.

Later, in the eighties, as part of his time at Westgate Baptist Community, Ross and a team of musicians produced the *On the Road* cassette and accompanying book. It was hugely time-consuming and cost so much that Ross laughingly noted that while others took on a mortgage, he made a tape in a professional studio. The high-end recording and sound world was not as accessible to nonprofessionals or Christian artists in Australia, and it took a great deal of work to make it happen in their spare time.

The group reflected the folk scene of the seventies, and the recorded versions of their music are set in media of another time, but their joy and messages still speak across the years.

Chapter 5

Marriage: 1973 to 1975

It is not your love that sustains the marriage, but from now on, the marriage that sustains your love.

DIETRICH BONHOEFFER

> *Well you came and stole my eyes like very few had done,*
> *And I well recall the night when you first did that to me,*
> *And the more I see the soul in your eyes the more I find*
> *That the stealing has begun, and I love you.*
>
> *Well you went and stole my mind; I just stood aside and stared,*
> *And I like you, but I felt a mile away, a mile below,*
> *And I often let you in, and I was proud you were my friend,*
> *And the stealing had begun, and I love you.*
>
> *Well you came and stole my heart; no-one else had found the way,*
> *And I'm praising God for all the feelings I've not known before,*
> *And I find, with some relief, that I'm just as much a thief,*
> *And the stealing's just begun, and I love you.*
>
> (RL, "Alison Song," 1973)

There was an urban myth around Melbourne that many Christian girls in the city had dated at least one of the Langmead boys at some stage. Ross had made good and lasting friends in his circle and met many wonderful people through his music. While they were still involved in the social scene with the Salvos, Jeanette remembers going on a youth group hayride and being asked by their mother to keep an eye on Ross, who was in his mid-teens. A little way into the ride, Jeanette turned around to check on Ross and discovered him with a lovely girl, a family friend, both covered in hay and clearly having a great time together. There would be quite a few broken hearts before he eventually found the one who won his heart.

Then came the Scripture Union years and Theo's coffee shops, but still Ross had not found the one to be his wife. Talented, friendly, kind, and handsome to boot; it was only a matter of time and intersections before he would meet his life partner. Once he had his precious but troublesome motorcycle and was free to travel, he explored friendships further afield which involved late night rides on the highway and mechanical breakdowns. He was looking for his partner, but wasn't sure just who would be the right one, nor how to decide.

Alison has clear memories of when she first met Ross. She was a member of the Portland Theo's team on the southern Victorian coast, and some of them had taken the young people they had been getting to know in the coffee shop for a New Year weekend camp. Because they had stayed up most of New Year's Eve, most had headed to bed early on the evening of the next day. So when Ross went out to the camp to sing with them, there were only leaders to talk to and share supper with. Alison recalls it as a lively conversation. When Ross returned to Anglesea along the coast where he was based, he told his mate Alan Austin that he had met a girl with lovely eyes.

At the SU teams' reunion later that year, where Ross and Alan were singing together, Ross pointed out the lovely-eyed Alison to his mate and said that whoever could get her phone number first would win a milkshake. Ross won because Alison asked him to sing at her school and he needed her phone number to plan the event. Things, however, did not move quickly at first because twice he had to cancel singing to Alison's class because he was not well. The year went by, and eventually Ross invited Alison to a Buffy Sainte-Marie concert in November to celebrate the end of his BEd exams. Buffy was an indigenous Canadian American singer-songwriter, artist, and social activist—not a surprising choice for Ross.

We don't know whether Ross was shy, unsure, or too busy, or all three, but the next development in his relationship with Alison was not until Easter in 1973, when Ross invited his new friend to go to the annual Belgrave Heights Convention meetings in the hills with him—not a particularly romantic date. As a result of generously offering to pick up two other friends from the city in their car, Ross and Alison talked nonstop for three hours, and a bond was formed. A few days later, Alison felt confident enough to invite him to eat with her family, and she recalls that although he made a good impression, he was a little overwhelmed with the more demonstrative style of the Wright clan, so different from his own family.

In May 1973, while preparing for a folk music camp, Ross invited Alison to a prayer meeting. This took her outside her own friendship circle and she sensed that Ross was awkward and uncommunicative and wondered if there was a problem. She later found out that Ross had made a shortlist of girls who fitted his criteria that he was taking out in rotation, because he was cautious about getting too serious. On that occasion, every single one of them was present in the room. No wonder he felt paralyzed.

Alison, meanwhile, had been that night to visit her "Ukranian nana," who told her she was praying for a good husband for her. On returning home, she sat down and wrote a letter to Ross and asked how he saw their relationship. He replied saying that he would like to get to know her better and began inviting her out. At a *Daddy's Friends* picnic, he reached out and touched her hand for the very first time.

From a quiet beginning, they were soon seeing each other most days for about six weeks, after which time, while on a camp, Ross wrote "The Alison Song." In June, he borrowed John Smith's (God Squad) Harley-Davidson motorbike, took her for a spin during which she encouraged him to go faster, literally and figuratively. That night he asked her to marry him. The shortlist had just shortened dramatically as Ross only had eyes for the girl who had stolen his heart. The engagement party was held in September, and the search for a wedding date began.

They wanted to get married immediately, but could see their full calendars stretching out ahead of them. Alison's mother, Joy, was supportive of an early date, but because of *Daddy's Friends'* gigs, the first free weekend was 1 December. That would give them time to have a short honeymoon and be back in time to lead the new Theo's mission at Rosebud after Christmas.

The only reservation for the excited couple was that Jeanette had become engaged before them and was planning her wedding for January 1974. Was it the right thing to pip her at the post by getting married so quickly? Ross was always thoughtful, so he made a long-distance phone call to his sister at Bible College in Adelaide to ask her permission; there was, of course, no problem, just a deal—that *Daddy's Friends* would still sing at her wedding as promised. And so it all came to pass and there was great excitement in the family as the first two Langmead siblings were married within weeks of each other.

If Ross had left his Salvationist heritage, he had moved into a family with long history in the Baptist church. Alison's father, Alan Wright, was well-known in many circles, but particularly for his period as chaplain at

Carey Baptist Grammar School, and for exploring more authentic forms of religious education. Since he had left the Salvos, Ross had been rather itinerant, often dropping in and sitting in the back of churches across the denominations. He visited the Anglicans, Baptists, and Churches of Christ, and in his teaching year in Wodonga had worshipped with a Baptist family. The intense busyness and commitments of *Daddy's Friends* after that meant that he was mostly performing or traveling at weekends, so he delayed commitment to a denomination.

His engagement to Alison helped him over the line and in August 1973 they began to attend North Carlton Baptist Church. As Ross and Alison considered becoming members, the issue of baptism came up. Philip Hughes remembers the unusual scenario of three very different people applying for membership at the same time: Robert, who had been sprinkled as an adult in a Methodist church; Hazel, baptized as a baby in a Congregational church; and Ross the Salvo, who had never been baptized. Ron, the pastor, called together the church elders and a robust discussion ensued, resulting in Robert's baptism being accepted because he was an adult, but requiring Hazel and Ross to be baptized by immersion to become members. Ross wrestled with this decision. He felt that he had taken his stand for Christ in every way possible in the Army since his childhood, and that the lack of sacraments had not been his own choice.

Ross returned to the leadership and asked whether they would accept him without a baptism, knowing that this created a dilemma for the church. To his surprise, they agreed to his request. Ross responded and told them that, in that case, he was prepared to be baptized. So Ross and Hazel were baptized on the same day in September. Ross wrote a special song, which Alison sang for him, with Alan on piano and Jill on bass.

> *When you say, "I am a Christian," you're not saying a light thing.*
> *You say to God, "I love you and I'll do, and I'll do anything."*
> *You say, "I'll leave the crowd." You say, "I'll not be proud."*
> *You say, "I'm not ashamed of the Lord."*
>
> *When you enter into the waters, you leave the past behind you,*
> *Just as Christ was buried and raised again, to the glory of God.*
> *You say, "Do you all see that Jesus sets me free?*
> *I'm baptised in the Spirit of the Lord."*
>
> *When you set your feet upon a new path, the way is very different.*
> *We're promised hard times but we'll face them with him there.*

60 | LIVING FOR SHALOM

> *The wonder of this thing would drive a man to sing,*
> *To sing to the glory of the Lord, the glory of the Lord.*

(RL, "Baptism Song," 1973)

The rest of the year flew by as Ross wound up teaching Math at East Preston, and Alison resigned from her teaching job at Preshil School. This was a time for making life choices—careers, churches, relationships, study, and life directions were to be negotiated in their coming together. Alison needed a change from the pressures of teaching and Ross wanted to pursue the academic path, so they made some big decisions together. Meanwhile there was a wedding to plan, a summer Theo's to prepare and lead, a Bachelor of Education for Ross to complete, and the ongoing commitment of his music group.

They chose the William Carey Chapel for the wedding, and Alison's father, Alan, led the ceremony. He had played a significant part in the design of the new chapel, and the setting fitted their desire for informality.

Family and friends gathered, delighted to celebrate with the couple in a service that was radical for its style at that time. Ross was resplendent in a safari suit and Alison's beautiful auburn hair was adorned with flowers. They were supported by Ross's brother, Leslie, and Alison's sister-in-law, Marijke; the three other members of *Daddy's Friends* sang "Hallowed be Thy Name," which were the words above the doors of the chapel, taken from Coventry Cathedral and set to music by Ross. The other music was quite traditional, but the vows were rewritten for simplicity: they each promised to love, comfort, honor, and serve each other, to be faithful, and to love unconditionally.

There was much joy for everyone, and the open reception was appropriately informal for the seventies. *Daddy's Friends* trio wrote a fun song to the tune of Australian folk song "Bound for Botany Bay" with verses like:

> *There were many who thought that I'd never fall*
> *For they said that I looked such a fright*
> *In my cap, beard, guitar, Theo's overalls*
> *But they're wrong, for I've just met Miss (W)right.*

(*Daddy's Friends*, December 1973)

The photos taken with Carey Chapel behind them soaring to the sky are a kind of metaphor: the sky was the limit. Those gathered to share and witness their joining in marriage all agreed that Ross and Alison had found each other in every sense, and that together, they would not only grow, but also contribute to the world and to their growing community.

They enjoyed a brief honeymoon in Merimbula before it was time to return for Christmas with the family and to lead the Theo's coffee shop in Rosebud before gathering again for his sister's wedding. Their married life had begun the way it would continue—with service and singing.

As Ross recommenced life in inner-city Parkville as a full-time student, the newly married couple moved into a flat at Ridley Anglican College, where Ross was to be a tutor. Well-placed in the education precinct adjacent to the University of Melbourne, they enjoyed the experience of living in a theological college and made friends that would last a lifetime. Alison was now the breadwinner, having upskilled herself with a secretarial course after finishing as a teacher; she obtained a series of jobs with SU and other organizations, settling around the corner at the Asian Bureau. She looked forward to working with the Jesuit organization as her teaching, faith, and leanings towards justice would fit well with the involvement with schools and churches in poorer countries.

Ross was fully occupied with his Master of Education studies and what would be the biggest year for *Daddy's Friends*. Combined with involvement in the nearby Carlton SU children's work, a round of family and friends' weddings, and a wide range of commitments, Ross's regular family letters recount nonstop events and people. In June 1974, his parents decided to return as missionaries to Taiwan, taking Grace, their youngest, with them. This departure marked the end of the Langmead family unit in Melbourne as there was now no home base and the older five children were living independently.

It also marked the first of Ross's family letters: he wrote regularly to his parents in Taiwan and to his sister in Adelaide, using carbon paper and adding personal notes. As the years went by and the family remained scattered, letters went back and forth between them all. The folder that exists today of every letter that Ross ever wrote is an invaluable account of facts, dates, Australian politics, world events, church history, stories from his community life, and his personal reflections on just about everything. As an example, one of his early letters commences this way:

> Dear Mum, Dad and Graciegirl (and P and J)
>
> How are our much loved ones? We are keen to hear how your first few days went (in Taipei). We think of you lots of times and pray for you every day, DF have adopted you in prayer too. We are very well and happy as ever. God is good to us and life would have to be a lot worse before we complained. Alison is a fantastic person to live with (and she insists that I write that "every day she is excited by the joy of living with Ross Langmead" Good grief). (RL, Family letter, July 1974)

Then would follow several typed foolscap pages of all kinds of news and stories, punctuated with cartoons, jokes, and wry comments about the latest family dating exploits, or car and bike bingle stories in the wider family. Combined with the other letters from siblings, this extraordinary record of family life is a rich source and confirmation of memories. For some of the family, hindsight arouses memories of feeling pressured to keep up such communication; the habit began with Jean in boarding school in China, where as a child, she was required to write home weekly. She then wrote every week to each of her adult children when they left home with news of everyone in the family; the replies from the children were not always so frequent. The reality is that once emails took over, we no longer have those records captured by letters.

Ross embarked on his Master of Education, which would focus on the philosophy of religion, a direction he had chosen after succeeding in this area of high interest for him. The reading and preparation took much of the first year, but by October he had written the draft of the first chapter. The timing seemed fortuitous, as the long-awaited Russell Report on Religious Education in Victorian Schools was released that month. It recommended that trained teachers employed by the government teach religious education, which was where Ross was heading with his thesis. In his own future, he was looking past the actual teaching of religion in schools to the need for teachers' colleges to train the teachers that would be needed for this subject: that is where he could see his role, a strategic one for Christians in education. He felt that the danger of the system was that if religion were not taught clearly and correctly at tertiary level, it would also be "fuzzy" at secondary level. He finally decided on his title: "The Epistemological Status of Religious Belief and its Implications for Education."

He set out to explore how we should educate in religion, and to find which part of religion causes the most difficulty in education. The associated question would be to inquire into which part of religion is the most suitable for philosophical consideration. As religious language, beliefs, rituals, and practices all presuppose beliefs, they need to be expressed in religious language, both systematically and reflecting the range of different meanings. Because truth is so difficult to discern in this arena, philosophers have traditionally argued that religion cannot be part of education. In eight complex chapters, Ross set out to propose a different argument:

> I will argue that religious belief interprets experience in ways not radically unlike comprehensive scientific theories, and that evidence and rationality play an important part in deciding its adequacy. I will defend its cognitive status and argue that its epistemological status (that is, whether it can be known to be true) is neither defective nor radically different from that of other types of belief.
>
> If the argument is successful, education in religion is possible. It will consist of helping a student to become more reasonable and understanding in the sphere of religion. It will present religious belief as possibly true or false. It will develop awareness of the implied dimension of religious experience as well as develop knowledge and rationality in considering explicit religious phenomena.[1]

His recommendations for religious education followed those of Professor Ninian Smart, who would soon become his supervisor in his next thesis. Religious studies:

1. Must transcend the informative;
2. Should not evangelize, but initiate into understanding the meaning of, and into questions about, the truth and worth of religion;
3. Need not exclude a committed approach;
4. Should help in understanding history and other cultures; and
5. Should emphasize the descriptive, historical side of religion.[2]

---

1. Langmead, *Epistemological Status*.
2. Smart, *Secular Education*, 97.

By this time, Ross had his eye on the next step: he had worked through education and philosophy; it was time for a serious exploration of theology. As a graduate, he would be able to enroll in the post-graduate Bachelor of Divinity with the Melbourne College of Divinity. His thoughts, however, were expanding to think about studying overseas, and he spent the next year following through on this dream. On the basis that three years spent doing theology might be better spent overseas getting a broader vision and better scholarship, he began applying to Harvard, Yale, Union, Fuller, and Princeton to do a possible Master of Divinity, and to the American universities, Harvard, Yale, Princeton, Columbia, Chicago and Emory, perhaps to complete a doctorate.

This was a serious decision with huge commitment and implications for their next life stage, especially financially. The practical barrier to all these plans was money; he would need to look for funding, and that was almost more daunting than making academic applications.

Part of this momentous decision was also whether Ross would pursue ordination in the Baptist Church. He was not sure then, and still not sure decades later about the validity of the ordination model. At this stage, he could not see himself as a pastor. He was clear, however,

> that God wants me to be a teacher in general, and of Christianity in particular. That still leaves the range wide, from lecturing in Religious Education, through lecturing in theology, through more grass roots pastoral work and straight evangelistic situations. (RL, Family letter, August 1974)

In October 1974, he sat for the American Graduate Record exams, essential for admission into US university post-graduate programs. The results of these were used to interpret his Australian academic record, so that his scores could be sent to three universities of his choice, and would show where Ross sat by percentile rankings in the world. That would help American colleges that were unable to make head or tail of Australian university results—who knows what they teach in those educational institutions Down Under?

When his results came back in January, they were world-class. His scores were better than 91 percent of candidates in the Philosophy Advanced Achievement Test, taken by those wishing to do post-graduate work in philosophy. In the aptitude test, taken by all candidates, his scores were better than 95 percent in verbal ability, and 99 percent of candidates in quantitative ability. In the world. Those results would have walked him into Yale or Harvard the next day, but money was still the big obstacle. He needed to have more in the bank or from other scholarships before they would award him any financial support. He began to plan to commence four BD subjects at home at Whitley College, while at the same time finishing his MEd. They would be relying on Alison's income for a while yet.

The intellectual and faith journey was not, however, without some road bumps for Ross. He tells his family about the doubts that arose in his philosophical explorations:

> I must admit that I have been tested recently, reading towards my thesis. I only get perplexed when a genuine problem presents itself in religious belief, such as the function of petitionary prayer. But it is not easy to find answers. I have been exposed to well-argued positions which claim that the main beliefs we have about God are incomprehensible, and when I need well written replies to help the honest debate in my mind, I do not always find them. The arguments are not always easy to follow, and so not easy to refute. Although I know we can never understand everything, and must live with some contradictions and even embrace mysteries. There are times when the problems with a view of how things are, seem to outweigh the rightness of it.
>
> My main areas of concern are not new problems: what prayer does, how to face unjustified suffering, and why God's "body," the church, is qualitatively different from other organizations. Anyway, I am working through these things in various ways, and hope to regain a positive perspective again. I would say that the main thing going for my faith is that I can find no other set of beliefs which has a message of hope for man. I know the quality of life possible in a Christian family and marriage. I don't see it in any other motivation.
>
> Alison continues to be a source of caring concern for not only me but all who come by this way. I am more convinced than ever of the profound influence on a man's direction made by his wife. When I have intellectual doubts on Christian things, her faith is a powerful strength. (RL, Family letter, November 1974)

Solid support from family and friends saw Ross through this time of wondering. His father wrote him a long pastoral letter of encouragement which Ross valued greatly. Alison's parents met with him and discussed the issue of prayer; he still struggled with unanswered prayer, but acknowledged that in the big picture, God is in control and he was at peace with that. He continually had to remind himself to place less faith in reasoning ability and more faith in faith. The troublesome area of how prayer works would be explored more fully in his next thesis the following year.

It is interesting that he only wrote one song in 1974. The demands of study, marriage, and the music group were high, and it is possible that the intellectual grappling squeezed his creativity during this period. He wrote the song for his brother Howard's wedding on his favorite topic of "Love":

> *We feel it growing stronger every day, It's sort of wider, deeper in a way.*
> *From deep within our hearts we want to say, it's love which we have found.*
>
> *And you already know the feeling too, nothing is a bind for you to do,*
> *You'll keep on finding depths of love quite new, your love will not be bound.*
>
> *We tumble out our praise to God our King, to him the promise of our love we bring,*
> *From deep within our hearts we want to sing, his love is all around.*

(RL, "Love," 1974)

Invitations were flying in for *Daddy's Friends* from youth groups, coffee shops, churches, and music events. Although he had made his decision to join North Carlton Baptist, he was seldom present because he was out and about with *Daddy's Friends* events. His new church had generously supported the group as missionaries, giving them both financial and prayer backing. This is his account of an event:

> Last night we did a youth service at Glen Waverley Meths where 250–300 turned up, all ages, many unchurched and vibrant in atmosphere. We work at a youth service which mixes unorthodoxy (applause for God), orthodoxy (a good old hymn straight), formality (read responses and read prayers from congregation) and informality (choruses, jokes, enthusiasm, preaching without notes and lectern). Last night was a winner with all types being provoked to reverence and enthusiasm. The after-church coffee shop was as usual good for our popularity if not big on communication. (RL, Family letter, August 1973)

The *Daddy's Friends* weekend in Adelaide in September 1974 was typical of the frenetic pace of life for the group. Ross's sister and brother-in-law had arranged quite a schedule for them: on Friday they went to multiple classes at a school, lunchtime and Scripture classes at a secondary college, followed by a visit to a remand home for troubled girls. The next day was a trip to an institution for delinquent boys and a Pentecostal outreach that night, followed by three sets at a Lutheran coffee shop. Sunday morning was a huge kids' rally at the Anglican church, a muso workshop in the afternoon, an appearance at a town hall rally, and finally an after-church coffee shop. Still apparently able to function, they caught a 7 a.m. flight back to Melbourne the next morning and went to work. The Tasmanian and Sydney trips were similarly packed with back-to-back events, squeezed between the work and home elements of their lives.

Ross's careful handwritten records of all their performances show that the mix of songs was tailored to the ethos of each event. At the Latrobe University Genesis Folk and Rock Festival, they sang twenty-six songs—a mix of Australian, justice, and popular songs, laced with Ross's gentlest songs of faith, like "God is Love," "Many Things," and "Bobby." At the Moe Christian Revival Crusade meetings, fifteen songs were performed over the weekend, all of them with clear gospel content, which would have been the request of Ross's second cousin, a Pentecostal pastor.

They sang fun songs at twenty-first birthday parties for friends, and love songs at weddings. The "Motorcycle Song" always went down well at schools, and coffee shop gigs usually included "Big Blue Frog," "Daddy Sang Bass," "Tarriers," and "Yesterday," interspersed amongst the carefully-chosen God songs. They almost always included "God Is Love," a round that would draw in the whole audience as they sang the circular words in four parts in a haunting minor key:

> *God is love and love is giving*
> *God gives me the life I have*
> *The life I have leads me to singing*
> *Sing that God is love.*

(RL, "God Is Love," 1971)

The records show that they were able to have the longer performing slots that they wanted, often multiple sets. That allowed them to change the mood and style of their songs and combinations of voices and instruments. Jill, for example, was a lead vocal, but also played piano and double bass, as did Alan. Pete often took the lead singing the Australian songs and Ross combined his singing and guitar with the Dylan-style harmonica. Theo's coffee shops were a major commitment for them; they would sing over sixty songs over seven nights, combining that with serving coffee and toast and chatting with the hundreds who came.

Daddy's Friends were popular with children, and they performed frequently at schools, rallies, Belgrave Heights Convention kids' programs, and children's homes. The simplicity of Ross's songs combined with spontaneous humor created an immediate bond with young and old alike.

For all the good responses, at times, Ross sometimes felt that he was well-received by everyone except his parents. They had dreamed of his future using his many talents for God, but things did not seem to be going to plan. Ross had made a commitment to become a Salvation Army officer when he was a teenager but had taken a different path. It was initially a disappointment for his parents that he had not become one of the next generation of dedicated Salvo officers.

When he began singing in all sorts of venues that were not necessarily churches or Christian in any way, Oliver had concerns about these decisions. Alan Austin tells of performing with Ross in an Eastern suburbs coffee shop in the early days and recalls that Ross was deeply hurt when his dad referred to these places as "dirty dives." It was a strange blind spot in someone who, in the spirit of founder William Booth, had a Salvo heart for reaching people who were not in churches, and yet was critical of Ross being involved outside the walls of churches. We can only surmise that these feelings came from concern that Ross would stray from the path of Christian service. Eventually, Oliver and Jean would be as proud of Ross as his many fans and became used to being introduced as "Ross's parents," although on one occasion, Oliver stood tall and replied that in fact, Ross was his son.

Significantly, the written record of gigs ends in July 1974. Life was taking over; married life was even more complicated for all the members of the group with their own commitments. Ross was feeling the pressure of needing more songs and time to rehearse, and by mid-1974 a decision had to be made. Jill was pregnant and it seemed to be a natural end to a wonderful phase. They all knew that to continue at the level of performance they had reached as a group was going to take more time and creativity than they could give. It was time to finish *Daddy's Friends* as a performing group.

The last two performances were Scripture Union events: a record was cut with a planned launch at an SU kids' rally when a thousand people would be at the launch of "*Daddy's Friends* and You." This time the record was produced by ANZEA and featured four songs: "Take a Good Look," "Jelly Bean Land," "Ballad of Jesus," and "Bursting to Say." There was actually a fifth song billed as "The Shortest Song in the World," which said ". . . yeah."

The very last event for the group was the commissioning service for the volunteer workers for the SU summer program. It was December 1974 and Jill was eight months pregnant. Ross was pursuing his Master of Education, newly married and leading a Theo's team. Something had to give, and, sadly for the Christian music scene of the seventies, it was *Daddy's Friends*. This was Scripture Union's tribute to the group:

> Their initial appearance proved to be only a beginning, for since then Daddy's Friends have appeared over 300 times. They've spent most weekends performing in coffee houses, rallies, folk/rock festivals, children's shows, and taking part in church services. They've travelled to country areas and they've gone interstate. A gifted group, they have combined their music with drawing, speaking, teaching and discussion—using whatever medium would get people thinking about their message.
>
> SU has been honoured to enjoy a close working relationship with Daddy's Friends and over the summer period they have helped at Theo's missions, CSSMs and ISCF camps. And now Daddy's Friends are breaking up. Three years is a fair slice of time to have all your weekends away from home. When the group was formed, it was recognized that such concentrated effort could be for a limited period only.
>
> The Francis family is about to grow. Ross and his wife Alison are looking to involvement in Carlton and Ross is completing his Master of Education with theology in mind. Alan will be working in accountancy and hopes to combine SU work with local ministry.
>
> The group's last appearance will be at SU's Commissioning Service on Saturday December 7th in Wesley Church where we will say our goodbyes and thankyous to Daddy's Friends. (*SU News*, December 1974)

One of the songs on this record was to become a firm favorite with children in many places. Even as early as 1974, Ross wanted to highlight justice in a children's song.

> *Jesus Christ was a Jewish man who lived a long time ago;*
> *Imagine a perfect man if you can and you've got him in your mind just so.*
> *Jesus Christ is the King of the world, and the Good Book says that he loves me*
> *Jesus Christ is the King of the World and he says that he loves me.*
>
> *He got angry in the church where the shopkeepers sat with their tables, a hundred or more,*
> *He tipped up their tables, said, "This is God's house," 'cause they cheated both the rich and the poor.*
> *Jesus Christ is the King of the world and the Good Book says that he loves me*
> *Jesus Christ is the King of the world and he says that he loves me.*
>
> (RL, "Ballad of Jesus," 1973)

And so it was that the group finished, leaving a legacy of many unforgettable songs and experiences. More than that, however, they had pioneered a new way of sharing the good news through music, or at least an old way in a contemporary style.

During these early years of marriage, Ross and Alison became involved in an urban version of beach mission, based at the church in Carlton. Known as Notlrac (Carlton spelt backwards), the kids' club drew large numbers of children from the surrounding Housing Commission areas in the suburb. It started with a summer mission in 1974–75 in which Alison was involved, and was so successful that it was decided to continue the style through the year as an on-going kids' club at the church. Ross and Alison committed to the venture as their main involvement, and Ross was appointed as the leader.

> Although I don't feel very confident, we are excited about the possibilities and I am glad to be back in children's work again. It's a great team and the church look like supporting it well. We are going to teach over a 10–15 week cycle and repeat themes with different stories to back up the points. The overall theme is the Kingdom of God = God's people, in God's place, under God's rule. (RL, Family letter, January 1975)

By this time Ross had moved out of Ridley College to nearby Brunswick and his life was well and truly based in the inner suburbs. Also, a long tradition of sharing their home had begun. All three of his brothers were living close by, and there were many house moves, both of locations and house mates. As the married couple of one year settled into life after *Daddy's Friends*, fixed on their main ministry, and moved into their first proper home, the creativity returned, and Ross and Alison wrote a song together. It was the first for some time and their first as a couple. Faced with singing a repeat song at a friend's wedding, Alison sat down and wrote "What is this springing?," which Ross described as "bluegrass style with close three-part harmony and gutsy voices and simple chords."

> *What is this springing, this leap of our hearts?*
> *What is this marriage of two separate people?*
> *The meeting and seeing, the learning and giving*
> *The knowing and trusting, the love of a friend.*

(Ross and Alison Langmead, "What Is This Springing?," 1975)

In the absence of any positive responses to his applications for overseas study, he had enrolled at Whitley College to commence his BD with four subjects alongside finishing his MEd thesis. He plunged into the New Testament Greek summer school in preparation. This was Ross's first involvement at the Baptist College, and the founding principal, Rev. Dr. Mervyn Himbury, was then running the college. Ross described him as:

> a genial Welsh chap, knowledgeable in Church History, and runs a free sort of show, claiming to have as few rules as possible. He speaks in extremes and can be annoying in his blanket statements, but is stimulating in discussion. (RL, Family letter, March 1975)

It was the dean who was to become an important influence in Ross's journey. Athol Gill oversaw the welfare of all one hundred and fifty students, and had studied theology for ten years. According to Ross, he was a specialist in just about everything. Ross was excited by the way he applied his insights to everyday life and resonated with his involvement with a youth drop-in center.

> He has good ideas on the church and how it must adapt for the twentieth century. I'm not sure how he will be accepted by the Baptists, as they are rather conservative, and he is rather radical. The thrust of the new idea is the NT concept of each Christian exercising the gifts God gives him. So one might preach, another might visit. I think I will really enjoy my contact with Athol. (RL Family letter, March 1975)

Ross, however, was still hoping to go overseas, and that made him feel unsettled. If he gained acceptance, he planned to drop everything, finish his thesis and go in time for the northern hemisphere academic year. His preferences were now Lancaster (PhD in RE), Yale and Fuller (MDiv), in that order. Life became a complicated limbo land of scenarios in two different countries, not made any clearer when acceptances arrived for the latter two prestigious American colleges, Yale and Fuller. Although the financial landscape was still unclear, it was finally definite that they would be going somewhere, and Ross withdrew from theology at Whitley to concentrate on finishing his thesis in time. An American stay would be for three years, a major undertaking in every way.

When in doubt, take a walk. That was Ross's philosophy, so he and Alison decided to walk at Mount Feathertop in the Victorian high country with six other friends, enjoying the stunning scenery, the rhythm of walking, and time to think. Ross knew that this decision would be another important pivot in his life story, but the right direction was not yet obvious. He did not want to take a wrong fork in the road, as they had done on their walk going down Diamantina Spur and had had to come all the way back up.

The year was a mixture of study, work, ministry, and family. Notlrac, the kids' club was a great success, although the children from the surrounding high-rise flats were rather wild.

"Some of these kids have only known the law of the concrete jungle, and it really tries your patience," wrote Ross. Nevertheless, they took over thirty kids away on their first camp, commenting that the team "outwitted and befriended them." Although they had broken windows and lost a kid at the police station, it was an overwhelming success. He knew now that he would be leaving later in the year, so began to work towards finding another leader. But there was still no news, except that Yale would not be able to help them financially. Ross decided to try again at Lancaster, applying for a one-year MA, instead of doing a doctorate in three years. This looked much more practical, and they took the decision to go under their own steam.

And then it came—a telegram, no less, from Professor Ninian Smart in Lancaster. He finally had a place in the university of his first choice in the whole world, contingent on successfully finishing his MEd. As that was always the plan, they finally knew the next step: they would travel to the UK in September. It had been worth the wait and the patient enquiries, and once it happened, Ross knew deep down what he wanted. It would be to study philosophy of religion first under a world-class professor, then a return to commence theology back in Melbourne. The decision was made, the offer accepted, and Ross started planning and making lists.

> I plan to study History of Buddhism, History of Islam, Philosophy of Religion and write a thesis in one of those areas. It is exactly what I want to do where I want to do it. (RL, Family letter, May 1975)

Ross pushed on with a tight timetable with his thesis, knowing he had to allow time for it to be typed—there were no computers back in the day. He wrote a family letter in June that was set out like a thesis with numbered paragraphs 1.1 right through to 4.1. He found out that there would be a very relevant conference in Lancaster before the term started, so that added to the excitement. The countdown was on, sorting and packing began around the thesis timetable, flights were booked, and arrangements fell into place, including a new leader for Notlrac. They were cutting ties and were ready for the next stage.

Chapter 6

Travel: 1975 to 1976

I am not the same, having seen the moon shine on the other side of the world.
MARY ANNE RADMACHER

Travel and change of place impart new vigour to the mind.
SENECA

After the long wait, the last weeks before departure were hectic. Ross and Alison's gear had to be ready to be shipped to Lancaster, using ten tea-chests to accommodate enough to set up a simple apartment; the rest they would carry with them to make do for a couple of months. What was left was lent out, given away, or stored. There is something very liberating about minimizing one's stuff to travel, and cutting ties with all the involvements at home. Ross did not even take his precious guitar, planning to buy and sell one over there. They were traveling light on this expedition.

Ross somehow managed to finish his thesis while packing up his life and handed it over to the typist with great relief. They planned a few days in Adelaide with Jeanette and Peter, which provided some rest and relaxation before departure, then returned to submit the three typed copies of his thesis before moving out of their home. That was it. Ross wrote:

> I have regained my balance after a week of intense pride in the thesis. I now see that it is one master's degree amongst thousands, and realise how little I know, and am content to leave it

behind and build on it. I consider it a very worthwhile thing to have done because it took me through many questions I would have had to face sometime. My basic faith in God is firmer for the experience, because it has stood intellectual fire; my ideas about specific doctrines are more tentative because I have not had time to decide which are right amidst a barrage of arguments for and against.

Debates seem to hinge most especially on differences in interpreting scripture, so I am getting keener by the moment to study theology. The whole business of sorting out what life is about will never end, but I feel I have de-bugged a few of the most disturbing questions. Their existential importance has been great—I can't ignore my doubts as others often do. I can see that it is both an advantage and disadvantage. (RL, Family letter, August 1975)

It would be December before he received his H2A honors thesis results. The examiner's report was positive but pointed out a flaw in the argument: Ross argued that "religion should be taught as possibly true or false," but based on his research, he should have included "meaningless" as another possibility. "Ah well," was his philosophical response, and wondered why this had not been picked up by his supervisor. They commented on the wide reading, good construction, clear writing and "philosophical originality of a high order." The first master's degree was filed away as he headed off to commence the second, which was just as daunting.

With flights booked and farewells planned, they moved in with Alison's parents prior to departure. Suddenly they received a message to say that their budget student flight had been rescheduled for a week earlier: Ross stayed up all night finishing his thesis, and they found themselves recovering in a Bangkok hotel on 1 September while their friends back in Australia had their farewell bush dance without them. The great adventure had begun.

Picking up camping equipment and a hire car, they set off for a week's drive following the coast around beautiful Wales, just drinking in the spectacular scenery. A few tourist days in London and then they arrived in Lancaster in time for Ross's philosophy conference, which was a mixed experience. It was worthwhile to meet the heavies and gain confidence, but some sessions were led by DZ Phillips, the Welsh scholar who headed up a school of thought that Ross had shot down in his thesis. Another "Ah well."

They were deciding how to fill the last days before term started when Ross suddenly became ill. Excruciating pain and vomiting turned out to be appendicitis, and before he knew it, he was trying out the National Health

Service and undergoing surgery. Not quite the start he was hoping for, but he was grateful for good care and a quick recovery. Always one to utilize his time, his letter recounting his hospital experiences has an unusual number of corrections as he was teaching himself to touch-type while he recovered, hoping to increase his speed before the course started. His goal was to exceed thirty wpm, which was his two-finger speed. With a long academic career still ahead of him, he rightly figured that he may as well use all ten fingers, which he did for the rest of his life.

Lancaster University is a collegiate public research university set in the countryside outside the city just twenty miles from the Lake District. In today's rankings, it comes eighteenth of the hundred UK universities included in a league table. Built in the sixties, the innovative campus was equipped with shops, sports facilities, pubs, and banks, all designed to integrate social, residential, and teaching areas. Ross and Alison were accommodated in Bowland Tower and appreciated the central heating and covered walkways of the colleges, especially through the stormy winter that was coming—one storm smashed their windows on the thirteenth floor. Ross and Alison began to attend various groups, including the Christian Union and some church services:

> Unfortunately the rock band was so out of tune, overloading their amps and murdering "There is a Green Hill" to "House of the Rising Sun," that I had to leave the Chaplaincy Centre (Anglican/non-Conformist) service. We liked the two pretty sane and unpretentious ministers (though they looked like a pair of priests out of the TV show Gas and Gaiters). We didn't like the "more Anglican than Methodist" format of the service however. Our alternative is the Baptists in the town, who are friendly, but oh so conservative and even simplistic (might be a bit harsh) that I don't know I could listen to the sermons. (RL, Family letter, October 1975)

Sunday worship would be a challenge, but there was plenty of other stimulation, with students from all over the world along with top class teachers. Ross was one of three studying Buddhism, and the only student who took on studying Islam. In addition to comparative religions and phenomenology, he hoped to choose a topic that would ensure that Professor Ninian Smart was his supervisor. With thirty-five books bought to start the course, his touch-typing improving, and new warm coats purchased for them both, he had the essentials to dive in. Before long he was up to his neck in reading and essays, and bewailing the fact that he knew so little about Islam. In fact, he was swallowing his pride because, although he was confident that he would pass, he was not sure if he could live with anything less than honors, like he had achieved with his first master's.

The flat they lived in only cost them $14 a week, but with food and weekend trips their finances were stretched. Ross recorded that it was costing them around eighteen a week to live, apart from rent, tuition, and holidays. Alison was enjoying joining in some voluntary activities but began to look for a secretarial job to find them some income. One that she applied for had seventy applicants. It was not going to be easy, but she finally managed to get a teaching job in a Catholic school, where it took some time before the little Lancastrians could understand anything she said. Although it was more demanding than she was looking for in a temporary job, the school was very relational, and she fitted in well and was much loved by the children and staff.

Committed as they were to community living, it was not all smooth in the accommodation they shared with two other couples. One couple seemed insensitive to the needs of the others and there were robust discussions from time to time about the kitchen. Ross and Alison found it hard to understand the lack of consideration, but had to make do and try not to hold grudges. These things kept Ross grounded while he wrestled with, for example, a seven-thousand-word essay on the work of a recent phenomenologist of religion using the writer's personal papers; when completed, it had a hundred and eight footnotes. The essays kept coming:

> 2.2.1 I think I'll write on why the Buddha deliberately left many questions unanswered, and deliberately leave it unanswered; and on the Muslim theologian who said that all speculation and argument was futile in response to God's revelation, and present it in a brief paragraph. Ah well, Alison loves me. (RL, Family letter, November 1975 [in a letter that caricatured essay style, complete with numbered paragraphs, footnotes and references])

Despite his reservations he quickly became involved in Christian activities, becoming the interim chairman for the Christian Association, developing a friendship with the Methodist chaplain, leading Bible studies, and joining in with the musicians. Ross used a two-dollar bush guitar for a while, and eventually bought a good one that he could sell when they left. He needed a decent instrument to feel genuinely happy in his music, whatever anyone else was playing. Significantly, he wrote no new songs during this period. There simply wasn't the time or the creative space.

> DF spoilt me for standards—our one or two practices each three weeks for the folk music service seem so sloppy and inadequate

(all amateurs find worse amateurs impossible to work with—I'm often no exception.) (RL, Family letter, November 1975)

The Brits are often amazed at Australians' capacity to cover vast distances on their overseas adventures: Ross and Alison fitted that stereotype. To save money, they often hitchhiked on their weekend excursions to explore the area, and even into town for weekly shopping. Their good friends, Bruce and Jean Rumbold, were in Manchester, so that was a frequent destination. Everything seemed so accessible, with distances much shorter to all sorts of wonderful places in contrast to long trips in Australia. They once caught four rides—covering two hundred and fifty miles in seven hours—to get home from London, having taken the tube to the outskirts to start the trip. A trip to Oxford in the freezing cold took them nine hours and nine rides door to door, one with a truck driver playing James Taylor's "Sweet Baby James" on repeat in his cozy cabin.

They spent a wintry Christmas 1975 with friends and were treated to the full British celebratory meal. In a hired car they explored Yorkshire, taking in Durham (Ross was very disturbed to find that the cathedral cost $9,000 a month to maintain) and then Hadrian's Wall in the dark, and Wordsworth's Lake District in the rain on their way back. Their British experience bank was filling up and overflowing. There was even peace in the shared accommodation as they all moved to mutual acceptance and enjoyed a meal out together. All required essays were submitted, and the mail was full of cards and greetings. The year finished well as they passed their second wedding anniversary a long way from home.

In 1976, Ross began exploring Buddhism. Professor Smart was back from leave, meaning Ross could be immersed in phenomenology and problems in contemporary Christian belief—of which there were apparently many. He was pleased to receive a rather mysterious grade of A-- for his essay on Islam: "a gallant attempt to clarify some of the most intricate problems of Muslim theology. A well-discussed and balanced essay." Meanwhile, the in-jokes ran like this: Jesus asked his disciples, "Whom do you say that I am?" One said, "Some say you are the Ground of Being, others the Absolute, and others the Existential Thou of the I-Thou encounter." And Jesus said, "Huh?"

Between weekend excursions to attempt long walks in the Lake District with friends (he was impressed that the British were better equipped for a day walk than many Aussies heading into the bush for weeks), playing competitive squash again, keeping up the communication with friends and family at home, singing at a local psychiatric hospital, getting major essays in on time, attending various boozy functions, taking in the Mystery Plays in York, and maintaining life in general, there was not much down time. By now, Ross was on first-name terms with Ninian, and enjoying highlights like a lecture from New Testament Professor CFD Moule. He was churning through the workload, with the final exams for coursework getting closer.

There was always the incentive of the next sightseeing trip to keep Ross's head down with his study deadlines. The next plan on the horizon was a car trip to Scotland's rugged west coast with new friends over the Easter break. Staying in hostels, they wove their way up through Glasgow and by Loch Lomond to charming Oban, ready to take the ferry trip to Mull and then to the Holy Island of Iona. After meandering through the rugged scenery of the wild northwest, they tackled climbing the 1,340 meters of Ben Nevis before returning through Edinburgh. Ross didn't quite finish his Islam essay, but was content with 85 percent from Ninian for his phenomenology assignment. He was able to leave it behind for a few days and be recreated in the beautiful north. They didn't get as far as the Inverness area, where tradition has it that the Ross clan fought the Vikings.

It was just as well they had an exciting plan for Easter, because on the home front, they felt keenly that significant family events were unfolding without them. Ross set the alarm in the early hours of 3 April so that he could wake and think of his brother Les's marriage to Grace. He was impatient for the first photos of his first niece, Naomi, born to the Woods in April. Even with multiple accounts in family letters and photos from every angle, they felt a little homesick and started to look at routes home. It was probably just as well they had not taken on a three-year course in America. After traveling around Europe with their friends, they would fly on, meeting Oliver and Jean in Taipei, Jeanette and Peter in Indonesia via Thailand and Malaysia, with SE Asian Buddhism as a focus. The return itinerary started to come together.

There was, however, the small matter of a dissertation to tackle before they finished. Ross's decision was that it would be on the subject of "A Phenomenological Approach to Christian Prayer"—why not do something easy, like tackling his personal chestnut? As he handed in his last essay, he was determined to enjoy the journey and not to be anxious.

> An aspect of Buddhism is very helpful here: Be aware of all things, don't be ensnared by your feelings, things are as they are. (And I add from a Christian perspective: things can be changed too, so get down and change them where appropriate). I am working through an attitude which can be called "philosophical but activist idealist. (RL, Family letter, June 1976)

End of term and exams arrived; Ross felt they were not too bad but may have brought down his average. As it turned out, his results were quite respectable. In fact, a lecturer ran into Ross one day and said that his exams and essays were of a high standard, and that his dissertation would likely bring him a distinction.

> In Phenomenology I wrote essays on Rudolf Otto, on Henri Bergson, and on the question of whether it makes any difference phenomenologically whether a religious object or focus like God or Nirvana exists if it is real to believers.
>
> In Buddhism I wrote on the development of the Buddha concept in early Buddhism, on a famous Buddhist called Nagarjuna, on the Tibetan Book of the Dead and on the Chinese influences on the Ch'an or Zen school of Buddhism.
>
> In Islam I wrote on Pre-Islamic Arabia and TS Eliot's theory of culture, on a brilliant medieval Islamic theologian called al-Ghazali, and on the hadith, or traditions surrounding Muhammad's life, and their authenticity or otherwise. (RL, Family letter, June 1976)

There were some who were puzzled, and even concerned, that Ross would put so much intellectual effort into studying religions other than Christianity. For him, the reasons were clear: he wanted to explore God's world, he saw the world as a global village with pluralism well-entrenched, and he felt that to understand Christianity properly, he needed to transcend

English cultural tribalism. These firm beliefs would continue to underpin his on-going study and life.

It was the end of the academic year, and Ross noted that regarding celebrations, he fitted many categories, which meant he was invited to many parties. Leaver, first year, final year, overseas student, post-graduate, married student, mature student—he fitted them all. Students were packing up and moving out, leaving a quiet campus, except for the possible distractions of Wimbledon (featuring indigenous Australian Evonne Goolagong), test cricket, and the Montreal Olympics. To celebrate, he shaved his beard off, but realized that he would have to grow it again to save problems with his passport photo. A trip to Old Trafford to watch cricket with his professor, and a holiday visit to Oxford and Cambridge, and they were feeling almost English. They headed off with Bruce and Jean in a van to explore the south, Norfolk and the Peak District, looking at many cathedrals on the way.

Back to the books. Ross gave a few weeks to reading while Alison took in a "Teaching English as a Foreign Language" course in London, and it was time to start churning out thousands of words, with a brief diversion to get his British driving license. With Oliver reminding Ross of simple truths like "Pray without ceasing" and "Prayer is the Christian's vital breath," and a headful of others' thoughts about prayer, Ross embarked on his fifteen-thousand-word thesis. Although sadly it can no longer be located at Lancaster University, Ross fortunately gave a useful summary to his wider family in a letter. His exploration covered the following themes: to whom we pray, prayer and magic, words, meditation, worship and living, and using conceptual analysis. His professor gave him the thumbs up for the draft and asked if he could borrow some ideas to use himself, which Ross took as a good sign. Ross and Alison typed it in relays, checked and copied it, submitting it with great relief on 20 September. His conclusion:

> Prayer is the expression of wishes or attitudes to a supernatural force or being with whom the pray-er has some relationship, and which is seen to have power to answer petitions when offered. (RL, Family letter, September 1976)

The Lancaster adventure was nearly over, but the long trip home was still to come. As their departure loomed, Ross looked back:

> Already we are appreciating our time here immensely, realising how privileged we have been in every way. The accommodation has been terrific, and economical. The course has matched my expectations and has taught me a great deal. Most of all it has gently widened my horizons so that I see Christianity in context, and know what issues are burning amongst scholars and

thinking people here as well as at home. It has been a sort of retreat, with not a lot of demands apart from study, and plenty of soaking up time, in seeing new places and meeting new people.

The value of this sort of informal education is hard to estimate, and I'm not sure I rate it quite as highly as many who advocate overseas study, but I reckon all the members of the families who have lived or travelled overseas know what I mean—it will probably only hit us when we settle back into routine at home, and find we look at things slightly differently. We'll see. (RL, Family letter, September 1976)

To Ross's great satisfaction, he did indeed receive a distinction for his thesis. None had been awarded in the year before; all his work had been worthwhile. He had completed his second master's degree with top honors, and now had a MA (Theol) from Lancaster University.

Within days they were packed and ready to leave. They sent thirteen tea chests home, which was three more than they took, mainly due to buying two hundred books and a typewriter. Vaccinations completed, they hitched to London and began the search for a serviceable van for the land trip in Europe. A few days to sort their gear and prepare the van and they were off.

Ross felt a bit queasy on the ferry crossing the English Channel in late October. He was also nervous about driving on the righthand side of the road in a Kombi van they had just purchased and finding their way around countries where they could not speak the language. He wished he had paid more attention in his French classes at school. All went well apart from getting lost frequently, and they were into a routine by the time Bruce and Jean joined them. They crossed rural France, alpine Switzerland, serene Venice, musical Austria, historic Germany, and then back across Belgium to Ostend ready to return to London by sea. Best of all, there was no study and there were no deadlines; the trip was a heady celebration with great friends.

It took a few days back in London to sell the van and repack before the next departure; that was when they realized with horror that Alison's passport was missing, probably stolen while shopping. With a series of miracles and split-second timing, she was able to get it replaced in time for the multiple-flight trip to Asia.

With Bruce and Jean Rumbold in Ostend.

They arrived in Taipei via Bangkok and Hong Kong to spend precious time with Ross's parents and younger sister, Grace. Jean had recently had surgery, so the family reunion was very timely. Oliver had a detailed plan for showing them around his work and the countryside, and the three-week stay was filled with interest and stories. It was wonderful to have time to care for his mum, catch up with little sister, visit some Buddhist centers, look at photos, meet friends, and help with cleaning and packing. The senior Langmeads were leaving Taiwan and would return to Melbourne before them.

In Taipei with sister Grace.

A few nostalgic days in Hong Kong, remembering Ross's childhood, brief travel overland in Thailand and Singapore and Malaysia, and they arrived in Jakarta, Indonesia in early January. Because the Woods had not yet arrived, Ross and Alison traveled on their own across Java, feeling quite overwhelmed by the poverty and population density. After a few days as tourists in Bali, they were back in Melbourne to discover what 1977 might hold for them. They were met by the family at the airport, including Ross's new niece; he cuddled her for a long time. Ross always loved babies.

Chapter 7

Commission: 1977 to 1978

The future is in God's hands, but he has given his people a part in shaping it. For this reason, we have taken time to ask of God, "How can we best live as the people of God in the western suburbs of Melbourne?"

Ross Langmead

The Executive Committee of the Baptist Union of Victoria was looking at the ailing churches in the western suburbs of Melbourne and wondering what to do about them. Like all good committees, they decided to commission a review to look closely at the small congregations located on the other side of the Westgate Bridge, hoping that the commissioner would be able to make practical recommendations. Peter Francis, member of *Daddy's Friends*, was on this committee, and his thoughts went immediately to someone he felt would be ideal and who would soon return from studying overseas—Ross. The invitation was sent to Lancaster and provisionally accepted. This decision was another watershed for Ross and the next chapter had begun to take shape, even before he returned to Australia. For Ross, the commission would fit well with his plan to study theology at the Baptist college, and would provide some needed income from a self-managed job with flexibility.

They had some settling back to do and moved into the vacant manse in Williamstown which they would share with friends Russell and Anne Deal. The family scene had been complicated through January since their return. With amazingly fine timing, thanks to the delay in Jeanette and Peter's visa to Indonesia, Oliver, Jean, Grace, Ross, and Alison had a precious few weeks' crossover time in Melbourne with the family before the next scattering. Grace commenced her nursing training, and Oliver and Jean were appointed to head up a Salvation Army retirement village in Perth.

The Woods eventually departed in February for Indonesia, so the letter-writing continued. Ross and Alison wrote every week or two, using aerograms with carbon paper, sending copies to Perth and Indonesia, and keeping file copies. Meanwhile, the five Langmead siblings in Melbourne enjoyed more frequent direct contact and shared many meals together.

Ross's long journey of study was not driven so much by the desire to achieve degrees, but by a genuine thirst for knowledge about the issues he really cared about. His education degrees confirmed the teacher in him and led to the focus on religious education. Philosophical questions followed, which he tackled in his MEd, which then led to his exploration of religion in his MA (Theol) in Lancaster. Now it was time to embark on theology, and he confessed to feeling more excited as he enrolled in the postgraduate Bachelor of Divinity through Whitley Baptist College.

The BD was accredited by the Melbourne College of Divinity (established in 1910 and now called the University of Divinity), which exists to "empower our learning community to address the issues of the contemporary world through critical engagement with Christian theological traditions"; it is Australia's oldest ecumenical theological institution. And so, in 1977, as an independent student, Ross embarked on Old Testament, New Testament, Systematic Theology (Christology), and Church History. Jeanette was chuffed when he asked her for advice, as she had completed her BD several years before. It was a rare situation when she could advise Ross academically.

Ross juggled study and his commissioner task while Alison explored teaching and tutoring jobs. The house was full already with two families living together, but they seemed to have a constant stream of extra people visiting and staying with them. They cared intentionally for younger sister Grace, on her own for the first time, and extended an open invitation for her to stay over any time. The diary records a rich history of hospitality given—sometimes friends and family coming for dinner several nights in a week, in addition to other meetings, church events, speaking engagements, and appointments. Their regular "Gang nights," which began at university, continued until the nineties. As time went on, these gatherings included children and were a social highlight for the young families. There were regular squash games, dentist appointments (a long saga resulting from a bad squash game), blood donations, holiday trips, and church camps.

In March, the same month that he began his study, Ross commenced his job as the commissioner for the western suburbs.

> I've received enthusiastic support for my Commissioner's job. I hope I can meet their expectations—I'm certainly not up to it without some divine strength. None of my previous responsibilities have been so wide-ranging, nor involved getting people stirred about deep changes. My tendencies to be a leader by reflection of the group's wishes, and an organiser of a task that is already agreed is to be done, will have to give way to a quality referred to in the job description as a "self-starter." I look somewhat vaguely at my first week in the job, and think, "Heck, what'll I do?" The answer, by the way, is to get basic statistics about the churches and contact the ministers and arrange a meeting, and start gathering info. (RL, Family letter, March 1977)

He had twelve months to come up with the report and recommendations, and knew that the change management would need to begin well before the publishing of the report. The plan was to seek feedback on each chapter so that there would be no surprises at the end of what he hoped would be a group project representing fourteen churches. Ross did not want a top-down distribution of a report that no one had read until the end.

He was open about borrowing ideas from literature on church renewal and radical discipleship, everything from Robert Girard's *Brethren, Hang Loose* to Athol Gill's *Discipleship Studies*. Most excitingly, Ross saw this project as a piece of genuine applied theology, which was close to his heart. The question he would address was: How can we best live as the people of God in the western suburbs of Melbourne?

In case he should fall into the trap of being so heavenly minded that he would be no earthly use, Ross decided to improve his knowledge of cars. This was a pre-computerized era when it was easier to service and repair one's own car, so he made a serious attempt to understand what was under the bonnet. To do this, he borrowed a library book called *A Woman's Guide to Fixing a Car*, and a few chapters into this most useful book, he realized that his car needed a valve grind and engine clean. On the basis that every hour of labor would save him $16, he proceeded with this handy manual to venture into advanced mechanics and to do just that. He resolved to face technical tasks head on and not to mystify them, which was just as well because his car continued to present him with mysterious challenges. He then tackled the tuning by adjusting the tappets and contact breaker points, changing the oil and air filter, and adjusting the fuel richness and brakes. To his delight, the Zephyr started without the choke and hummed along beautifully as they set off for a break in Hall's Gap in the Grampians, a national park some three hours from Melbourne.

All of this kept Ross very grounded as he ploughed his way through Greek exegesis of chapters of John and Romans, studied Genesis, led services, and preached. He found that his newly learnt exegetical perspectives were changing his sermons, and his challenging role as commissioner was keeping him close to people. In May, feeling rather vulnerable, he presented his first report to the Western Suburbs Church Conference; it was well-received by the forty-five people present and he was encouraged to press on. The idea of a questionnaire was accepted, and it was suggested that he deal with each of the six congregations separately for a start.

This was the time when he built strong networks of friends and colleagues. Athol Gill, the Dean at Whitley at the time, was heading up The House of the Gentle Bunyip at Clifton Hill Baptist, which Ross enjoyed visiting to extend his ideas on creative worship. Marita Munro had met Ross before Lancaster and would also work with him later; Philip and Hazel Hughes worshiped with Alison and Ross at North Carlton Baptist, and in 1978, Philip followed in his steps by studying in Lancaster. Paul and Jan Hopkins were independent students from Sydney who were, like Ross, looking for the open approach that Whitley offered. Graeme Garrett and his wife, Pam, became good friends in these years in his role as theology lecturer. Ross was drawn to his thoughts on Richard Neibuhr and had great respect for him as a person. Graeme writes:

> I would call Ross a "communicating friend," a person who knows you well, listens to you carefully, shares with you the challenges, perplexities, mysteries and mistakes of your life (and his) with kindness, understanding and forgiveness. A person who shoots straight, who just doesn't reinforce your own tendencies to self-deception, but gently tells it like it is. A person you can trust, who intends goodness to you and for you in the best sense of the term. A person who enables you to see and become the person you are meant (and want) to be, especially in times of stress and confusion. (Graeme Garrett, 2020)

Friends were important to Ross and he was a faithful friend to many. He valued those who were open to questions and who nurtured his questioning. He was sensitive to judgment, yet accepting of those who saw things differently from him. Hospitality was to become a key theme right through his life, and the Langmeads were known for their open house and table. Their commitment to simplicity meant that they were happy to share without fuss or pretension. The bone-handled cutlery set they rescued from the family home is still in use today, and homemade soup with crusty bread is often the menu.

From his days at home with his family, Ross was very willing when it came to chores; while his siblings were arguing over the turns for doing dishes, he would just start. Many remember his habit over the years of jumping up from the table, clearing dishes away, and starting the washing up before anyone else could get to it. It may have been part of his almost obsessive love of order, but it was also part of his practical service.

This commitment to sharing and simplicity led Alison and Ross to think seriously about what it meant to live in community. The decision to live with Russ and Anne and their baby daughter was not taken lightly, and there were many discussions about the practical aspects of sharing. For Ross that meant sharing the laundry roster, and he wrote once of his debut on the diaper-washing. They shared many values and enjoyed each other's company, so they did not find it difficult to share their lives but they did discover that it always needed review and honesty. The Deals' decision to train a guide dog puppy took them to the edge of friendship, but the puppy's cuteness won them over. When Russ and Anne moved to the country later that year, they felt the loss of good friends, and baby April asked for Ross for a quite a while after they left.

That spring feeling in the air is bad news for university students: it means that exam season is nigh. Ross felt anxious and daunted by the vast amount of material covered in first-year courses, despite his impressive academic record to this point. He had, however, learnt how to prepare for exams, and focused his preparation on the topics he wanted to write on.

Incredibly, there was a mistake on the New Testament exam paper, with the passages from John for exegesis being taken from outside the prescribed chapters. As a result, Ross and the other students were forced to write on all the Romans excerpts and felt rather stretched. He and others complained, and the mix-up was considered, but he felt pessimistic. He needn't have worried: his results were all honors, two first-class and two second-class.

The Western Suburbs Report progressed through the year. Firstly, Ross looked at the facts of life in the city with its benefits and problems. Then the focus was on the western suburbs, where the problems of disadvantage, poverty, loneliness, and powerlessness were amplified. There were urgent needs in every area of human welfare, with housing, employment, education, family support, childcare, youth welfare, aged care, and migrant welfare being paramount.

Looking at the churches in those suburbs, he saw that their middle-class nature amidst working-class suburbs was clearly incongruent and had led to a bypassing of the working class. There was a need for an urgent Christian response which would offer help to the neediest, strengthen networks, foster self-help, and work with others. His Salvo upbringing came through, as Ross echoed many of the things that William Booth had emphasized a century before. His review of the fourteen Baptist churches in the region showed that membership had decreased along with effectiveness as God's people.[1]

This study raised big questions about the nature of the church, and we see in Ross's writing the seeds of what would become his signature theology: that mission is part of the nature of the church; or, rather, that the church is part of God's mission. Ministry and worship would follow in the members' relationship to each other and to Jesus.

> The mission of the church is to proclaim and live out the Good News that the reign of God has begun in our lives. The Good News is power for liberty and love amongst those men who allow God to rule. A striking thing about Jesus' ministry and teaching is his strong emphasis on the poor, the needy and the outcast. We in the western suburbs live in an area where there are many such people, and our mission should reflect the urgent needs of the area.[2]

Although the report would encourage the congregations to tease out their own responses, Ross's suggestion was that the church needed to recover its sense of community that would enable them to engage with the needs of those around them. This was the part that Ross knew would not be easy to achieve. In some ways, he was pre-empting the Church Growth Movement of the eighties that was on its way from North America. It brought a willingness to apply research to attracting members, including quantitative methods, and introduced the term "seeker sensitive" to describe church activities that would bridge the gap to non-church people. He was, however, concerned with the quality as well as the quantity of the church, and saw success more in the changed lives of the community members and their motivations for reaching the needy.

The fourteen Baptist churches in the western suburbs[3] were all founded by 1915; the growth period of these churches was, however, in the twenty-five-year period prior to 1915, and there had been little growth in

1. Langmead, *Report*, 1–2.
2. Langmead, *Report*, 4.
3. The churches in 1977 were: Aberfeldie, Altona, Essendon, two in Footscray, Glenbervie, two in Kingsville, Moonee Ponds, Newport, Sunshine/St Albans, Tottenham, Williamstown, and Yarraville.

numbers after that. In the same period, the population had increased threefold. The number of Baptists per thousand people in the west had decreased from 5.2 to 2.7. With nine ministers looking after fourteen churches due to lack of finance and too few experienced ministers willing to live in the west, the situation was unlikely to improve. Add the traditional style to which most of these congregations were captive, and the future was not promising.

The Baptist churches in the east, in contrast, had shown growth, and had an average congregational size of 197, which was larger than any other area: the denomination was thriving in middle-class areas. Even in the west, the differential was apparent within the region, with the more middle-class congregations in the Essendon area being larger with more full-time ministers than the others. For all these reasons, it was apparent to Ross that his report would need to disturb those living comfortably in the leafier suburbs. Given that working-class people tend to believe in God more than other classes, he believed that there was a problem in a church that does not attract them. To add to the issues,

> As lower middle-class Christians get "better" jobs, they look for better homes, and move to middle-class suburbs. One church in the west has dropped in membership from 120 to less than half that number in twelve years, mostly through migration to those suburbs.[4]

Ross pinpointed the verbal and abstract nature of much Christianity and saw it as a priority that Christians work at communicating simply and through actions as well as words. He felt that when people saw God at work in everyday lives, they would make this known to each other. This was a central point in his conclusions and would drive many of the recommendations:

> It is to do with making the Good News visible in our lives and interpreting it in simple words.[5]

For all Ross's education, he had a gift for making things understandable that many have remarked upon. Even the report itself is very readable, attractively set out with the line drawings of designer/artist David Wong.

---

4. Langmead, *Report*, 63.
5. Langmead, *Report*, 64.

He wanted the report to be collaborative and so presented the chapters progressively for discussion through the year; a weekend camp for some of the members drew them closer together and created a context for honesty on what would be a challenging journey for everyone.

> My latest sermon is based on Matthew 25:40, about helping the naked, sick, and prisoner, and as I sat outside a church last Sunday after preaching, waiting to be picked up for home, I read how George Walker (his grandfather, a missionary in China) was challenged by this verse. I wish the churches could catch a vision of the relatedness between caring action for the needy and the gospel, even half as vital as Grandpa had. (RL, Family letter, November, 1977)

There was a conference meeting in late November at which Ross proposed that the six Footscray churches that were all within a two-kilometer radius should combine as a regional church, and that the other churches make some changes. He was surprised at the level of support for the plan, but equally unsurprised at the objections of the diehards who wanted things to stay as they were. He decided to spend the rest of the year interviewing key people while writing his final report to be completed in the new year.

Ross had a small insight into how people differ when he spent an evening with his brother Les and his wife, Grace: Les was about to move away to the country as a school psychologist for a region with eighty schools.

> I came away aware of how brothers can grow so differently—I had to come to grips (with tolerance) with Les's approach to Christianity, which stresses simply being God's people (the covenant people, like the Jews of the OT, called just to be God's). My approach stresses mission, the doing, especially the action side rather than just words. Of course, we can both learn a little from each other. What impresses us about Les's house is the ability

to read a book for sheer pleasure or relax doing very little. (RL, Family letter, November 1977)

Ross's father, Oliver, had been unwell when he and Jean arrived from Taiwan and moved to Perth. After many tests he was diagnosed with an acoustic neuroma and underwent significant surgery in May 1977. With Jean still recovering from back surgery, this was concerning for the family. The operation was a success, although Oliver was left with a dropped face on the side where the tumor was removed, and that affected his confidence in public for the rest of his life. Ross and Alison had gone out of their way when returning from Lancaster to visit their parents in Taiwan only months before, but they wanted to see them again and began to plan to travel across the Nullarbor Desert for Christmas in Western Australia. In the heat of mid-summer, in the Zephyr that had proved to be capricious in its performance, and with siblings Peter and Grace on board, the trip was always going to be a challenge.

The car needed several things attended to, including a new battery, before they could attempt such a trip, especially in the days before mobile phones. Ross decided not to put in a reconditioned engine before they left but resolved instead to travel in the cooler parts of the day at a lower speed, hoping to delay the need for a new engine or to deal with the problem if it happened. The mechanic told him that the car was fine, as long as he wasn't planning to drive across the Nullarbor! Ross reassured Oliver that he planned to carry jerry cans of water and petrol, and plenty of spare parts. He even fitted venetian blinds on the back window for comfort in the days before air-conditioning.

The exciting news was that Alison was pregnant, and they looked forward to sharing the joy with the Perth family. She had emerged from morning sickness and felt confident about managing such a big journey. They would be up early every morning to leave at 4 a.m. in the cool of the day, which would be more comfortable for everyone, including the intrepid car.

It would have been surprising if there had been no car problems. Breaking down somewhere on the Nullarbor with what they thought was engine trouble turned out to be trouble with the fuel pump, and two separate wheel problems left them short of a spare, meaning that Ross had to draw on his hitchhiking experience to get to the small town of Eucla and back. Then there was trouble with the points, and electrical malfunction in the taillights in a storm. With the engine cutting out frequently, they limped into Perth, rolling down the hills without a motor, and push-starting to get going each time. Ever enterprising, Ross stripped a few parts from an abandoned Zephyr he found in Caiguna and was optimistic that they would make the return trip. He noted that his was the oldest car they saw in the remote outback; there was probably a reason for that.

The momentous year ended with a joyful family gathering over Christmas in beautiful Perth, and with summer sightseeing and swimming in the Indian Ocean. Oliver and Jean lavished hospitality and outings on them, and the return trip was fueled by gratitude. That was quickly eclipsed when Alison's parents lost their home to a devastating fire—Ross was fortunate to retrieve his fire-blackened thesis from Lancaster. As he held the volume, it must have seemed like a metaphor: philosophy refined by fire. *The Western Suburbs Conference Report* would be one of the most important projects of Ross's life, and certainly the one with the widest impact.

Chapter 8

Parenting: 1977 to 1978

The Word became flesh and blood, and moved into the neighborhood.
JOHN 1:14

There were two significant deliveries in 1978: The *Western Suburbs Conference Report*, and a baby.

While Alison prepared for the birth, Ross continued to battle with the car, this time with replacing the clutch. His main task, however, was to complete his report, and, as he wrote, he knew that he had to make some decisions. One immediate outcome was regretfully to inform the North Carlton Baptists that he and Alison would leave the church to worship in the western suburb churches. This was something that Ross needed to do as part of his own recommendations.

> It's a strange beginning to a year for us, partly because it is starting with a busy climax, and partly because it contains so many unknowns. It is easy to feel a bit apprehensive about moving into a little church and committing ourselves, especially after publishing for everyone to see my opinions about the "ideal" church and its attitude to the local community. (RL, Family letter, February 1978)

Community life continued, now with Newton Daddow and Alan Witt sharing their home. Every week was very "peopled." They tackled the coming birth as Ross and Alison did with everything, with extensive research and a great deal of anticipation. They chose the new LeBoyer birth style as their plan, and Alison became involved in The Nursing Mothers Association. So many of their friends were having babies and the conversations now ranged from theology to parenting styles:

> I'm feeling the support of our little community here very positively at the moment. It seems that for every demand there are many hands—not only in housework, but in things like if X rings, someone else can go on making the fruit salad or finish sweeping the floor. I think to have more people genuinely sharing their lives means there is a bit less tension between jobs, chores, service to others, rest and relaxation. I am grateful to Alan and Newton and to God who is our Lord. (Alison Langmead, Family letter, April 1978)

Newton appreciated support too, and the deep friendship continued after he left the house:

> I'll never forget the day when I'd claimed unemployment benefits following the breakup of my marriage and struggling to balance all the demands. I sat down at the kitchen table and crumbled into tears. I will never forget Ross's gentle compassionate response. Ross knew me very well in many ways through the various times of personal turmoil and struggle. He was never judgmental. He is an outstanding example of grace. In this regard he was an embodiment of Christ likeness. (Newton Daddow, 2020)

As the time ticked away for the report to be finished, Ross and Alison approached the South Kingsville church about the possibility of them moving into the empty manse. This was it: they would literally move into the neighborhood. Ross would become a living part of his own report and include their own lives as a key part of the working out of the recommendations. In hindsight, there is some irony in the fact that at that time it was a downward socioeconomic move, which has now reversed, with South Kingsville becoming gentrified with the associated property boom. Although they wondered at the time whether they would stay there more than five years, Ross would live the rest of his life in the Kernot Street home, which they were able later to purchase. He began to live out his practical incarnational theology well before he wrote about it.

The move went well and helped Alison to embark on serious nesting. They were showered with gifts for both the house and the baby, and they reckoned he or she would be the best-dressed child in the region. Both Ross and Alison had read the birthing books, been to their classes, worked on the exercises, and felt excited when the practice contractions began. They moved into their new home just weeks before the baby was due.

Benjamin Ross arrived without much fuss a little early and changed their lives forever. Ross spent many hours at the hospital with his new son and loved being involved in caring for Ben in those first few days. They were blessed with gifts from their wide circle, and as it was for many new parents, the most practical one was the gift of a diaper wash service. As Ross recalled those days:

> Well, it feels great to be parents, and Benjamin already shows little signs of being a unique person. My confidence in Alison's maternal instincts has been more than justified so far, and we can already understand a bit of the depth of love that parents are said to have for their children. We are grateful to God for this gift, for the quality of the birth experience, for the love he has given us to share, and for the joy which lies ahead. (RL, Family letter, June 1978)

Then he raced back to play squash for Whitley, where he had been number-one player for the past three years.

The *Western Suburbs Report* was being published, which for Ross was like his own birth experience. It was now up to the participating churches to make their decisions about the way forward. Ross needed to get back to his theology studies after all the excitement, and life settled back to some kind of routine, but with the constant demands of a young baby added to it. The family letters are full of stories about Benjamin's antics, growth, and cuteness. They admitted to going out and buying a pacifier on one particularly stressful occasion, but that was recounted in the same letter that told of the baby's first smiles. With another cousin born just weeks after, there were now six Langmead cousins and the new generation was gaining strength and numbers.

One of their near neighbors was Jen Shields. Jen met Ross and Alison when she was invited in to share his birthday celebrations. She found it a pleasant change to meet males who were "not overbearing" and moreover, who actually baked bread and hung out diapers on the clothesline. Jen would become a lifelong friend with the Langmeads.

Ross needed to make time to consult with the churches in the *Report* and to help them make decisions. He spent many evenings meeting ministers, deacons, and leaders and carefully considered the responses. Some members were not keen on the idea of being visited in hospital by someone "from another church"; others were really attached to their buildings and facilities. As the year progressed, it became clear that it was unlikely that the six churches he had suggested would all want to combine.

Somehow between all his activities, Ross found time to help people out. Family and friends seemed to move house continually and he was always there to help. He spent time coaching his younger siblings in study methods when their exams approached, while needing to do intense work himself; two of his BD subjects were not offered by the college that year, calling for self-management by Ross. He continued to mow the church lawns and a neighbor's, just because they needed help; he always went the extra mile and trimmed the edges as well. He offered to look after the regular newsletter distribution for the Woods, who were now living and working in West Papua. It is said that if one wants a job done well, ask a busy person, and that person was Ross.

Newton (who was one of the people who moved at that time) comments on "the blue trailer":

> An unsung contribution, but very important, was the way Ross maintained the blue trailer. It was used over and over, always

available for loan and Ross would maintain it by always keeping the rust away, repainting it periodically, and maintaining all the wear and tear bits. And it is still used today. (Newton Daddow, 2020)

The small groups began almost immediately, as a key recommendation in the *Report*. The Langmeads began one in their home on Wednesday nights, starting to get to know each other and to explore the local needs. Ross joined a "Companionship group" at Kingsville, that visited people having hard times. The Kernot Street group would continue to meet there for the rest of Ross's life.

> All is exploratory at the moment, but I feel pretty strongly that our move to South Kingsville is no mere whim. God is bringing things and people before us constantly, whether it be Christian couples not sure where to live next year while studying at Whitley or others seriously considering moving east to west, like Alan Marr and family, whose sharing group in Blackburn say their commitment to each other is such that they either all ought to be out there or they should all move over here. (RL, Family letter, July 1978)

With the *Report* finally accepted officially in August, he felt relieved that it was no longer his responsibility, although he would be personally involved in its outworking. It had taken longer than he planned, and he was now left with ten weeks to start almost from scratch in four BD subjects. The Baptist Witness that week had a front page spread with photos and a headline, "Radical Remedies for Western Suburbs Churches," setting out all Ross's conclusions. He reflected with some apprehension that it certainly looked rather radical.

There was a rocky path ahead, between congregations unwilling to compromise and a denomination seeming not to be genuinely interested in the west. The *Report* did not even make it on to the Annual Assembly agenda that year until determined lobbying achieved that.

> Oh, I come home exhausted after a long day of study. I must confess that scholarly pursuits are aesthetically far more pleasing than gently nursing aggressive Baptists to some minor step forward in their understanding of church life. (RL, Family letter, September 1978)

He just pressed on with Mark's Gospel in Greek and with Kierkegaard, marking off the weeks in his diary. By late October, he was working at college from 7 a.m. to 10 p.m., six days a week, giving new meaning to cramming. Alison just prayed and supported until exams were over. Before long, Ross was complaining about the sixty-cent toll each way on the newly-opened Westgate Bridge, which has since become the lifeline from the city to the western suburbs. It was, in fact, to open the way for commuters from the area, raise the property values in the region, and gradually add appeal to life across the bridge for the aspirational. The West was changing.

With another set of exams out of the way, Ross, the father, took his little family to Tidal River for a break to try to recover before an influx of visitors. With Oliver and Jean over from Perth, and the Woods home from Indonesia, that Christmas was the first time the family had gathered together since 1974.

Chapter 9

Community Work: 1979 to 1980

He makes sure orphans and widows are treated fairly, takes loving care of foreigners by seeing that they get food and clothing.

DEUTERONOMY 10:18

The family needed income. With the commission complete, Ross was on the search for a job as he embarked on his third and final year of theology studies in 1979. This was the year he would turn thirty, and while the academic road had been long, he was still young, full of energy, and ready to make the rubber hit the road.

He had an ongoing tutoring position in philosophy of education at the University of Melbourne but was ready to connect with the community and use his teaching skills in some way. He applied for and was appointed to the Educational Program for Unemployed Youth (EPUY) as the numeracy teacher in the inner western suburbs. The government-funded job aimed to help long-term, poorly-educated young people. They were aged from sixteen to twenty-four years and had generally been unemployed for a year or two. The goal of the course in the first year was to build confidence and improve literacy and numeracy, establish better life habits, and experience some enjoyable, healthy recreation along the way.

A house was rented and prepared for the group and staff drove around with a trailer on council hard rubbish day to look for furnishings. Ross began to connect with local schools and community groups to scout for possible employment for the youth.

> I am pretty excited about the job right now, feeling it's where I ought to be, and that I have something to contribute and to learn in this situation. I've been interested to learn this week that some of the key people behind the project are Christians, while at least two others are Communists—it seems that one must have a strong sense of cause to bother with these youth. I'm impressed with some of the themes of lifestyle, co-operative living and coping with future society that I've already heard coming through. Of course, the area where I differ most in terms of expectations is in my analysis of human nature.
>
> Sometimes I think others think the poor and oppressed are really great people, just trodden on, while those in power and government are all evil monsters. I have a firm realization of the good and evil in each of us, and the oppressive nature of the structures we get locked into. Already I have had to question their one-sided vilification of government/education department/ACER/local council and question the Robin Hood ethic which prevails in places like this. It has come out in suggestions such as pinching bricks from building sites for our use in building bookshelves and fiddling the accounting to get more funds. (RL, Family letter, March 1979)

And so Ross, the pure math honors graduate with two master's degrees and in his final year of theology, began to figure out how to teach the boys the new metric system, how many grams are in packets of food, whether a thirty-degree day is hot or cold, and how many liters of paint they would need to coat a wall. Those boys had no idea how long Ross had studied to teach them.

He had many stories to tell as he became involved in the lives of these young men. Dean had been "inside" more than out at thirteen, living with a girl with seven children at twenty-two, and with another girl pregnant to him. He was working at the market to pay off a fine for stealing three cars and escaped custody on the grounds that he was in the EPUY program. Covered in tattoos, he was diabetic with poor insulin management. One week they had five homeless boys in the course; they ended up in court for smashing police station windows, allowing rape to happen in their house, and for owing thousands of dollars for false pension claims. They were drunk all night and slept all day; sixteen security guards were unable to control one of their parties. That's why these boys were in the program.

> But they treat us well because they regard us as fair dinkum, and the more I get to know them the more I like them. I'm pleased that all my study hasn't made me unable to relate to them openly

and aggressively and accepting their ignorance and prejudice on so many things. This acceptance is the key to gradual change. (RL, Family letter, May 1979)

The participants were mostly in unstable accommodation, involved with the law and drugs, and in poor health.

> Three are obese, four have sight problems (unattended to), six appear to have nervous problems, two have severe mental health problems, five have very poor personal hygiene and all but a couple suffered from very poor self-esteem.[1]

Camps were both highlights and challenges. The boys had no outdoor experience nor inclination, but some were persuaded to try. Between fear of heights and lack of fitness, the trail that Ross had reconnoitered in three hours took the group eight long hours. One part of the group went ahead of them and burnt two of their essential maps to start a fire, then consumed all their food on the first night. The camps became popular and regular, and Ross often took Ben along for the ride; it was humanizing for the young people to have a baby with them who accepted them with his big smile.

When the job was readvertized for a second year, Ross applied with success; at the same time, he became a member of the government's State Youth Council, questioning why a stated priority like youth unemployment was receiving so little attention from the government. His natural sense of

1. Langmead, *Evaluation Report*, 3.

justice as well as the information in his *Report* had been fueled by his experience with the EPUY course and he was increasingly passionate about the need for resources in the west.

Another area of need that he and Alison decided to be involved in was emergency accommodation for needy children. Their first foster child, Michelle, was a four-year-old whose mother had tried to commit suicide; they embraced her figuratively and literally and helped her through her tears. A little later they took in Caroline, whose mum had cancer. She was harder to manage and not so used to doing what she was told. They realized then that fostering would require deeply committed focus which their lives would not allow as they explored and gave leadership to the community. They withdrew from the program and soon Alison was pregnant again. They knew that they would eventually be able to include their own children's friends from families in the district, many of whom were needy.

Around this time, Llew Evans, an old friend of Alison's family, began staying a few nights each week so he could participate in the Wednesday small group and do some odd jobs around the place. He had been recently widowed and was wondering what God had for him in this next phase of life. He heard of the Westgate explorations of Christian community and was keen to be involved. It wasn't long before Ross and Alison invited him to join them and he remained part of their extended household for the rest of his life, even though he purchased the house next door for community use and purchased a bungalow to put in the backyard for his own space. Inevitably Ross, Alison, and Llew's wider families sometimes felt that they missed out on the close contact that the community enjoyed. That was a balancing act that would always be sensitive.

During this period, a group of committed Baptists began meeting to share concerns and issues of social justice. Described as Baptists of mostly conventional theology but with progressive politics, influential members included Athol Gill, Terry Falla, Alan Marr, Catie Inches, Newton Daddow, Graeme and Pam Garrett, Alan Austin, and Ross. Alan Austin was drawn in as a journalist with social justice connections, especially with some remote indigenous communities. They met monthly for many years, and prioritized poverty, unemployment, indigenous affairs, and homelessness. Alan recounts that the group organized three visits to North Queensland indigenous communities and published reports after each; they were one of many voices lobbying for land rights and the formal apology that came years later.

These few years between the publication of the *Report*, and the formal launch of Westgate Baptist Community were important as the small groups grew in several churches. Ross's group started a fund that brought in nearly $30 each week (equivalent to about $160 today), pooled for use for those in need. Over the years, many people were assisted from this common purse. The members grew accustomed to honest sharing, worship and music, acceptance of children, and the joys of hospitality as they shared meals together.

The Kernot Street group increased in size until they felt too big to interact personally, and in 1980 they went through a challenging division of the group. Ross tried to listen and act democratically in these issues, and a working group within the community was charged with making the decisions. After over six weeks of combined gatherings of the new groups, they had an evening of renewing their covenants, accepting new members, sharing communion, and a footwashing ceremony. The groups became increasingly significant in the life of the members and were the catalyst for people making decisions to move into the area, and to live in proximity. Community was emerging organically, almost in spite of the structures of the old churches.

At the same time, there was movement in the eastern suburbs as negotiations began with Rev. Alan Marr to come to the west and become their pastor. The process was prolonged, but, significantly, Alan and Jenny, his wife, made the decision to make the move anyway: it was their Acts 16:9 moment, as they responded to "Come over to the west and help us." They like to point out that their "Macedonian call" was also because the Yarraville Baptist Church happened to be next door to the local Macedonian Reception Centre.

In due course the appointment was made, and Alan was inducted as pastor of the Yarraville Baptist church in February 1980. A move from the east had started, as Ross had hoped. The Jacksons were amongst those who made the big move with the Marrs towards the end of 1979, purchasing a new home in the area. They sold the house they built in Blackburn and brought with them computer and teaching skills. The reverse migration had begun.

Alan Marr met Ross first on SU beach mission at Tidal River in the 1970s. He recalls their first gig when, together with Bruce Tudball, they were to be a pirate crew, goose-stepping across the footbridge singing, "Yo-ho-ho and a bottle of jungle juice." Alan notes wryly that over the many years to follow, Ross never asked him to sing with him again. It was when they heard Ross present the *Western Suburbs Report* to the Baptist Assembly that Alan and Jenny knew clearly that God was calling them into a grand adventure. It was to be the beginning of a lifelong friendship.

> Ross was probably the most gifted person I have known—teacher, musician, poet, cartoonist, preacher, prophetic leader but he

> was also heaps of fun. Just when I began to see him as an austere, uncompromising, prophet type, he would have me rolling with laughter. (Alan Marr's Eulogy for Ross, July 2013)

The church and the small groups were reaching out more widely as time went on. Clearly, the west was under-resourced in services, so the dream developed to open a holistic medical center that would bulk-bill and be accessible to all. In November 1980, The Doctors' Place was opened, a clinic staffed by Christian professionals, with Ross Dyer as the first medical practitioner. It was the first and continues to be the only general practice owned and run as a health care cooperative. Kristine Glasby was one of the clinic's doctors in the early days when she her doctor husband Michael moved into the area to renovate their house.

> The remarkable nature of the clinic was its Christian nature and that many of the doctors were also involved in the Westgate church. Its focus was on health care being part of an individual and community concern, run on a subscription system. The sense of the GP needing to be patient-centred was being articulated by authors in our medical degree and I believe Westgate was already onto it more than other clinics at the time. Indeed, when we left and I started various jobs in GP elsewhere there was nothing like the community involvement and ownership I encountered at Westgate. This framed my career, particularly to patient centering. And I look on it as part of the Westgate experience which was very much community centred, social justice oriented, and the leaders were solid at the core of their teaching. (Kristine Glasby, 2020)

Anne Paltridge, a member of the community, coordinated volunteers and recalls the pastoral team's availability when counseling was needed. Community members assisted with transport for appointments when needed, and everyone felt part of the initiative.

There had been a long drought in Ross's songwriting, with almost no output since 1973. It was a sign of his renewed creative energy that the music began to flow again. "The Great Physician" was written for the opening of the clinic:

> *Jesus healed both body and mind, disease of every kind,*
> *And most of all made whole, with Love, the ready soul, the broken life,*
> *And when he gave his life for us, the wholeness he released was offered to us all.*

We have seen the cure begin, His love at work within,
His Spirit will restore, make new, bring harmony,
And yet our hearts are moved to see the suffering still,
The need for wounded lives to know the balm of Love.

Make us whole in every way, your kingdom come, we pray,
And as we grow we'll share this health, this energy,
This news that you're the Great Physician,
and your Love for us includes our mind, our body and our soul.

(RL, "The Great Physician," 1981)

Part of the struggle of birthing a song was that, at times, theology and philosophy challenged Ross, and delayed the music.

> The song on healing for the opening of the Doctors' Place required quite a bit of study and reflection on my part before deciding what line to take. Do I expect God to heal us physically as part of His restoration of our lives in love? I decided to say that God's love includes our mind, body and soul; that His Spirit has begun working in our lives and in others; and that we long for His Kingdom to come in its fulness. In other words, healing does occur physically through faith and love, but that we can't expect it confidently until the Kingdom comes fully. I'm not a disbeliever in healing miracles (how could I be?), but I'm reluctant to ask for them. Is this lack of faith, or not putting God to the test? I don't know.
>
> Anyway, once I'd struggled through the thought and prayer, the writing of the song flowed better than usual (with the tremendous assistance of the rhyming dictionary Alison gave me for Christmas—how did I get on without it?). People seemed to really like the song. (RL, Journal, February 1981)

It's a wonder any song was written with this lengthy reflective process, but it was always part of the composing for Ross, especially when songs were commissioned or written for public occasions. He wanted his songs to be authentic.

Ross pressed on with his study and completed his BD with honors at the end of 1979. There would be a break in formal study for a few years, although he had not finished yet. He was enjoying working out his beliefs and reaching out in his community. Politics depressed him:

> Fraser's Razors have slashed $560 million off the next two years' budget. Medibank is now totally dismantled—most people will now have to insure at $10+ pw for health costs, the Melbourne City Council was sacked yesterday, replaced by a $100,000 p.a. administrator; Australia promised 0.7% GDP for foreign aid in 1976, but it has gone down from 0.54 to 0.45 and falling—the worst record of any OECD country. (RL, Family letter, May 1981)

It is tempting to ask what has improved in forty odd years. It is unlikely that Ross would have entered politics, although there were those who encouraged him to think about it as a way of effecting change.

> 1979 has been a significant year for us. We're both 30 and my study is now complete. I've spent the year working in an entirely new field and felt very much at home. It's the first year since we were married in 1973 that we haven't shifted house, and we are involved in a local church with some prospect of stability. It's been our first full year of parenthood, and we have begun to face the challenge of being moral educators. I'm very aware that the

end of study means no more pressure from that area, but that small vacuum will fill up quickly.

I see next year as a critical year in establishing family patterns of involvement, balancing work, parenting, church, wider Christian ministry, wider family, friends, rest, music and entertainment, house maintenance. We've been too busy, but our ability to say "No" grows only as fast as the demands placed upon us.

I'm really glad I did Theology, partly for the resolution of some issues of faith and doubt, partly so that I am no longer at the mercy of competing theological viewpoints, not knowing who to believe (Francis Schaeffer or Bultmann or someone in between?). I feel that the intensity of my doubts has had two effects, apart from taking me on a long and fruitful detour through philosophy and history of religions. One is to make me place less store on doctrine as such, due to concluding that our knowledge is so imperfect that we see through a glass darkly.

The second effect is in contrast: I am strongly convicted that the life of faith must be all or nothing, dedicated to exploring life in Christ in all its dimensions, particularly of love between people, and the structures which allow love to be expressed best, both in the church and in society. So my theology tends to be liberal in doctrine yet evangelical in its implication. (RL, Family letter, December 1979)

The shape of the emerging new church was fluid in the early days. Yarraville and South Kingsville had met together informally, and both were without pastors. Kingsville had a part-time pastor. Ross and Alison visited these congregations and led services and shared music and discussion. It was these three churches that combined to call Alan Marr as their new pastor, although he came believing that six churches might combine.

In the end, it was two and a half that came together, using both the Yarraville and South Kingsville buildings. Those involved at the time found it confusing and energy-draining but recognized it as a crucial time as the new struggled to emerge from the old, like a butterfly pushing out of its chrysalis. Ross worked his way around the leaders, the groups, the youth, and the deacons, and went with the flow as the connections began to strengthen. Ross persevered and ran courses for all six churches on how to make small groups tick.

> On Sunday we started our new worship format, with praise and sermon followed by cup of tea, then small group discussion and group prayer, all taking 1½ hours. I have led the first

two, though we have had visiting preachers. Yesterday Yarraville joined us and it was great to have a full church for a change. There's a fair bit of pressure for me to preach regularly, but time doesn't permit at present. I've agreed, however, to take a series on relationships and sex for the Yarraville youth. They apparently have never discussed anything at all related to this, though most of them are dominated by it in their thinking. (RL Family letter, July 1979)

This was the period of learning to be parents. In June 1980, Kia Marinna was born on the day of Benjamin's second birthday, which fitted in with Ross's high sense of order. Unfortunately, Ben had scarlet fever at that time, so no visiting was allowed, but when the new baby came home, the family of four had a feeling of completeness. The children would be brought up also by a wider community, who all delighted in these little ones and would influence them into adulthood. Ben and Kia only ever lived in the Kernot Street house until they left home as adults. They were true "Westies."

There were more cousins being born at the same time as their children, and many friends were also enjoying a productive period of pregnancies and births. As life became busier, they worked on freeing up time for Alison without the children, and Ross was able to take them on for half a day a week for a start, as well as sharing the household chores. They also felt the need to practice what they preached to other house groups and instituted weekly house breakfasts for discussion and prayer.

Ross and Alison felt blessed with their two little ones, and as part of their responsibility for the world's resources decided not to add to their family. Anne Paltridge recalls how, a few years later, when Kia asked Ross about a possible little brother or sister, he answered her by explaining his vasectomy in detail. We know from Ross's diary that he used the recovery hours after his operation to read the thesis of his friend, Philip Hughes, and later agreed to supervise his doctorate. As in Lancaster, there would be no time wasted on convalescing.

They still shared their simple home with various friends and needy people, and Ross was combining work, groups, children and daily needs. The car continued to be a saga, draining money and time, but there was no possibility of buying a new one. Through all of this, they had a continuous trail of people in their homes and lives. This is one paragraph from one letter, one of many like this:

> There are real ups and down in our church. Mandy is a teacher who has had deep depression due to low self-image, is finally doing very well in Vic Psych Unit. Bill got a job as a cleaner at a hospital, but couldn't cope and lost it after a week. Sarah has had a traumatic time, had a court case and a friend stacked her car. Bruce, the recently converted drug addict may be back on heroin again and his housemates are understandably uptight. (Names changed) (RL, Family letter, July 1981)

The annual Western Suburbs Phillip Island Family Camps over summer are fondly remembered by many, with many of the friendships made and support offered continuing to this day. These camps included a good sprinkling of Westgate families and singles but also Christian families from the West who could participate and enable precious relief to single parents who had had no down time from their kids in years. Social workers referred families who would otherwise not have had vacations, and struggling local families Westgate members were getting to know could also experience the joy.

The churches accepted Ross's economic sharing proposal, which would support the poor in the community to the level of the poverty line. Each person would receive $20 from it and the rest from subscriptions. They were the first church to do this systematically, which encouraged Ross. Ever the prophetic voice on social needs, he presented a paper at the Baptist

Assembly on poverty in Australia, speaking on income security and economic sharing in the church.

There was growing pressure for Ross to join the pastoral team in the community church as it moved to combine. With study finished, the EPUY job complete, Ross began to consider seriously what it would mean to be a pastor, and, more importantly, the nature and definition of ordination. If he were to commit, it would be with some reluctance combined with a sense of calling.

Chapter 10

Pastoring: 1981 to 1985

Now it's up to you. Be on your toes—both for yourselves and your congregation of sheep. The Holy Spirit has put you in charge of these people—God's people they are—to guard and protect them. God himself thought they were worth dying for.

Acts 20:28

There has possibly never been a more qualified but less confident pastor than Ross when he accepted the invitation to be part of a new team in the west, with Alan Marr and John Strugnell (who was already at Kingsville). He did not like the term "full-time Christian work" yet acknowledged that there was plenty of work to fill the role. In fact, if he multiplied out the demands on his time of the Kernot Street group to those of the whole church, it looked daunting. He did, however, respond enthusiastically to the opportunity to work in his neighborhood and to follow through the recommendations of the *Report*.

> As I look forward to full-time work locally this year, it looks pretty busy from here. I worry a little bit about week-to-week accountability. I have never wanted to be a pastor because of the unreal expectations of multiple-gifted performance, but gradually my job takes on the same feeling.
>
> Maybe there is an underlying guilt about whether I will work hard enough. I have always been a bit of a clock-watcher on my past jobs because there have been so many other things

> I have wanted to do. But here my job and my interests coincide a fair bit. Will I overwork as a result? What activities constitute work? Should I work a 40-hour week plus the time a normal lay-person puts into the church? I really don't want this Christian community to swallow me up. I do want to continue study, write occasionally for other concerns, play squash, work on my marriage, spend lots of time with Ben and Kia, work on the car etc. (RL, Journal, January, 1981)

As it turned out, his first week involved buying an office chair, helping Newton put in a fence post, regular committee meetings, the State Youth Council, visiting his probationer, and trying to make sense of the last year's finances: welcome to pastoral ministry. One exciting aspect was that the flow to Westgate from other suburbs had begun, although not without its issues. He saw that varying reasons motivated the trend, including the buzzword "community," employment, and the perception that something new was happening. Some brought their middle-class attitudes with them. Alan and Ross spent some time actually dissuading some prospective members from coming, telling them that in fact, the reality was all rather ordinary.

Ross had several reasons for remaining unordained as he took on his pastoral role. He did not feel called to lifelong pastoral ministry, which he saw as the model in many churches. Nor did he believe that the permanent ordination structure seen in many denominations was biblical. The clergy/laity split engendered by that concept was not how he saw the use of the gifts in church, and he sensed that the status of clergy was not all positive in the community. In fact, what he was moving into was perhaps a pragmatic "ordination" for a time, need, and place. Being paid to do the job meant that the church was setting him aside; he was to wrestle with how that would all work out.

> (A highly personal reason:) I'm not sure I would pass through the heresy net of the ordination process. My theology, having survived some pretty heavy knocks from my study of philosophy and other religions, would be called liberal by many Baptists. I would prefer to be accepted or rejected due to my behaviour rather than due to my beliefs alone. I'm not finding many hassles in my present position. (RL, Journal, February 1981)

Alan Marr was very keen to draw Ross onto the pastoral team, so he drew up a tailored job description that would allow Ross to operate within his passion and gifts. He, for example, never officiated at weddings or funerals: that was Alan's role; what he did was to write songs for these occasions and sing them. Ross's areas would be leading small groups, spearheading community development, teaching and preaching, social justice issues, and music. He was a "recognized pastoral leader," according to the Baptists, with authority to pastor at Westgate only. That suited Ross as well as Westgate.

The immediate challenge was to work through the overlapping nature of the groups in community with the new group of combining churches. There were now four small groups, including about forty-five people and their children. They amounted to about half the embryonic church, but how to merge? And would it amount to a takeover or abandonment of identity? Ross feared factions if they continued as they were but was not sure how to proceed.

For him, the issue raised questions about the theology of "the church"; after all, community was a central recommendation in his *Report*. Ideally, the local church(es) would form a Christian community; what they actually had was three churches, some members of which were exploring community and some of whom were already in groups, living in proximity.

In the public worship services, Ross was pondering the "limited usefulness of preaching," acknowledging that he fell into the traps often of reading things into the text, spiritualizing what couldn't be directly applied, making obvious things sound profound, going on too long, not applying texts to their lives, and speaking earnestly but boringly without humor or interest.

> It all adds up to a message going out from the pulpit and heading straight out the door or ceiling, but not into the heads of the congregation, who can be seen with eyes glazed or heads nodding, or minding kids with relief. Is preaching The Word as important as protestant[sic] churches make it out to be? Is the verbal, instructive approach necessary? Can the preacher claim such authority as to do it week after week without opportunity for the people to challenge him? I must cultivate the art of seeing the essential issue, of asking the obvious question and of saying simply what I am thinking. (RL, Journal, January 1981)

Before long, the preaching demands were too much for him. Rotating between three churches and visiting some others meant that there was no continuity or planned teaching. He felt that he was shooting into the dark without knowing either what went before or what the current needs of any congregation were.

Ross admired Alan's preaching and found it easy to listen to, and wanted to be less didactic himself, more interactive and humorous. He began to focus on South Kingsville, suggesting that he took a series every few months. Ever the provocateur, Ross suggested to the group looking at a draft constitution that the words "by immersion" be omitted from the requirement for members to be baptized as believers. That idea, not surprisingly, caused controversy in a Baptist church, and was not accepted.

The "community of groups" was growing and bonding, and there were always people needing support. Then suddenly Ross and Alison discovered for themselves what it was like to be helped through a crisis. Kia, not quite a year old, ended up in hospital for an extended period, very ill with septic arthritis. The family was plunged into emergency mode. They had to rush her to hospital, have an IV drip inserted into her little arm and prepare her for surgery the same night. She was in hospital for two weeks and it was traumatic for everyone.

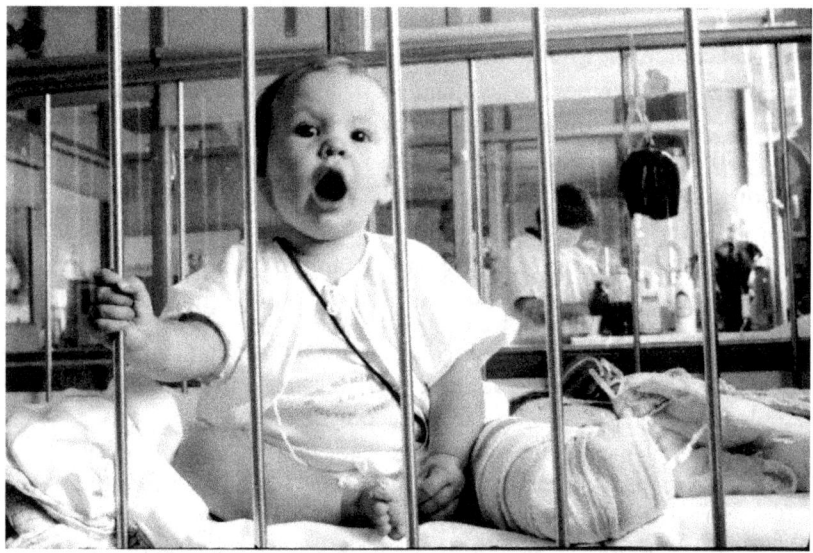

> The practical support offered to us by both small group members and other church members has been overwhelming. We not only plug into supportive family connections and live with a bloke who picks up the tab often, but are surrounded by an army of concerned people who have offered and given childminding, shopping, casseroles, relief at the hospital, house cleaning and release from obligations. I'm excited by realising that this is what community is about. We have never been so dramatically on the receiving end before. (RL, Journal, April 1981)

He understood community to be a quality of relationship, a sense of commonness of purpose and daily life which could grow best when there was intentional commitment to love each other, and work through the hurts and differences. Ross saw it as an ethos of togetherness running against the tide of individualism. God's free gift of reconciliation, experienced among themselves. That, he believed, could only be experienced in small groups. The mix of people in the groups mean that there were inevitable clashes of culture, lifestyles, and personalities. Ross was always on a learning curve.

> For someone so comprehensively living a life of Christian discipleship, Ross was surprisingly and refreshingly lacking in judgement of those whose lives were a more complex mix of practices. The first time he invited us around to dinner, aware that we were not as good Baptists as the Langmeads, he encouraged us to bring wine if we wanted to. We didn't, but we sensed that it would have been totally fine to do so. (Laurie Krepp, 2020)

Not everyone felt positive about the early explorations of combining the churches. One church questioned whether Ross was even doing a pastoral job, because he didn't attend every service at every church. Others asked whether he should be a social worker instead because of his work out in the community. Ross was being financially supported by the groups to free him up to do what he was already doing, and to work with the leadership to bring about change, but it was never going to be smooth.

Ross knew, however, that those who had sacrificially given money had done it with confidence in him as a person. Those into church politics were worried that his appointment gave South Kingsville an extra vote. These were very real issues, but are not unusual when churches merge and change. There were even arguments about whether so-called secular events such as the "Walk Against Want" should be advertised in the church bulletin. All of this sent Ross into despair at times, and he developed abdominal pain that his doctor suspected might have been from ulcers.

> We obviously have a long way to go. Sigh. (RL, Journal, March 1981)

His frustration with those who were not as committed to the vision as he was may have been what Rex Glasby, the retired minister of one of the other churches, meant when he said to Alan Marr as the community was launched: "Take care of Langers, Alan. He is too pure for the ministry." Perhaps by inference, Rex thought Alan was tougher. The remark, however, did recognize Ross's role as the vision caster, and, even today, Alan affirms Ross's leadership in this area.

By 1981, there were four thriving small groups, and people were beginning to choose to live in clusters near each other. Llew bought property and renovated it for the community. The Marrs bought a place nearby as well, and the vision of an interdependent group of people, loosely connected in the area, but sharing their lives, started to develop. The growth of the community, with all its challenges, was a critical part of Ross's model in the *Report*, which began in the family, the group, the church, the region, and ended up with the denomination.

The consultations continued. Ross could see that he needed to clear the decks to focus, and resigned from EPUY and, later, the State Youth Council. After three years of work and the goal in sight, he was willing to weather the storms, take on board criticism, and persevere with the coming together of the communities. In July, he listened to Newton preach what Ross called "the most brilliant sermon I have ever heard," on Jesus appearing to his disciples after the resurrection. Newton reminded them that in the winter of their experience, Jesus comes and says "G'day," with all the dimensions of that greeting, and transforms us. It was not only a call to mission, but a "sermon of strength": it moved Ross and gave him courage to go on. "G'day" became Ross's signature greeting.

The Baptist Social Justice Working Group continued with Ross heading up the Ploughshares taskforce. Their goal was to educate Victorian Baptists so that they would take a clear stand against nuclear weapons. In 1982, they gathered support for a peace rally and produced a resolution for the General Council, which was passed. The BSJWG organized a delegation to visit and spend time with both the indigenous people at Weipa South and the mine operators at Weipa North in the Northern Territory. The group eventually sponsored three visits to several North Queensland indigenous communities, and published reports after each. The outcomes were practical changes as well as real moral support. Ross continued his supervision of probationers, which kept him in touch with needy youth as well as with the corrections system they were part of.

By 1982, it was clear that the combination would be made up of just two churches—South Kingsville and Yarraville—plus part of the Kingsville congregation. In March that year they began a six-month trial period of combined worship that would move them towards becoming one church.

The new worship style demanded a new collection of songs, so that was another project which would take some time to complete. What it did was to inspire Ross to write more songs; the celebratory occasions in church life as well as the sad ones presented opportunities to write. One such song was "Rachel's Song," written for the dedication of Rachel Jackson. The family had been through so much to have this child, finally going the way of international adoption. When they returned from overseas with Rachel, Ross and Alison were among those from the community that welcomed them home at the airport. This profound song became so much part of the history that it was used for many children, and is still sung today.

We bring you this child with our hearts overflowing,
We thank you, we know there'll be joy, there'll be tears,
We thank you, we praise you, how can we repay you?
O Lord of life, we'll learn your love through the days and years.

We share the joy, we all say thank you
We'll all take our part in leading her, surrounding her
In the way of Love.

We bring you this child with a prayer that you'll guide us
In caring and sharing through childhood and youth,
We pray that our lives will be beacons to guide her
In search for Joy, for Peace, for Love
On the path of Truth.

We bring you this child in our quest to be childlike
And pray that we'll learn from her smile round the place,
For Jesus said, "See them, of such is the Kingdom,"
O Lord of Life, we learn of Love in her trusting face.

(RL, "Rachel's Song," 1981)

Music was still what touched Ross's heart. He went to hear Handel's *Messiah* that Christmas, after having had six nights out in a row, and with an unfinished sermon for the next morning due to a crisis of confidence about whether Christmas had made any difference to the wretched, foolish world. He wept through most of the first half, moved by its powerful scriptures, and felt cleansed. He regained his perspective, seeing that sorrow and pain were set in the context of joy, hope, peace, power, and love. He remembered again the ministry of music.

Ross saw economic sharing as a broader concept than income pooling or equalizing incomes. The church developed its common fund and continued to distribute to those who needed support for all sorts of reasons. Ross heard Jim Wallis speak when he came to Melbourne, and was challenged to see the church as radical, prophetic, distinct in its values, and not locked into success, wealth, militarism, materialism, or crushing or ignoring the poor.

> This involves my internal conflict and a desire to express a world view which conflicts with the prevailing one. The pastor versus the prophet. The peacemaker versus the stirrer. Maybe the gutless versus the brave. Where I differ from the John Smiths, John Hirts, Jim Wallises and Athol Gills is in my unwillingness for a radical viewpoint to be translated into an angry prophetic message for our time, distancing itself from the world, from the lukewarm church, accusing, berating, talking in opposites. The philosopher in me sees two sides. I see the evil and ignorance in me and hesitate to cut myself off from the Mrs. Hs of this world. (RL, Journal, June 1981)

For the Langmeads personally, there were decisions to be made that would balance trusting God while making provision for the family's future. They were committed to living simply but wanted the children to be able to have extras like music lessons. Oliver questioned his son about plans for the future, further jobs, and owning a home—this from a man who had lived on the poverty line all his adult life as a Salvo and never owned a house. Ross felt that if he were offered another job that paid more, he would accept and save the extra money for the future as well as sharing with others.

These years of moving towards being one church in the west took their toll on Ross. Some of the turbulence was just the outcome of change; some of it was very personal. He and Alan talked, prayed, and worked, and sometimes just had to stand their ground as a team. Ross made the decision in 1982 to decrease his time as pastor and earn some money by doing casual teaching locally and some tutoring at the university.

Significantly, in his journal at the start of that year, he decided to pray for joy:

> I have decided to pray regularly for the fruits of joy and peace. I don't care if it is theologically balanced or not to do so. I would like to be freer within myself about myself, to be able to really laugh more, to be able to sit quietly, to live without incessant activity, to be able to rank retreat times up there with attack times, to be less of a frowner, doubter and knocker, to be the sort of person who leaves others with a little hope, joy and affirmation. Then next week... (RL, Journal, January 1982)

Most people who knew Ross in those years and through his later life, have actually described him as exactly this sort of person—fun, humorous, good-natured, optimistic, cheerful, positive, encouraging. One could say that God did answer his prayers, but also sense that his internal struggles were ever present for him over the years that followed.

> Ross was always very glad to see us in his warm but undemonstrative way. He'd emerge from his study to be present in the kitchen and an immediate family-type connection was reliably there, and he would delight in us and our news. And yet there was almost always a sense of an invisible burden on his shoulders, which he would only allude to. What that burden was I will never really know but it seemed to me it was a combination of the sheer responsibility of his workload, stresses in the workplace and a kind of world-sorrow for all the suffering, oppression and corruption he saw but couldn't fix. This is merely an impression of mine, which I also saw lightened by laughter and especially song, but he carried a lot on his broad shoulders. (Fay White, 2021)

The church pressed on to respond to the needs around it—homeless youth being a priority. A group met and prayed for the provision of a property and were blown away in June 1982 by an offer of a five-bedroom house and bungalow rent-free by a grateful local builder whose wife had been ministered to by the Westgate pastors. Thus began the Lanigiro Housing Group. For the opening of Lanigiro, Ross wrote this song:

> *We are pilgrims, we are strangers, we are orphans, we are widows,*
> *Is there anyone who will shelter us in this land?*
> *On the hard road, in a strange place, needing comfort, feeling lonely,*
> *Will we find a roof and a welcoming hand?*

> *We're restless till we find our home in you, O Lord.*
> *Find our resting place in you.*
> *A place we're never alone, a place where we are known,*
> *May we find our home in you.*
>
> *If we're hungry, if we're thirsty, if we're shivering, if we're prisoners,*
> *Is there anyone who will take us out of the cold?*
> *If we're wandering like a lost sheep without shelter or direction,*
> *Will we find a shepherd and sleep in the fold?*
>
> *You were homeless and rejected and you send us into byways*
> *Calling anyone who will take on what you went through.*
> *Yet you call us to your mansions, to your fireside, to your ballroom;*
> *Will we come and celebrate living with you?*

(RL, "Finding our Home," 1982)

There also was a need to bring people together to share activities, so the idea was born that became Learning for Life. Headed up by Cherry Jackson, it was an opportunity for people to share craft skills and to reach isolated women in particular. They launched with over fifty responses and were able to offer a dozen courses; the idea obviously tapped into a need and the numbers grew. Everything was on offer, from macramé and weaving, to word processing, from woodwork to detailed ceramic painting. Ross taught guitar playing in a twelve-week course.

> I began to think of ways to involve the local community in a craft program based at the South Kingsville Church, including myself. Interest grew and Ross became involved, designing the logo for "Learning for Life." This became such a valuable resource and such a wonderful way to involve locals as many people—men as well as women—offered to teach their amazing crafts and skills. (Cherry Jackson, 2020)

Around the same time, the School of Christian Living commenced at Westgate with over forty registering for the opening course on the Old Testament. Held after morning tea on Sundays, teachers were drawn from a wide group to ensure the quality was high.

Westgate Community Initiatives commenced during these years, a group concerned with unemployment and job creation. Its first project was a delivery service, using an old truck and unemployed men as drivers. As Ross noted, it had its hassles; it wasn't a great idea to send rough, untrained blokes around to pack and move someone's wine glasses. At times, the pastors had to step in and become drivers, which was definitely not in their job description.

Being too busy became a recurring theme at this stage of Ross's life. In his journal he recorded his average nights out each week in 1982 from February to October: four or five were usual. When combined with about ten shared meals per month either at home or out in the same period, the program was obviously too full. Some other people were also burning out and needing space, while the programs were attracting more needy people who needed help around the clock. It was a conundrum that would probably never be solved. They had more available supportive accommodation than ever yet struggled to find places for those in need. Ross and Alison's home was at times a crisis hub and always very much a place of hospitality.

Leslie-John Newman was a member of the Kernot Street group from early days and experienced a great deal of love and support as he battled unemployment and ill health. With encouragement, he managed to get back to study and was one of the very first adult full-time secondary students in Victoria. He tells how he was unable to type and therefore could not submit his assignments as required. When Ross became aware, he offered to do it for Les, who found out afterwards that he had stayed up most of the night typing the assignment. Later he spent some hours introducing Les to his first computer and teaching him basic skills. Les says that today he remembers Ross when he "copies and pastes," which was one of the first things he learnt.

> Ross was like a mentor to me, walking with me in both the good and the bad times. My life is not perfect but what I have achieved is down to the constant support and encouragement Ross and Alison so willingly and freely gave. Not a day goes by that I don't stop, even if only for an all too brief few minutes and think of Ross and the impact he had on my life. Even after all these years, I still miss Ross. (Leslie-John Newman, 2020)

Lyn Kroker met Ross in 1978 after reading the *Report*. She had studied church history at Bible college but was left feeling a little depressed about the state of the church. The *Report* filled her with hope, and when she finished college, she was one of the people who moved to the west, and later became a member of the pastoral team.

> I think that his most important contribution was the way he lived, holding the words of Jesus and the state of the world together in one life. Others grew in faith, justice and compassion by being around him and so he has left an amazing legacy. His genuine way of life and his friendship still reaches out from the singing of his songs. (Lyn Kroker, 2020)

Ernest Vladica married Kay, a doctor at the clinic, and many remember Ross's rendition of the song he wrote for their wedding at Westgate. Ernest writes today:

> The text Micah 6:8, "to do justice, embrace faithful love, and walk humbly with your God" always reminds me of Ross. He was great at preaching his message in clear, simple terms and set a strong example of conducting himself patiently, faithfully, simply and consistently. We had the privilege of him writing the song "Different Eyes" for our wedding and performing it himself at the jam-packed ceremony at Westgate. (Ernest Vladica, 2020)

> *Seeing the world with different eyes and finding God is deep within,*
> *We're going deeper.*
> *Oh surprise. Different eyes.*
> *Things that grow seem greener now.*
>
> *Looking beyond what happens now and finding God is greater still.*
> *Let's walk together.*
> *World unknown; not alone,*
> *Hear the song-bird calling now.*
>
> *Glimpsing the pain beneath our lives and finding God is suffering too,*
> *Not always easy.*
> *Hopes and fears, lots of tears,*
> *But blue's a different colour now.*

(RL, "With Different Eyes," 1988)

There were many stories like this, and we know that Ross's heart was to love and support, but his time and strength had limits.

> I wouldn't be in academia now if you paid me, nor paying a mortgage on a new house in outer suburbia, nor ordained and "running" a church by myself, nor living in isolation, nor closing my home to others, nor working away from home 12 hours a day and wondering why my kids cause trouble, nor travelling the country speaking to important gatherings, nor writing books with the latest vital clue to an improved Christianity. If I ever had "grand delusions" I am having them less now. I'm happier now overall than I can remember for a long time. (RL, Journal, October 1982)

Westgate Baptist Community was finally and formally constituted in October 1982, and became one entity. The long-awaited amalgamation had happened. The focus of the community was to witness to the good news of Jesus in the local area, which had a large sector of disadvantaged and working-class people, and a limited availability of community services. Ross wrote a song to celebrate Christian community and to mark the occasion:

> *What grace, to make us your people.*
> *What love, to call us your own.*
> *What power, to make us your body.*
> *What care. We're never alone*
> *Because you have called us together.*
> *Oh, incredible love. We're in God's family.*
>
> *What pain we surely must give you.*
> *Such lives. We're covered in shame.*
> *How sad, we go to our corners.*
> *What stain we bring to your name*
> *Because you have called us together.*
> *Oh, be patient we pray with all your family.*
>
> *Father, your vision will lead us.*
> *Jesus, your love is the way.*
> *Spirit, creatively guide us.*
> *We'll meet to serve and to pray*
> *Because you have called us together.*
> *Oh, Lord help us to learn to be God's family.*

(RL, "In God's Family," 1982, vv. 1, 2, and 4)

The following year, the pastoral team changed, and Ross looked for work. Ben started school locally and Alison joined the school council. Ross was still involved in the nuclear disarmament movement and saw it as an important part of his faith's activism. The community experience was a roller coaster, such as when a drug addict staying in a share house wrote off someone's car then absconded, leaving a debt. The community rose up and raised $1,000 to repay the loss of the car. Ross agonized over this drama but saw it as bad news and good news all in one event.

Groups grew and divided with inevitable angst and relationships grew through the struggles. The groups diversified, with some being geographically based and others mission-oriented. Ross and Alison celebrated ten years of marriage by buying some new sheets and the ailing Zephyr sent

Ross back to hours of research. Llew turned seventy and became a permanent member of the household.

Ross wished to free the church of the cost of supporting him, although he still wanted to be involved. So, after discussion and thought, he signed up for casual teaching two days a week at the local Williamstown High School, and experienced all the highs of good pay and no preparation, and lows of challenging discipline, low involvement, and little relationship building, while earning some needed cash. He knew that he wanted space to be able to stay close to Alison, write more songs, read more deeply, and to invest in his own health and fitness. He wrestled with the dangers of being an activist at the issue level but not the personal level. No one would have seriously accused him of that failing.

The following year, Ross returned to tutoring philosophy of education, at the University of Melbourne, which he enjoyed; it was a little more sessional income and he marked papers over the summer break to supplement it. Becoming involved in Whitley again by being elected to the College Council probably indicated that Ross had not abandoned academia forever. The pastoral team at Westgate now consisted of Alan Marr, Ross, Kaye Cameron, and Ron Miers. It was the year of the first community camp and the first Westgate Paper, the idea of which was to respond to the need for information about Westgate for visitors, newcomers, and members in general.

Despite writing an entire dissertation on "The Concept of Prayer," Ross continued to struggle with this spiritual discipline:

> I have tried praying with Alison often, without being able to keep it up. Prayer is very natural to Alison. It can be intellectually-made-sense-of for me. Why not make it the altar of the shared commitment to spiritual values and guidance by the Spirit? Well, it hasn't worked yet. Why? I have a resistance that makes me unable to take part actively; it robs us of intimacy—Alison feels it, I feel awkward and it has been affecting everything—our communication, our relationship to Llew, our sense of love for each other. I can't avoid it any longer. We are partners, lovers, married. We want to want each other and to talk deeply so our intimacy is going to have to be spiritually based. (RL, Journal, May 1984)

There was no easy solution to this dilemma. They tried various forms of prayer, acknowledging that God was in it all. Ross wondered whether he lacked discipline in that area; in October he wrote that he still had not been able to share his thoughts on prayer with Alison. He knew that it was a spiritual battle too, and that he could never take the growth of Westgate for granted. Although he had written six songs in five months, he sensed a diminished creativity in the new church, and agreed with Llew, who felt it was becoming like any other church. That insightful observation was not a compliment.

The year 1984 reads as one of struggle in Ross's journal, yet one suspects that his journaling was helpful in processing and provided somewhere to vent, and was thus not necessarily representative of all his thoughts. He was frustrated with the challenges of getting older, and also of seeing people in whom he had invested time and love who seemingly did not live out the lessons learnt that he taught over and over. This is the complaint of many a pastor, yet Ross took it to heart and agonized over these perceived disappointments and his own failings. Soon after this, he decided to share his written ponderings with Alison, which was an important step in their desire to stay close and transparent.

In all of this, Ross appreciated Alan Marr as a friend and colleague. They resonated as kindred spirits and shared the Westgate story from the inside. Alan embraced Ross's incarnational mission mode, and they worked it out together in the nitty-gritty of pastoral ministry. Alan saw Ross as a role model:

> He was always there, doing the right thing. He always said he wasn't much of a pastor but over the years he has been a very good pastor to me. I have kept a quote from a sermon Ross preached at Westgate in the 80s: "Entry to the kingdom of God is free. It just costs a fair bit to live there. But we live eternally on credit in God's kingdom. We are forgiven before we enter, and we are forgiven every day we live there." (Alan Marr, 2020)

Pastoral team: Ross, Lyn Kroker, Ron Miers, Mavis Conway, Alan Marr.

The world of computers was opening up, and, not surprisingly, Ross was keen to buy one. He struggled over the cost but could see so many advantages: speeding up all his writing with word processing, the ability to edit, the use of databases, and being able to share documents with others for a start. His mathematical mind was attracted to the world of computing, and he was able to buy a discounted Kaypro II (an eye-watering $1500 in 1984), while promising Alison that he would not succumb to addiction. Adding a printer made the technology his single most expensive investment apart from the car. From the wider family's point of view, especially those who had scored the bottom carbon page of his letters, it was the end of blurry, light type and correction fluid and the start of a new era of clearly printed letters from the computer.

The theological crises kept coming, especially on a Saturday night when Ross was often preparing a sermon. He wrote half a page in a family letter explaining his difficulties in preparing to preach on Romans 5, bewailing the fact that he thought too much about issues like the atonement. The letter then set out various theories and demolished them, concluding that his theological studies had left him with no robust explanation of what Jesus did on the cross. He decided that his philosophy had helped him to find the language needed to explore the concept with "critical realism" and that he could accept the mysteries of what God did. He ended the letter with, "Strike, the fatal fourth page is over. And how are you all?" That would have been a sermon worth hearing.

On retreat with his colleague, Ron, he read a bestseller book, Sheey's *Passages: Predictable Crises of Adult Life*, that caused him to reflect on his family of origin yet again, especially considering the challenges of each decade. He identified with the section on life in the thirties, finding the fit of life "awkward": pursuing new goals, denying them and then broadening, and men wanting to develop their feeling side while women worked on their careers.

> In the light of all this, where am I heading or coming from? Leaving the Salvos was certainly part of "pulling up roots," though the evangelical scene was hardly a rebellion relative to the whole spectrum of views one could have had. So 19 was an important passage. Externally I rejected my father's hold on me. But the "inner custodian" remained with me, though diminished by the way I had always approached Dad, which was fighting him with reasons, rather than going around him, as (others) did.
>
> Why is it so hard for me to think of talking to Dad still? I'm averse to conflict and inflicting pain. Is it better to leave him be into old age? Or tackle the issues we have between us, such as the

way he treats Mum, his covert materialism, his giving in to the SA despite the way they have treated him, his unacknowledged deafness and even his apocalyptic and fundamentalist theology and right-wing politics? I can see that some talking is necessary for me to resolve at least our ability to talk at all. How do I start? (RL, Journal, October 1984)

It would be another three years before he gathered up his courage to talk meaningfully with his father. He concluded after reading about the thirties that his career choices were not driven by status or money, but that influence was his main driver, and identified that he and Alison had legitimate ambition to influence others for good. For the first time, he began to look more widely than Westgate, although he would remain a vital part of the church community for many years. He felt the weight of some people's immaturity and therefore their inability to serve others over their own needs. There seemed to be too many leaners and not enough lifters to balance it all out. Meanwhile his own commitment was costing him dearly in lack of self-care, especially in his health and family life. He recognized now his need for a mentor/spiritual director to help him make good decisions at this life stage, yet felt ambivalent about being made accountable.

At the start of 1985, he was able to look back on the launch of the Westgate Papers as well as satisfying services and songs written and arranged for the growing songbook for Westgate, and successful annual family camps. So many good things were happening, but for Ross it sometimes became a downhill spiral of discouragement that he was rarely able to share with anyone.

By April, his journaling while on Westgate staff retreat is revealing. There was quite a disconnect between his chatty family letters, full of news about the children and stories of Westgate, and his raw journal entries. He regretted not reflecting enough and felt overwhelmed by the tasks facing him. His overbusyness was affecting his feelings about marriage and family life, and he had little success in dealing with his issues with his father. His own health was concerning him; most importantly, he was unhappy on the inside.

> Basically, I'm not coping in my emotional life. I've regressed—repression, overwork, over-eating, bland exterior. I'm losing authenticity. Don't know what to write when I sit down. I'd like to summarise books, but it doesn't seem important compared to facing myself. (RL, Journal, April 1985)

It was a lonely journey for Ross, and many of the people he saw all the time had little idea of how low he felt. Spiritual disciplines deserted him, and he felt powerless to take control back in his life. Although he believed that he had thrown off that inner custodian of his father's influence, he was, in fact, driven by something he probably had inherited from his dad: a high sense of duty. When others may have collapsed in a heap, Ross refused to let people down and pressed on, despite the storm he was weathering on the inside. At the end of the retreat, he recorded:

> Last night I told Ron, Kay and Alan about my depression, my avoidance and my sense of helplessness. It felt good to have shared honestly and they received it well. In a sense I couldn't avoid saying what is uppermost in my mind. But I also felt pretty vulnerable. (RL, Journal, April 1985)

There was no more journaling until October that year and the family letters give no hint of how hard things were. Ross took time to write individual letters complete with hand-drawn cartoons to his niece and nephews who were now living in Central Java. They were so popular that he wrote an illustrated book of limericks about all the cousins, called *Morning Tea in Java*, and printed copies for the family for Christmas. They are still treasured family heirlooms today. He was a much-loved uncle from a distance and received cards and letters in return. Somehow, he managed to connect personally with so many people, both near and far. His diaries have long birthday lists in the front, and lists of all his friends' children's names, with their birthdates.

Ross's much-admired lecturer friend at Whitley, Graeme Garrett, resigned, leaving a faculty position vacant. Graeme had suffered from ill health and Ross had helped him out at times, but now Graeme was moving on and was irreplaceable, according to Ross. Ross was invited to take on some of the load the following year and to be that replacement. He wrote that he was in turmoil about teaching Theology 1. Obviously, he would have to make time if he were to do it, but he even felt unsure about the importance of doctrine for Christian living. On the positive side, he knew he was the best man for the job, and it would earn some money to support his music recording project. The most persuasive argument from Alan was that this was an opportunity to influence future pastors, and that Ross could reduce his pastoral team time to make space. And so the decision was made, and a new chapter would begin alongside the Westgate story.

Meanwhile the inner battle continued:

> Feeling pressure inside again today. Symptoms: Anxious thoughts that I'm not keeping up or catching up, and can't, without putting in some late nights, which I rule out on lifestyle grounds. Tight feeling in my chest and a fluttery feel and flushed head. Hits me when I'm planning which of many things

to tackle. Has been going on for months now. Don't know what to do. Have noticed stress symptoms occur when I don't have a list, when I am thinking trapped-type thoughts and when I am trying to achieve a ridiculous amount in a day. (RL, Journal, October 1985)

At Westgate, projects continued. An important audiovisual about disarmament was presented to the Baptist Union of Victoria, and work on the church songbook continued. The annual family camp had over a hundred people present, and Ross noted that with only one ping-pong ball destroyed, it was a calmer event than previously. A music book called *Praise for All Seasons* was released for wider church use at special events and included eight of Ross's songs.

Somehow, he pushed through and turned his attention to the events of the new year. He would become an Adjunct Lecturer at Whitley College, continue tutoring in education at the university, be a part-time pastor at Westgate, and work towards a recording of his songs. He started the year with a long list in his journal of why he had been too busy and an analysis of which he could do less of, but there simply were not many areas he felt he could cut down. He sensed that while he was really encouraged by Westgate, it possibly needed him to step back a little for others to grow. He began to run through the possible directions: schoolteacher, research, welfare, BUV. Were any of these more important than building the church?

Chapter 11

Diabetes: 1986

So I wouldn't get a big head, I was given the gift of a handicap to keep me in constant touch with my limitations. Satan's angel did his best to get me down; what he in fact did was push me to my knees. No danger then of walking around high and mighty. At first I didn't think of it as a gift, and begged God to remove it.

2 Corinthians 12:7

Most people can point to a time when there was a major disruption in their life. In October 1986, Ross was diagnosed with Type 1 diabetes, and would have to monitor his blood glucose readings for the rest of his life to minimize the possibility of a range of complications.

Latent auto-immune diabetes in adults (LADA) these days is understood to be Type 1 diabetes, triggered in an adult rather than a child. Ross became ill and was diagnosed relatively late at thirty-six, and had probably been unwell for some time, both physically and maybe mentally. Research shows that for some, depression is part of the unwellness before diagnosis, which throws some light on his struggles of the year before.

Ross had already begun swimming to help his sore back, enjoyed the exercise, and was happy to lose some weight. The weight loss, however, was probably one of the signs that his pancreas was not working well. Although stress may not be a direct cause of this disease that lies latent in a person, it does lower the defenses of the autoimmune system, increasing vulnerability to viral and bacterial infections that can become triggers.

Unlike juvenile diabetes, the onset can be gradual as the adult pancreas uses up its stored insulin, but the outcome is the same: it will result in dependence on insulin to create what the pancreas cannot. There is a honeymoon period until the residual insulin runs out, and the patient can feel hopeful that exercise and medication will halt its progress, but diabetes is inexorable and life-changing. Until the early twentieth century, it was untreatable and used to be a death sentence.

There are no journal entries in this onset period from the end of 1985 until four weeks after his diagnosis in October, which is probably significant.

> I feel burdened, fragile, tired. Westgate's problems are depressing me: criticism, polarising, money, anti-leadership feelings, failure of Lord's Supper paper, lack of volunteers, Lanigiro's future, low attendances, comfort and affluence.
>
> The diabetes is exacting in time, acquisition of knowledge and discipline, but deep down I don't feel bad about it. After four weeks I can already see the positive sides to it: health, care of the body, fitness, right weight, compulsory overcoming sweet tooth. I'm fragile but hopeful. My spirits rise and fall daily as my sugars fall and rise. (RL, Journal, October 1986)

Diabetes requires round-the-clock monitoring of blood glucose levels to counteract that rise and fall; the aim is to keep the level stable, but the reality is difficult. So many factors affect the readings—exertion, food types, emotional levels, especially stress, and lack of sleep. At any given moment, some or all these things can be in play but only understood in hindsight. People with diabetes generally feel tired of thinking about what they eat, and how to counteract the disease with a failing pancreas.

In the 1980s, diabetes research and treatment was nowhere near today's world of insulin regimes, efficient monitors, and pumps that deliver insulin directly in response to wirelessly transmitted information from a sensor. With all that technology, there is still a constant element of guesswork involved; for Ross it was a daily journey of trial and error. It was early days for blood testing strips but much easier than the urine strips used prior to that. Biosynthetic human insulin was approved in the eighties, with fewer allergic responses, and in 1985 the first insulin pen was introduced, meaning that Ross's diagnosis was at the start of a new era in treatment options.

Glycated hemoglobin tests also became available around that time, making it possible to measure blood glucose average levels for the previous three months or so. Ross always marveled at how this test worked, at the same time dreading the results from his HbA1c blood tests. Finely calibrated medication followed from these innovations, and Ross was keen to monitor his readings carefully to try to avoid the inevitable complications that can develop with this disease.

His response was initially sanguine: he would measure, record, and control this beast. There was some appeal to his mathematical side as he began detailed spreadsheets, finding averages, noting the variations and their possible causes. He observed the effect of exercise in lowering the readings and increased his cycling, swimming, and running, knowing that this would all contribute to better fitness and, hopefully, weight loss.

Some newly diagnosed diabetics plunge into denial and do not want to know what is happening to their blood glucose. Ross was the opposite. For his whole life to this point, knowledge had meant understanding and therefore power to act, so he was determined to understand the disease that had come as this major disruption to his life; he chose to see it as an enemy with benefits.

Sue Garner, a friend, recalls observing Ross's approach to recording his blood sugar readings:

> When he became a diabetic, he showed me his mathematical charts of his readings, as we were both mathematically minded, and I was amazed and impressed, but worried it would engulf him. I followed his lead and graphed my own peak flow readings for asthma for a while, but it became too obsessive for me. (Sue Garner, 2020)

It is significant that in the early days there were few mentions in letters and journals about his diabetes. He would persevere with the running and cycling. Later that year he was unwell, and tests showed a low white blood cell count, with advice to avoid infection if he could; infections are always serious for a diabetic who heals slowly.

A couple of weeks after diagnosis, Ross's diary shows a dietician appointment, and a list of calories and carbohydrates and the "exchange" rate: he was starting every diabetic's lifetime project of calorie and carb counting. That night he went out to dinner to celebrate the end of the year's lectures—no doubt the calorie count went out the window on the first night. Alison remembers him commenting wryly on their lovely dessert. Soon after that he paid a deposit on a glucometer, added lancets and strips, costing him $100 for starters. It is expensive to have diabetes, as it is for any chronic illness. Ross saw several medical practitioners that year and joined Diabetes Foundation Victoria to gain information and to share with others with the same disease.

The appointments continued, and undoubtedly were a source of stress in Ross's busy schedule. After seeing a hematologist in July, he had eight appointments in a few weeks, presumably to find the sweet spot between medication and blood glucose. To keep a tight rein on his readings meant increasing and estimating medication over against exercise and food variables. He joined the local Altona Swim and Fitness Center and felt the benefits of his exercise regime which lessened the need for medication.

After a while, the honeymoon period was over, and medication and exercise were insufficient to keep the readings stable and low. All Type 1s will end up being dependent on insulin, as did Ross. In March 1988, it became evident that oral medication, diet, and exercise could not compensate for a failed pancreas; Ross was admitted to the hospital to learn how to self-administer insulin by injection.

He was treated and observed by nurses, doctors, dieticians, and his endocrinologist. He was dreading the first shot but felt much better when he had managed it; it became clear, however, that the nuisance factor would increase with swabs, injecting, and keeping the insulin cool. To get exercise in hospital, Ross ran up and down eleven flights of stairs five times, which made his blood sugar plummet, and, ironically, he didn't need insulin that night. His health professionals affirmed that he was healthier, more active, and better educated than most diabetics.

Kia, his anxious daughter, sent him a lovely heart-shaped letter, full of eight-year-old empathy for her dad:

> When I first heard that you were going into hospital, I was very sad. I hope you get used to putting needles into yourself (and it is not hurting). I really didn't want you to be going into hospital because sometimes at night I can't get to sleep if you are not here. Another reason is that you help us a lot with our piano practice. Piles and piles of love, Kia. (Kia Langmead, Letter, 1988)

Although he had some difficult periods with his regime, he never had to go to hospital again for his diabetes. In May he wrote:

> My insulin regime is gradually improving. After a fortnight recently when I averaged a hypo a day, I have sorted it out much better. My next step is to mix my insulins so that the morning reading is low. I might have to knock off having supper. Meanwhile I'm feeling so fit I am dangerous. (RL, Letter to Grace, 1988)

The more controlled the readings, the more likely he was to have hypos, which then had to be reversed by consuming sugar (the famous jellybeans) followed by slower acting carbs. When the readings fall below a certain level, a diabetic will start to feel dizzy and weak; without reversal this soon leads to confusion, disorientation, and ultimately to a dangerous condition which can be life-threatening. All diabetics despair at times of maintaining a healthy diet as they "chase carbs" after hypos and reverse all the calorie counting, and the goal of losing weight becomes very difficult to achieve.

The familial aspect of diabetes is evident in the wider family: Ross's niece who was born while he was in Lancaster was diagnosed with Type 1 at a similar age as he was, and her daughter now also has Juvenile Diabetes. Naomi and Ross were to talk about their shared journeys over the years and encouraged one another. Naomi recalls that Ross refused ever to use the more convenient disposable needle pens on the grounds of saving waste.

For Ross, the public nature of his illness was hard to handle. Having to inject insulin before eating a meal with friends or colleagues drew attention to it, which he hated but could not avoid.

And he still struggled with his theology of healing:

> When Alison said this morning that Peter Woods wants to make a time to pray for me, my reaction was typical—silence, a civil nod, an intense internal reaction and an hour later, "Why not?" At first I feel, "If it happens then I get better the next day, what do I make of it? Was it the increased medication or the prayer? Hang on, I don't think of prayer as a physically causal agent. What do I think?" Now, three hours later, I can readily acknowledge that prayer is a mystery, that we are encouraged to bring these things before God, that people like Peter do appear to have healing gifts, that psychosomatic illness in particular (and both stress and depression are involved here) is susceptible to healing through prayer, in my opinion. (RL, Journal, July 1987)

From this time, all Ross's travel involved carrying insulin, keeping it cold, and making sure he was never without emergency rations in unpredictable situations. When he stayed with people or went to a conference, he reluctantly told his hosts that he needed regular, low-sugar meals, but was always worried that he sounded fussy. Despite improved community education, very few people understand the life-and-death nature of living with diabetes; it never lets up.

Chapter 12

Lecturing: 1986 to 1989

The trouble with a lecture is that it answers questions that haven't been asked.
ALAN ALDA

Mid-1986 was Ross's transition to lecturing at Whitley College as an adjunct lecturer in theology. His subject was "Introduction to Theology," but he had reservations about how well it would prepare young people for pastoral ministry. If he had been a reluctant pastor, he was now also an uncertain lecturer. After a summer of family camp, holidays, taking Ben on the train to Wodonga in the country and both children to Learn to Swim lessons, as well as undertaking a bushwalk with the cousins, the year began. He identified his needed course preparation and worked on making a tape of his music. Those projects, along with finishing the church songbook, would be his major challenges for the year. Ross realized, however, that there were several other daunting tasks demanding attention.

Tutoring at the university continued for another couple of years and the ups and downs of the Kernot Street group kept Ross and Alison occupied. Various children stayed with them for temporary care, Ross sang at weddings, and the car needed a new engine. One of Ross's young probationers ended up in jail, despite all the support that had been given. Ben and Kia were both learning Suzuki method piano in the hope of encouraging some latent musical talent, with chequered success.

There were now eight small groups at Westgate, rearranged with the usual challenges. "A difficult process but bloodless in the end and working well now. I'm very pleased."

The community projects were humming along, with Lanigiro, Learning for Life, and the medical clinic all thriving. The deacons ratified the policy of allowing little children to take communion, and discussion was even under way about whether they should consider a building program or go to two Sunday services, or perhaps to go out and renew another little church. With a pastoral review under way for Ross and Ron, he wondered which of all these directions would happen. Although his own choice would have been to take a sabbatical, he was nevertheless encouraged.

> Building the church directly does seem more important to me. But then, can I do it for life in one spot, without running dry myself or damaging my community? I'm really encouraged by Westgate at the moment. The camp, to which 96 people came, was characterised by lack of factions and a warmth of spirit. I have detected growth in people. The Social Justice nights are going to lead to a stronger social stance. I feel I belong. I am confirmed in my view that I wouldn't fit easily anywhere else that I know. (RL, Journal, March 1986)

The Social Justice nights were bimonthly, and the first was on chemical hazards in the Melbourne's western suburbs, the second on disarmament, and the third tackled education. Each night had three speakers followed by a long question time, and they were lively events.

This year was also the beginning of the Compuskill program, and the Westgate Community Initiatives Group became incorporated and gained funding for the program. His dream of providing services and resources for the western suburbs was slowly being realized.

On the family front, Ross was busy coordinating a major family gathering to celebrate his parents' fortieth wedding anniversary; it was to coincide with the return from Indonesia of the Woods family and would be the first complete family event for some time. Held in the church hall, it was a wild reunion for the twelve grandchildren and the family and friends of Oliver and Jean. Ross managed to coordinate a family musical offering which was possibly the first and last time ever when the whole extended family sang together. It was probably not a coincidence that Ross was reading *Escaping from Fundamentalism*[1] as he was drawn back into his family of origin.

He began working early in the year for his mid-year start as a lecturer, excited that his old friend, Bruce Rumbold, would join also as a pastoral

---

1. Barr, *Escaping from Fundamentalism*.

studies lecturer. For someone with Ross's academic record and honors in theology, he seemed unduly anxious about commencing as a lecturer. After an introductory lecture, he started with "Faith and Understanding," followed by "Revelation," "Narrative Theology," and "Reason."

In his lecture notes on factors in theology, which referenced Tillich, he summarized his many years of study in both philosophy and theology, noting that philosophy deals with being-in-itself, whereas theology asks the meaning of being-for-us. Therefore, he concluded that philosophy and theology are neither in conflict nor capable of synthesis. Because of the opaqueness of reason, he continued, revelation is necessary; reason is a necessary grid for understanding but is not to be considered absolute.

One of Ross's past students, Jason Goroncy, wrote in a blog about the challenge of theological education. He posed the question of why there is such antipathy to theology, such that pastors eschew being called theologians. He notes that in Germany, the term "theologian" actually means the local church pastor. The dichotomy in our churches between theology and practical Christianity is, he says, a false one. Church leadership should provide theological direction.[2] This was the praxis that Ross was looking for and he would have agreed wholeheartedly with Jason.

Numbers of students in theological institutions in the eighties and nineties increased: Whitley College went from around twenty-five in the seventies to as many as four hundred in the nineties, many of whom were seeking theological education but not necessarily ordination. These were students seeking to study their Christian faith beyond what their local church had offered them. Thus the teaching of theology was changing direction and the shape of pastoral ministry with it, and Ross himself was an example of this.

Alison commented in a letter that the preparation was heavy, equivalent to reading for and writing a six-thousand-word essay for every two-hour lecture. She saw him staying up into the early hours preparing, drinking copious amounts (with his increasing thirst a sign they had not yet recognized as diabetes), and knew that it could not continue that way.

> He's had to face all the inadequacies he feels about it all and remind himself that he feels it a whole lot more than the students who are basically enjoying it a lot. The hardest part for him is that it cuts out almost all his extra-curricular activities and keeps him in his study hour after hour, in between Westgate and Melbourne Uni tutorial commitments. So he really has two jobs at present. The family are bearing up OK, missing him but

2. Goroncy, "Theology for Ministry."

> knowing his level of preoccupation will not last forever. We've had a great deal from him over the years which creates a generous spirit in us all when such a demand arises. (Alison Langmead, Letter, May 1986)

This combination of roles, which was more like three jobs, would continue to create tension for Ross, with the part-time fractions of time always adding up to more than one full-time job, and the busy patches not always coordinating between his various tasks. Finding a work-life balance was a continual quest because he valued all the parts of his life, but like many busy people, was often forced to attend to the urgent rather than the important. His pastoral review was nevertheless affirming, and he was encouraged to press on at Westgate while finding his way in the world of tertiary lecturing.

It was a time of change for Whitley College. The founding principal, Mervyn Himbury, had retired, and Ken Manley was appointed as the new principal. He would become a lifelong friend and colleague.

> I first met Ross when I came to Whitley College as Principal in 1987. He was in that year lecturing in theology as we were waiting to appoint a permanent lecturer. I was most impressed not only with Ross's undoubted teaching skills but with his positive and uniformly cheerful contribution around the place, even as a visiting teacher. The more I learned about Ross, the more I was so grateful that he was part of our college life. I was amazed at his musical skills and the creative way in which sound theology was linked with eminently singable songs. Again and again across the ensuing years I saw how these songs added to our worship as a College community, and, as any good hymn, they also taught us sound understanding about Jesus and called us to our mission as his disciples. (Ken Manley, 2020)

Ross and Alison attended Ken's induction in the city as principal, at which everyone was wearing their colored academic robes, except Ross. Trappings were never his thing.

Fitness was not an optional extra for Ross; his diabetes was ever present, and exercise was a high need. In 1987 he entered in his first triathlon with community friends Newton and Michael, finding the swim leg horrible because of the interference and not being able to see, but caught up on the bike ride and the run with a tailwind, finishing in about three hours.

> There will not be a next time. Though a fun run or biathlon maybe. Training for the triathlon has certainly helped me manage my diabetes this year, with increased exercise and a general feeling of feeling trim and fit. It's ironic that as a result of "getting

sick" I am fitter than I have ever been before and back to my target weight. (RL, Letter to Grace, March 1987)

Ross, Newton Daddow and Michael Glasby.

He also managed to sign up for an adult education class in pen and wash art, finding it relaxing and enjoyable; this is the first mention for a long time of something that Ross did just for fun. Most of the time, the demands of everyday living and the needs of the small groups filled his spare time.

> I spent two hours today trying to paint the Airey's Inlet headland and lighthouse. Very frustrating for a beginner. I'm not sure when it becomes relaxing. I can't get the colours I want, and I lost my white lighthouse in my last bits of fiddling around. Clouds and water are hard too. I don't know whether I'm shirking the discipline, but at the moment I feel more like doing impressionistic sketches—not realism. (RL, Journal, April 1989)

In April 1987, the pastoral team went on retreat as they did regularly, and this gave Ross an opportunity to read, think, and journal. He even fitted in a sketch and a run. Significantly, he chose to read four books on stress, and summarized them all in his journal. He concluded that he hadn't learnt a lot over the years about stress, and committed to developing his hobby, limiting work hours, putting family high on the list, using time off on totally other things, keeping out of some clerical expectations, and having an attitude of gratefulness. To achieve that he planned to, yes, work on prayer and to limit social engagements. He planned to tidy his study, structure his week to save wasting time, and he would try to work ahead of deadlines. He proceeded to draw up a grid and allocate his time, at least in theory. He noted later that month that he had cleared his in-tray for the first time that year—that was Ross's way of dealing with stress.

The recording of the album *On the Road* was a huge undertaking and occupied a great deal of his thinking and planning time. With pages of lists of what had to be done to bring the dream to reality, he pushed through with choosing and arranging songs, gathering musicians for rehearsals, and calculating the financials. Jenny Marr played a big part in the musical arrangement of the songs for the tape, and then many other songs later on. At times, Ross lost motivation and the task loomed like a growing mountain in front of him. By July, however, the tape was done, and it remains one of the best productions of Ross's music.[3] Complete with an illustrated book of the lyrics and settings, it included sixteen original songs, "shared with others on the Christian journey in the confidence that we all experience similar struggles and joys." The title song was written for the wedding of neighbors and encapsulated Ross's understanding of the Good News. The title came from Luke 10:33: "But a Samaritan 'on the road' was moved with compassion."

> *On the road, on the road, oh we're together on the way*
> *We're finding love, finding love, show us how to walk, we pray,*
> *Because in you we see this love, and we long to live it too,*
> *You can lead us, lead us forward.*
>
> *Oh, growing in love, oh, helping each other to grow,*
> *Oh, learning to share, learning to give.*
> *Growing in care, growing in God, growing in love.*
>
> *Room to grow, room to grow, to be creative, to be free,*
> *To be ourselves, reaching out, but in growing harmony,*
> *In tune with you, and in your power, with your people by our side,*
> *You can free us, keep us growing.*
>
> *Stepping out, stepping out, though it's a risky thing to do,*
> *When others fail, we'll forgive, and remember we fail too,*
> *And when we're down, we'll turn to you, and we'll bear each other's load,*
> *You forgive us, make us stronger.*

(RL, "On the Road," 1985/arr. 1987)

Many of the songs on this recording became firm favorites, including "Lord, let me see," which can be found in various songbooks and still sung

---

3. Langmead, *On the Road*.

in many churches.[4] Ross was asked to lead fourteen thousand people singing it at the Baptist gathering called Genesis 88, where there were massed choirs and a wide variety of musicians and participants; he felt honored, and it probably fixed the song in the memories of many people. Other songs still sung frequently include "Servant Love," "God Is Love," and "We Are Not Alone in Suffering," which cover all the big themes of life.

There were disappointments and sadnesses for Ross as some couples whom he loved, and for whom he had written special wedding songs, separated. Some of those were in the community and others in his closest circle of friends and family; the pain inevitably affected those near to them and Ross and Alison struggled with divided loyalties in their friendships.

The children were growing, and Ross was enjoying the lull in the storm between the drain of infancy and of teenage years. Kia was passionate in her relationships and was devastated to lose her classroom teacher, piano teacher, and swimming teacher all at once. She fronted up bravely to her swimming lesson, jumping into the pool with tragic tears running down her face. Ben, meanwhile, was motivated by milkshakes for swimming laps and was saving for a penknife.

In his wider family, it was finally time to summon up courage and arrange to meet Oliver for intentional talks. It had taken a couple of years since his resolve to do so, but Ross followed through, hoping to bridge a gap that had been there for twenty years. Although it wasn't easy, he made the first lunch appointment in May 1987. He felt nervous and wondered whether he could be up-front with Oliver after all these years. How do you tell your dad that you feel distanced from him?

He decided to say it directly: "In my recent praying and journaling I've realized that some of the distance and walls I made between you and me in my teenage years have stayed, and now I am thirty-seven it seems silly. I suppose I am talking about getting to know you again."

Oliver responded warmly and did not take much prompting, beginning with his parents' childhood and spiritual journeys. He wished he had talked to them about many things. He then shared about having to leave school in the Depression to work for the family, about his marriage, and about time in Hong Kong. Ross could feel that they were edging closer to the question that had remained unasked for so long; if the Hong Kong experience was so amazing, why did they not return after the first term?

Ross was stunned when Oliver replied honestly that inappropriate behavior, self-confessed, had led to suspension from ministry. Ross felt bad that he had unsuspectingly dug out this skeleton, but Oliver had determined

---

4. For example, Hymn 681 in *Together in Song*.

that he would be transparent in this second meeting and not procrastinate. It was a watershed for the father-son relationship.

They then moved on to his years of Salvation Army service after Oliver returned as an officer: the hard work, the satisfaction, and the struggles, how he felt he had been overlooked because of internal politics. They discussed his breakdown in the sixties and the eventual poor health that resulted that no one seemed to be able to diagnose. Oliver put it down to the suppression of his feelings: "There is a cost involved in following the Christian approach to ambition." Eventually low blood pressure was blamed for his mysterious spells.

> Dad's experience probably explains the almost paranoid advice I got as a teenager on the temptations of sex and the wiles of the devil. It really does change my view of Dad, in that he seems more human, but doesn't lower my respect for him, strangely. The emotional effect of it all is feeling a bit bad for Dad and for uncovering it, but good that he had decided to tell me and did. Mum says on the phone that he felt better last night—great. (RL, Journal, July 1987)

After this remarkable meeting, Ross wrote to his dad, who responded with this reply:

> My dear son Ross,
>
> Thank you for your special letter, written so sensitively and full of love and understanding. It brought confirmation of the kind of mature love and understanding that I hoped for yet had no right to presume would be the reaction to learning of human failure in one you have always loved and respected. Your wholehearted loving response has made a most difficult situation into a time of rich blessing and has removed a barrier. Your response is more than I could have hoped for and has opened the way for mutual trust. We love you very much Ross and are so proud of your accomplishments in life and thankful to God for your dedication to working for him amongst people with great needs.
>
> Ross, by far the greatest part of our lives has been richly blessed by God's love, guidance and provision, and dark times have only proved his father love in more clarity like the stars on a dark night.
>
> Thanks Ross, and may God bless you and your lovely family.
> Your loving Dad (Oliver Langmead, July 1987)

A month later, Ross met Oliver again, this time to talk about the parenting years and about the kids. His dad admitted to regrets about being too busy and not relaxing with the family, but said he was the practical type. He observed that he felt the children had not been mollycoddled and, as a result, just got on with life. Although Ross wondered if he should have spared his father, he stopped short of raising the issues of the struggles of each of the siblings. Oliver recognized that he had not always shown appreciation to Jean but felt that he was making it up to her in these later years.

It was on this meeting that Oliver told the story of Ross and Leslie's first decision to follow Christ, still recalled by Les today. They were aged just six and five and were attending chapel in the King's Park orphanage in Hong Kong. Their dad watched their eager faces when the invitation was given and prayed that they would respond. Eventually remembering that parents bring their children to Jesus, he came down from the platform and asked them if they wanted to "make a decision." When they nodded, he took them to the front to kneel with him. He recounted this story with great emotion. In the light of his own failures, it was almost as if he wanted to be sure his children were safe, and expressed his love and protection for them in this way.

That custodian voice inside Ross was diminishing in power and growing in love. Each of the siblings has had to find their own way in understanding and separating from their family of origin, but Ross was the boldest and, for him, it was worth it and opened the way for a better relationship. He reflected in his journal that the problems his brothers and sisters had with their parents were for them to settle and not for him to raise.

Oliver and Jean retired from their Salvation Army ministry in 1988, and to mark the occasion, Ross wrote a song:

> *Come celebrate love, Give thanks to our God.*
> *Oh tell us the stories of love through the years.*
>
> *Thank you for those who have taught us the way*
> *Who have followed your call wherever it leads them.*
> *Thank you for those who have loved, who have cried*
> *For the world, a world that needs love.*
>
> *Love in the home, in the church, in the world.*
> *We see love in the poor and the orphan.*
> *Spirit at work in the joy, in the pain.*
> *It's the path; it's the tried and the true.*
>
> (RL, "Come Celebrate Love," 1988)

At Oliver's suggestion the following year, Ross was able to have meetings with his mother, and found them similarly helpful.

> I feel good to have got to it last. I've known that before my parents died, I wanted the chance to sit with them as adults and talk about them. I felt great deep down that I can. It is far more healing to give them the gift of my time and interest, non-judgmentally, than trying to re-order my relationship with them by confronting them or setting conditions for the sake of my survival. After lunch today I felt elated. I felt newly adult, like in middle-age. I know who I am, and have the power to do what I want to do. (RL, Journal, November 1989)

Perhaps in the light of this reconnection with his upbringing, Ross ran a monthly series of discussion groups at Westgate called "Rebuilding Faith," advertized for anyone who "has a background in very conservative theology, has found it inadequate for life and wants to re-mold a faith that is open and liberating." They tackled the basic questions of theology, including heaven, hell, and pagans. That would have been an interesting discussion, and it has to be said that while Ross majored on love and shalom, he never avoided the tough topics.

Opportunities emerged outside the college and the church to share his growing thinking about the wholeness of the gospel. Evangelicals were still divided in their understanding of what this meant, and despite a rich historical tradition of an integrated approach, the contemporary emphasis seemed to be on the word of God being more important than people's physical needs.

In a presentation at a Scripture Union Training Day in 1988, Ross set out his argument very fully. Starting with the coming of the kingdom with Jesus, he spoke of the "upside down" nature of it, where people are included rather than excluded, where it is not about trying to be good but about trusting God. It is an invisible kingdom. He grouped the spiritual, intellectual, and emotional dimensions together, reminding his audience that he was a mathematician and philosopher as well as a social being with physical needs. He then restated what became the bottom line of the *Western Suburbs Report*: the mission of the church is to make the good news of God's love visible in our lives, that is, to incarnate the gospel.

He followed on with how this could happen, based on his experience: community, including hospitality, sharing, care for the poor, simple living, clear communication, inclusion of the arts, and servant leadership. His message was not only for pastors, but also for ordinary Christians who were seeking to live out their lives for Jesus; he made it sound so simple and compelling.

Ross began to think about his musical directions after completing the huge project of recording *On the Road*. He felt stimulated to write more songs. He envisaged songs with fewer words, songs that were more metaphorical and pictorial that would meet specific needs. He was especially keen to write more in the area of praise and social justice. There was now a conflict between piano and guitar—he seriously considered learning to play the piano properly but knew that the guitar was more portable and playable for him, even though he felt limited by it.

Alison and Ross had lived sacrificially for their ministry years at Westgate, but it was not always easy. Choosing to receive 20 percent above the poverty line as a standard wage came with constraints. In 1988, Ross reflected on the pressure of financial instability: they were in debt to family and had invested in the tape, were part-time at Westgate, and had not yet received any payment for university tutoring or emergency teaching that year. Things were tight and budgeting was challenging on an irregular income. Ross was keen to take a major break but could not see any easy options on limited finances. In the end they decided to take some space and go north for a couple of months in a friend's caravan.

Families tend to remember significant road trips, and a major six-week holiday to the far north of Australia would become more memorable than the Langmeads intended. They set off in mid-November towing the borrowed caravan, heading for sunny Queensland, which is a rite of passage for many Australian families. On the third travel day, after staying at Parkes and Moree and about 1,400 kilometers into the trip, disaster struck, and they had a serious accident. At Croppa Creek Bridge in outback New South

Wales, sixty kilometers south of Boggabilla, the caravan began to "fishtail" behind the car and could not be brought back into control; it overturned and smashed into pieces, scattering everything in it all over the road. With six weeks of carefully planned holiday ahead of them, it was a very low moment, saved by the fact that, miraculously, no one was injured.

Recovering in an overnight stay, they pondered what to do. They had literally to regroup, rescue their belongings, and replan how to continue without their mobile home. While Alison and Kia went ahead by coach to Brisbane, Ross and Ben drove their car, jammed with their gear, with Ben feeling nervous after the shock of the accident. In Brisbane they stayed with friends while they bought a trailer, tent, and towbar and they were off again. Five days later they reached Cairns in Far North Queensland, thrilled to have made it in spite of the mishap. The return trip took them back south through McKay, where they stayed with cousin Ernie, whom Ross had visited up north in 1967; as they toured Ernie's sugar factory, Ross observed that it was not the place for a diabetic. Then it was home just in time for Christmas, having covered a total of nearly 10,000 kilometers on a memorable holiday.

Westgate community continued to support many needy people with projects like the casserole bank to help those who were either sick or under life pressure, fridge bank (people could rent and then pay off a fridge), learning for life, Compuskill, and the health clinic. Lanigiro and the community housing group combined, with the use of five houses, two bungalows, and one caravan. In 1989, the Westgate Trust Fund was established, set up by a group of interested people who supported Westgate financially over many years. The fund offered help to achieve long-term objectives and continued to encourage and support the community. Alan Marr continued to visit churches on behalf of the Baptist Social Justice Group and found that only some were open to following up with action on the issues he presented.

The only song Ross wrote that year was called "A Song for the Children of the Poor," which was never performed. The opening lines are significant in the light of Ross's adult renegotiations with his parents:

> *Loving us more than a father or mother*
> *God is here loving us*
> *Can we love, oh can we nurture each other*
> *We can care, we can love, we can love.*
>
> *May your kingdom come we pray*
> *Take the children's pain and suffering away*
> *And yet we are watching the poor getting poorer*
> *Without a word, without a word.*

Was it you in need of food
Poorly dressed or sick or absent from school
And when did we visit or work for some changes
Oh was it you in suffering too?

Let the children come to God
Let them grow in love with all that they need
We'll speak out and open our lives a bit wider
The Spirit blows to change the world.

(RL, "A Song for the Children of the Poor," 1989)

1989 was a year of consolidation; Ross was happier with his diabetes management, although always balancing out the inevitable hypos when he tried to eat less food. Benjamin graduated top of his primary school and was gaining confidence; he was off to an SU camp in summer. Kia's piano playing was progressing, and she planned to go to Suzuki music summer camp. The family had a good holiday in Hall's Gap in the mountains and prepared for Christmas.

In the year that Ross turned forty, he had some downs, but on balance the ups won in his reflections.

> I have had the privilege of being happily married, being an enthusiastic parent, finding a Christian community, finding a great job, being educated, discovering myself a fair bit, enjoying a lot of physical activity, savouring the world of ideas, having some great, close friends, living overseas, finding a creed to live by, being able to live out that creed with some integrity, being loved as a leader in my community. I am, objectively, one of the most privileged people I know; and, subjectively, I experience life as grace-filled. If I couldn't, who could?
> Turning 40 does remind me that although I will always be a student and learner, I do have a responsibility now to guide and teach with more authority but I will never become authoritarian, and my style, hopefully, will be that of a midwife, but my inferiority complex about what I know is melting. I can contribute to others; and I ought to. (RL, Journal, September 1989)

Ross had a review every three years which resulted in a six-year reappointment at Westgate, and he felt affirmed and optimistic. There were big invitations for the next year that would take him beyond the western suburbs of Melbourne and stretch him well beyond his comfort zone.

Chapter 13

Adventure: 1990

Only those who risk going too far can possibly find out how far they can go.
T. S. Eliot

World Vision International invited Ross to travel to the USA in March 1990 to lead the music and worship at their conference in Los Angeles. This was a wonderful opportunity, but Ross wanted to explore further, so decided to extend his trip to Central America to balance the experience in a poorer adjacent region. His goal was to become a better-informed partner in the struggle of Christians in those countries, and he was supported by Westgate and sponsored by World Vision to do this. Undoubtedly the contrast would be striking, but both parts of his travel would present him with challenges that would stretch him; it would be an adventure.

At the front of his detailed trip diary there are two pages of research comparing Australians and North Americans: he was well-prepared to cross the cultures. It makes for entertaining reading. His list of American characteristics that are similar to Australians included: frontier, practical, inventive, low value on intellectual and spiritual pursuits, forthright, informal, gregarious, mobile. He noted, however, that compared to Australians, Americans have wider social circles, more violence in their lives, respect achievers, know very little about Australia, and are seriously friendly, needing to be liked. He especially noted that there is a big difference in sense of humor, and that Aussies need to tread carefully with their jokes. That was a good reminder for Ross.

Having prepared himself culturally, Ross was busy getting away right to the last day; he had a long list of vaccinations required and needed to spend time preparing his music. His biggest challenge was to work out how to travel abroad for the first time as an insulin-dependent diabetic. Because he would not be in control of his circumstances, this trip was full of risk.

He departed for the United States on 13 March 1990, with Ben waving a goodbye flag at the airport; that sight brought tears to his eyes. Five weeks would be the longest separation he had ever had from his family. He read their beautiful farewell cards and letters in the transit lounge in Sydney and shed a few more tears. On arrival in Los Angeles, he immediately faced his first diabetic challenge when he had to walk over a kilometer at the airport to find some food to stave off a glycemic low. He stayed with good friends, Ken and Joy Luscombe, as they all prepared for the conference.

His most urgent task was to buy a guitar. Without his own transport, he borrowed a ladies' bike and rode nearly forty miles roundtrip checking out music shops and finally spotting the guitar he really wanted. That night, he lay awake, jet-lagged, trying to decide whether to buy the guitar and ended up with a hypo in the early hours.

In what he called "the sweetest moment of my week," he bought the guitar the next day, along with a strap, picks, and a set of bongos. It is hard to imagine how he carried all this extra luggage for the rest of the trip. The conference began at the Forest Home Conference Centre in the San Bernadino mountains of California, right on the snowline at 1,524 meters above sea level. In the rarefied air, Ross felt puffed just walking to his cabin. He did some great walks as he became stronger, including one to Point Inspiration, enjoying watching squirrels and crested honeyeater birds in the stunning forest.

Breakfast was a diabetic's nightmare, he recorded, with sweet cereals, cupcakes, and buns, but he found some scrambled eggs to start the day more safely. He did not want to start his ministry feeling sick.

The silence periods were challenging for everyone, but participants brought back to the group what came to them in those times, and for Ross, it was refreshing. He reflected one time on the Syro-Phoenician woman, realizing that he ached for the broken people he knew, just as she did for her sick daughter. He determined to be as cheeky and bold as she was, demanding to be included for her daughter's sake.

As he mixed with the crowds at the conference, talked, and led songs, Ross also reflected on his own personality and ministry.

> I have taken on this trip as a next step in my growing towards
> a more rounded personality. I'm trying to accept that although

introverted, I can relate successfully to people. Although I am not a natural performer, song-leading with the occasional semi-performance is something I do well. Although I am inhibited in using my body in worship, I am in a position to encourage movement in others. Although I struggle with faith and doctrine, what I can affirm I can inspire others with. In these respects, I feel like Moses, who felt he couldn't speak to Pharoah, but managed very well as conscripted leader. He had been very well prepared in his earlier life, in fact. Me too.

All this means that if I do continue in this direction, I need to do a little less, so I recover each time. I need to decide deliberately to develop in these areas so I grow in confidence. And I need to let go within, so I relax into the roles. (RL, Letter to Alison, March 1990)

The conference continued with great affirmation of his music ministry, and with opportunities to draw out people from other cultures. From Ross's perspective, the evangelical theology of most of the speakers was conservative, yet he was grateful that their gospel included the poor and involved great risk and courage. He observed people from places like Zimbabwe wearing suits and ties, carrying large zippered King James Bibles and sounding a bit preachy, yet admired the strength of their testimonies and the cost of their commitment. He met outstanding people from many countries—Bangladesh, Zimbabwe, Zambia, Malawi, Hong Kong, the United Kingdom, and India for example—and often found that cautious humor offset any discomfort with their theology.

He felt a strangeness that his song-leading was thought to be worth a $2,000 air ticket, when there were so many other talented people there. He also realized that he needed to prepare more simple songs with actions to draw people in. World Vision bought copies of his tapes and book for each of their offices, and it pleased him to think of his music spreading so widely. He was even besieged with autograph requests, which was a novelty for Ross the introvert.

Ross was refreshed in the spectacular mountain scenery by taking long walks and runs, finding waterfalls and gullies, steep paths and rocky lanes. His fitness made him feel good and alive and more able to give out. He ran in some areas known for rattlesnakes but tried to be reassured it was not the season to encounter them. He did one run with a Mexican friend who had run the New York Marathon twice, but found Ross's pace too fast—he was very chuffed at that. He also practiced some techniques to calm himself when he felt too much adrenalin: observing himself, breathing, understanding his feelings and then handing it all over to God. "It's OK, it'll pass," he would say. He was even happy to learn from Buddha if it helped.

All the time he had to be aware of his blood sugar levels which were a roller coaster reflecting his feelings, food, and exertion; he could not afford to collapse from low readings somewhere in the San Bernadino mountains on a solo run. He could have chosen to stay home where his situation was more controlled, but having embarked on this undertaking, he determined to be vigilant and stay well.

> There was only one occasion so far when I was over 15 and getting up at night. It's hard to turn down Brownies—an American choc fudge slice—or other desserts, but in general I have done. Part of my method has been to talk openly about my diabetes, which then acts as a social brake on me indulging. (RL, Letter to Alison, March 1990)

He finished well, feeling more energetic than when he arrived. The leaders were thrilled with the music and felt it was the glue that bonded the group.

His big encouragement was World Vision's new initiative of "Urban Advance," which was intended to get them into urban ministry through things like building networks, training community organizers in slums and squatter areas, and empowering the poor. Some of the participants were field officers looking to move in this direction, and he was warmly received as someone with a resonating vision. His earlier feelings about "western gloss" dissolved as he heard people's stories and learned about their families. He heard about their travel away from home for long periods; he saw their commitment to the poor, and felt their challenges with lifestyle. Ross understood and felt connected; it warmed his heart to reflect on how to meet the needs of the poorest people in the cities.

It was time to leave after one more long run down the valley. He basked in that satisfied feeling of a job completed and a network of new friends formed. It was snowing lightly as he left Forest Home camp, heading for Chicago where he would join a gathering called a Seminary Consortium for Urban Pastoral Education.[1]

Visiting Chicago was a heady experience for Ross. He loved the vibe of the city with its soaring towers, daring architecture, and beautiful apartment blocks fronting Lake Wisconsin. He visited Al Capone territory and the massive Museum of Science and Technology, wishing he had Ben and Kia with him. He called the city "urbane, liberal, gracious, wintry, windy and wealthy." The hotel Bismarck was right in the center of town, walking

---

1. SCUPE is now called Omnia Institute for Contextual Education, an interfaith organization.

distance from everything, and close to good public transport. All that made Ross happy. He was not, however, comfortable with staying in what seemed to him like a luxury hotel, while the congress would focus on urban poor. He railed at the expensive restaurant and long waits, as well as the unfamiliar system of tipping; he soon bought cereal and milk to have in his room for breakfast.

His first run was in one-degree cold and falling snow, which required gloves and scarf, but was helped by the stunning misty views of the Sears Tower. Running was definitely his way of staying well and centered through this experience. The sessions were absorbing and worthwhile, but for Ross, the highlight was listening to Ken Medema, the blind gospel folk singer. An amazing performer and speaker, Ken says that his disability helped him to have sympathy for the disenfranchised, whether politically oppressed or for any reason. Ross was captivated by his music, his message, and his down-to-earth humility.

> His theology is great and he breathes joy, humour and compassion. It was worth coming to Chicago just to hear him. (RL, Letter to Alison, April 1990)

Perhaps there had been a little too much conferencing, but Ross had some serious misgivings about how he fitted in by the end of the week.

> I am meeting lots of Christian leaders on this trip and methinks they travel, lecture, write, report, "network" too much. That is, because their career structures are undefined, there is much huffing and puffing, much telling of their own situations at home, much office-bearing in coalitions/consortiums/institutes/networks, much name dropping, much conference going, much dressing up and much domination of conversations and Bible studies. How else can they feel they have status, or feel they are doing something important?
>
> I see it in many of the World Vision staff who are simply executives in a corporation—Ken couldn't get enough families to host our group of 25 visitors for a weekend from 500 WV US staff and over 100 WV international staff. They work as an aid agency and live like executives, with big expense accounts and staying in good hotels. WV staff travel amazingly frequently. They think globally, jetting in and out of countries for a week. I'm on a different journey from most at least. Westgate feels unique. No-one else here is in jeans or looks poor. (RL, Letter to Alison, April 1990)

This little outburst in Ross's trip diary seems uncharacteristically judgmental, but it does express his deep discomfort with what felt like a disconnect between the conference and the situations it was meant to be focusing on. Ross was never at home in a four-star hotel—he was a backpacker and hitchhiker at heart. On the other hand, he was encouraged to meet people like Ken Sehested, from the Baptist Peace Fellowship of North America, whose workshop was creative and confronting. The conference finished on a high note, led by Ken Medema on piano and synth.

Ken Sehested would later get to know Ross and Alan Marr when he came to Melbourne in 2000 for the International Baptist Peace Conference which was held just prior to the Baptist World Alliance Convocation that year. Ross and the Social Justice group sponsored the event. Ken wrote recently:

> Ross was among the Christian leaders the world over who have been returning to Jesus as the principal lens through which genuine biblical vision is developed. Instead of the "crib-cross-crown-glory" vision of much theology (including the church's historic creeds), Ross was among those advocating Jesus' concrete life/teachings/healing work. (Ken Sehested, 2020)

Snow fell softly again in Chicago as Ross prepared to leave, acutely aware that if a comfortable conference center and a good hotel had taken him out of his comfort zone, the lack thereof in the next part of his travel would be even more confronting. With that in mind, he trimmed down his luggage, and flew via Houston to Guatemala. The next stage had started.

For the next two weeks he traveled through Guatemala, El Salvador, and Nicaragua, feeling as though he was in an alternative universe. Ross's reason for visiting Central America was to understand the politics and human rights situation, particularly in El Salvador. He wanted to hear directly what it meant to be a Christian amidst poverty and conflict, so that he could return a better educated, more passionate, and more committed partner of Central American Christians in their struggle to apply the gospel. All in two weeks.

Easter was an amazing time to be in Central America, with extraordinary religious and cultural events to experience. Hosted by Central American Mission Partners and Baptist missionaries, he met many workers at the forefront of the ecumenical groups that stand with and for the poor in their country. One example of the people he met was Jim Morgan in El Castano.

> Jim is working an agricultural plot with local campesinos to demonstrate techniques which care for the land and look to the future. We visited the local Baptist church where local villagers

were preparing for the advent of water-on-tap. I heard stories of a massacre which occurred in the region early in the 80s, aimed at crippling the work of the local co-operative—very sobering. I was told of the ways the government is undoing the little land reform which has occurred. I saw a composting latrine designed by Jim and suited to local conditions. I saw soldiers at all major intersections and stopping vehicles on main roads. I was deeply impressed with the model of missionary work demonstrated by Jim, who has worked alongside the campesinos humbly for years. (RL, Report of visit, September 1990)

He met a youth pastor, who, as well as running Bible studies and rallies, ran a Protection Center helping families to retrieve sons forcibly recruited from the streets by the army. He heard about the six Jesuit priests who were murdered at the University of Central America only months before, and saw a squatter community formed by refugees from the 1986 earthquake. His very detailed trip diary has pages of these stories and conversations.

The atmosphere of fear and the cost of being a Christian, the critical political state, and the deep level of poverty he saw everywhere struck him continually. Yet people were resilient and found hope in liberation theology. As he saw Christian workers identifying humbly and long-term with local people, he wrote: "What dedication. How mundane. How specific. What a level perspective."

In Nicaragua, Ross visited a clinic in Achuapa that had become a partner with the Westgate clinic. He was able to carry in a carton $300 worth of over-the-counter supplies like iron tablets and bandages, as a gift. A token perhaps, but a satisfying connection with home. He saw an open society in a precarious situation with collapsing currency and lack of basic goods. The Christians there were politically aware, and most were living in "rice and beans" poverty. It was all disturbing and difficult to respond to on the spot with little space for reflection.

Ross was challenged by his inability to communicate, apart from learning a few Spanish numbers and phrases, and experienced some tricky moments in his travel. At times he had to grab whatever he could find for his dietary needs, like warm coke from a small supermarket. As he arrived in the city of San Salvador, one of the most murderous cities in a very violent country, he had the double worry of getting not only the large carton of medical goods he was carrying to the Nicaraguan clinic, but also his own medications and syringes.

"Estan medicinas para un amigo, un medico en una clinica en Nicaragua," he managed to stutter to the customs man. He was so nervous that he didn't understand the reply, thinking he was being told to leave it there. In fact, the official had said he was good to go. Under the watch of gun-toting soldiers, he tried to tie the box together again, dropping and breaking his watch as he did so. He was trembling, having barely recovered from a hypo just moments before. Relief washed over him as he was met by the friends who would look after him for a few days. As he expected, the uncertainties of travel continued to push him into difficult situations:

> I had forgotten my Novo insulin pen, and we had Salvadorean breakfast on the way—tortillas, curried mince, fried soybean, fried banana and cream. Only after did I remember I could use syringe and bottle, which I did. But we carried no water, and my readings went up over 15. I got so desperately thirsty and had to ask for water while we were standing on the hot hillside talking agriculture. I drank three big glasses and had mineral water for lunch and drank coconut juice from the coconut.
>
> I went for a 45-minute run and didn't feel bad during or after it, though it was hot, humid, hilly and therefore hard. But I must have dehydrated, because I was thirsty all morning and most of the afternoon. I think I wrongly interpreted it to be high readings, until my thirst coincided with an almost hypo at about 3 p.m. I was still juggling readings and having bananas and butter scotches. D and R probably think my diabetes is a fussy thing because they seem to go long stretches without food or water, and are having to adjust, which they are thoughtful about. (RL, Letter to Alison, April 1990)

At last, it was time to return to his beloved family and community; he arrived home as the children were returning to school for the new term. Ross felt unsettled by what he had encountered in Central America and was burdened with awareness, yet conscious that he knew too little to be an expert. He reported on his trip and attended some events organized by concerned groups. His decision was to join one group that would give practical support: Comrades Australia, that supported relatives of the disappeared in El Salvador. He became part of an urgent response network in cases of human rights abuses.

This trip gave him a global perspective, a feeling for what many two-thirds world Christians experienced daily, and joyful memories of resilient people. What he found most challenging was how to relate his concern for Central America to daily Australian life. While acknowledging that he couldn't save those people, neither did he want to ignore them.

Community life at home had not stopped while he was away, and many issues were waiting for him. Pastoral staff meetings, catching up on the crises, singing at weddings, and speaking at events about his trip filled his time. An Urban Mission conference in June was a perfect opportunity to share his experiences, and several churches invited Ross to speak. These were also a way of selling his tapes and books, and hundreds were sold during this year.

The serious business for the rest of the year would be his next big adventure: running the Melbourne Marathon. There is a long lead time to any such event, and Ross had already run some fun runs and triathlons, but never the forty-two kilometers of a marathon—his furthest distance before this was seventeen. Was it possible for an insulin-dependent Type 1 diabetic to pull it off? That was an even bigger challenge than the actual endurance factor. To add to the pressure, Ross set out to complete it in a personal goal of under three and a half hours.

The Melbourne Marathon is the largest in the Southern Hemisphere and the 1990 event attracted runners from the largest-ever number of countries, with twenty-two nations represented. Out of a total of 3,881 entrants, 1,146 were first-time runners like Ross. Apart from training runs, his first move to prepare himself was to see his specialist. Before he commenced serious training, he sewed a pocket into his shorts to carry sugar cubes and telephone money and wore an identity bracelet for safety's sake.

For Ross, keeping blood sugar at the consistently right levels for such a long event would be a matter of trial and error, so he experimented on his training runs with taking less insulin beforehand, thus starting with slightly higher levels. If he miscalculated the amount of insulin, he would have a hypo. One day, he did drop too low and discovered that he had forgotten to carry his sugar; he had to find a chemist shop to beg for glucose and phone home to be picked up. He was in a cold sweat, shaking, panicking with a severe headache, had numb feet, and was walking as though he was drunk. Each run involved an estimate of how much energy he would put out; if he were wrong, he would wake up at 3 or 4 a.m. suffering a hypo.

About two hours into a run, Ross would need a carbohydrate, so on a training run would drop into a milk bar and buy juice, even though it reacted in his stomach. He then tested by running around a large block, testing his sugars every time he passed home. With help from experts, he calculated that he needed about thirty to forty grams of carbs per hour. This was mathematics meeting sport.

All was going well until he did a trial thirty-two-kilometer race in September. Taking his specialist's advice, he used no insulin at all before the run, but his levels shot up and he could not push his body without energy. He was so discouraged and doubted that he could run the extra distance. In fact, he was dehydrated—extremely thirsty and fatigued, with leaden legs and his spirit crushed. He was worried that he just wasn't tough enough.

Fortunately, he tried again and felt good on the next twenty-eight-kilometer run. It was a puzzling balancing act between insulin, initial blood readings, carb intake, temperature, and pace. He finally felt that he could make it and now had two basic goals: to finish in a respectable time for a forty-one-year-old, and not to end up in hospital.

The day of the race was a beautiful spring day in Melbourne. Ross's support team was ready: his family, his dad, and some friends. Newton Daddow recalls having Ben on the back of his motorbike so that they could keep up with Ross and see him at each of the drink stations. Ross had woken with a hypo at 3.30 a.m., which was not a good start and he knew he would feel a bit seedy. He set off at 6 a.m. with Alison and Kia to take the special train to Kananook Station in Frankston for the start. There were bands playing, queues for portable toilets, people warming up, boxes for the runners' supplies of drink bottles, and lots of sunscreen being applied. Ross tested his blood sugar; it was ten, which was perfect. Steve Monaghetti, the long-distance running legend, started them all off and within thirty seconds, Ross was on the start line and through the first challenge.

His plan was to take the race at an even pace, rather than start fast, aiming at a steady five minutes per kilometer. It worked and he felt terrific for the first twenty kilometers. Then the wind kicked in and the temperature went up and the muscles began to tire. He pushed and hit his lowest point at thirty-five kilometers; he was not at all comforted by the fact that there were only seven kilometers to go.

Alison and Kia missed him at the southeastern suburb of Mordialloc, which was partway, and he did not see them until the finish. He "prayed to Monaghetti, the patron saint of marathoners," he pretended to like the pain, he looked at others dropping out, and ended up just putting one foot in front of the other. He missed the drink at forty kilometers that had been placed by Newton and Ben, so they were rightly worried.

Oliver said that he would be near the War Shrine in St. Kilda. There he was, offering a drink and chocolate. Ross knew then he could make the last kilometer, although he wished afterwards that he had taken the drink; he just did not dare break his rhythm. Then he saw the 500-meter sign and finally walked over the finish line. A jump for joy was impossible, even though he was euphoric.

Then his legs gave way and he swayed, as his blood sugar plummeted. A helping arm and jellybeans, minerals, and fluids in the first aid area restored him before the cramps set in. When he recovered, he relaxed with his team with a picnic in the park and allowed himself to feel a bit proud of his achievement.

> Over all, I was really pleased that nearly all the factors that I had to work out came together on the day. I wanted above all to finish, and did. I also quite wanted to beat 3 ½ hours and did it by about two minutes. I feel great to have done it, and doubt very much I will ever do it again—I've climbed that mountain. (RL, A Story About Special Circumstances, October 1990)

An article in the *Diabetes Association of Victoria* magazine a few months later featured a photograph of Ross receiving a trophy for the Courage Award, presented by the Lord Mayor at a town hall reception as a municipal award. The photo was also included in the official glossy *Melbourne Marathon* magazine, and in the local newspaper. Ross made the point with all these articles that he wanted his fellow diabetics to know that it was possible to be active and enjoy life and even achieve sporting goals that may push them well out of their comfort zone. He didn't just do it for himself.

Many years later Ross spoke to UNOH supporters at a celebration supper and based his thoughts around lessons learnt from running the marathon fifteen years previously. He learned to pace himself: in his Christian life, that meant setting boundaries and living life sustainably. He also discovered it was not good to miss a drink stop: he related this to his need for spiritual nourishment and the need to locate the spring of living water, with retreats, prayer, journaling, and reading. His last thought was that he needed to run with a group—we all need to be with community to keep us going for the long haul. With this extended metaphor he encouraged the UNOH team to care for themselves in their demanding ministry.

Ross wrote a couple of songs in 1990, with one of them embracing the fullness of life in the Spirit, in all its aspects. The song is a benediction, imbued with joy, and written for the wedding of friends Lyn and Steve.

May you live in the Spirit of the evergreen God
In the sun and the showers of blessing.
May you draw your life from the flow of God within,
From all the tender times you bring each other grace.
And for love and for energy be thankful.

May your roots go deep in the warm, dark soil
In the heat and the drought of the summer.
May you stand and trust, knowing God is in it too.
The seed lies in the dark, the night before the day.
Letting go in your growing, still be thankful.

May you grow in the beauty of a colour-filled life
In the joy, in the flowers of creation
When you sing, when you paint, when you laugh and when you taste

May all your senses know that you create with God.
Let the artist within you now be thankful.

May your leaves give shade to the creatures of God
And may birds find the shelter of justice.
May your life together be open to the world,
Embodying the love that springs up from the deep
And transforms all who feel it and are thankful.

(RL, "Evergreen God," 1990)

Chapter 14

Advocacy: 1991 to 1992

I spend half my time comforting the afflicted, and the other half afflicting the comfortable.

WESS STAFFORD, CEO OF COMPASSION

Sometimes the road will head uphill through terrain which may be strange for some of us. But if we are following the stranger from Nazareth it will be an exciting trip—a journey full of hope, for us and for all humanity.

ATHOL GILL, NT PROFESSOR AT WHITLEY COLLEGE

It was time for a change of rhythm, so Ross took off the whole of January 1991 with his family. Ben and Kia and their ten cousins were now old enough for some outdoor expeditions, and this became the first year of the now-fondly remembered "cousin hikes." Twelve children aged fourteen and under, accompanied by their parents, uncles, and aunts, going hiking and camping through the high country. What could go wrong?

Ross's brother, Les, was the expert on hiking in the high-country region, so he planned the expedition carefully and they all met up at his place in Wodonga as a launching place. The heavy rain that night should have been an indication of what was ahead, but they set off optimistically for Harrietville with packs sorted and weighed, and the adults carrying the bulk of the load. Ross records that "Ben re-dammed the Ovens River" among other feats, and the fitter cousins raced ahead, leaving the little ones behind.

As they set out, kitted up for a hike from the caravan park, the storm broke, lashing them with rain, hail, and sleet. After a set of keys locked in the car was retrieved, they retreated to the church hall in Bright to regroup. A tire puncture and a snake sighting later to add to the excitement, they made another attack on Mount Hotham, this time reaching Dibbins Hut for the night. A campfire with damper and marshmallows and a good night's sleep re-energized them to get back to base, where Ross noted that "lilos seemed bliss." The cousins, now in their forties, still talk about the annual hikes, but especially this first one.

This was the year that Ross sought out a spiritual director. He liked John at the first meeting, and they clarified that their purpose was to facilitate Ross's relationship with God: this was not therapy. John would be a "privileged onlooker, a listener and a prodder." Ross wanted to feel more at ease within, more aware of God-at-the-center, able to overcome blocks, taking steps on his journey, and linking daily grace events to God.

John helped to draw him out, although Ross was always conscious of his verbal skill, and that he could choose how to present himself in each session. He raised his relationship to Jesus as a crucial area of exploration in these sessions. He was encouraged to read out the words of some of his songs: could the songwriter minister to himself?

John tried to help Ross to steer a path between relaxing more and not being down on himself, while at the same time staying organized to get through what he had to do. He experimented with allowing his journaling to lead into prayer, but still found silent retreat difficult. Even when he managed his to-do list, there were constant pressures like people needing help, counseling of couples who were breaking up, not being able to sleep, weight gain and insulin management, feeling flat, and being anxious that they had no money. They are all common stresses but difficult to escape from.

Ross was always deeply drawn to the marginalized and disadvantaged, whether they were within the church or not. He saw firsthand the severe lack of services in the west, and his *Report* had uncovered the confronting statistics of unemployment in the region. He felt conflicted when the demands of pastoring left him little time or energy to reach out, and his drive to advocate and act was sometimes frustrated. His journals are filled with the stories of those demands—a pastoral role can be simply defined but not simply contained. He had been part of Compuskill since its inception in 1986 and his diary shows his ongoing commitment every Friday in this period. Teaching, empowering, and encouraging the participants was his way of advocating. Not just words, but actions and connections were his language.

Youth Pathways helped young people who were disengaged from education and employment, which was always an area of great interest for Ross. It partnered with Melbourne University to research not-for-profit employment services and began to establish social enterprises; it has grown exponentially and won major awards. And this all began with a local response to unemployment by the Westgate Baptist Community.

> On Thursday I visited a Sudanese friend who is doing a course at Compuskill. He is a political refugee brought to Australia by the United Nations. He had heard that two weeks ago the Sudanese military had strafed an airfield in Sudan where 250 refugees were waiting for UN food supplies, killing 117, and wounded the others. He lost an aunt and an uncle, and a sister and two brothers were wounded, one critically. This week he sold all his furniture, borrowed $1000 and sent his total unemployment cheque, totalling $2,300 in all, so that his brother would be treated at a hospital in Nairobi. He has a vaguely Christian background, and when Westgate was able to help him a little, he thanked God for it and said my availability was an answer to prayer. He is presently asking God why this suffering occurs, and I am too. (RL, The Westgate Pilgrimage, October 1991)

The church celebrated its tenth anniversary since its amalgamation, and it was time to review. The congregation gathered together to consider its direction with the theme of "Meeting the Future," reflecting on the strengths and weaknesses of Westgate and how to work towards a vision statement. One outcome was that the community purchased a property in Yarraville to use as a multifunction site, even though there were concerns that the finances were well under budget. The pastoral issues were increasing, and the difficulty of balancing out his various roles was challenging; Ross began to consider his basic discomfort in the role.

The outcome of this reflection was that Ross told the deacons that he would reduce to half-time on the pastoral team, and that he would actively seek another job in line with his desire to research and advocate. His tutoring role at Melbourne Uni had come to an end because of funding cuts, and he would continue his lecturing in theology at Whitley.

Deeply impacted by his trip to Central America the year before, he began applying to development agencies for jobs that would put him more in touch with the poor in developing countries, as well as in his own neighborhood. They would have involved travel, which is interesting in the light of his criticism of the World Vision staff traveling a lot, but he was becoming clearer about his transition out of pastoring and counseling. This decision was not a rejection of his commitment to his local church and community; in his early forties, Ross was feeling the need to be more intentional in his advocacy to expand his influence.

In early 1992, he was offered two jobs: the Overseas Service Bureau interviewed him, but wanted him full-time, and the Footscray Council offered an appointment as community relations worker. The latter was a thirty-week, funded job for two days a week and was an ideal opportunity to influence local government policy. Ross accepted immediately and was briefed the same day on how he was to improve access by ethnic groups to the Council and municipal services, as part of the social justice strategy of Footscray. It was based in his own western municipal region and felt like a great opportunity to advocate for marginalized migrants.

The elements of Ross's new work week were coming together: half-time at Westgate, half a day at Compuskill, and the new project for the other two days. Of course, there were still church camps, pastoral retreats, a course to present on writing skills for VCE students in the western suburbs, speaking and singing opportunities, church rosters, and a new songbook to tackle. Keeping the time fractions balanced was always a challenge, but somehow the peaks and troughs worked out on average.

Partway through the council project, Ross submitted his report.[1] In 1990, Footscray Council had issued a landmark Social Justice Report with 122 recommendations on access and equity for non-English speaking residents. With $10,000 worth of funding to spend, they wanted information and action. Ross's role was to provide opportunities for non-English speaking local groups to connect with local government, and to assist the Council

---

1. Langmead, *Footscray Project*.

to understand the makeup of the local community better. In addition, he was to explore ways of providing improved information on services available. Lastly, he was to ensure that there would be on-going consultation.

In 1986, Footscray was one of the most multicultural municipalities in Australia, with 43 percent of residents being born overseas and speaking another language at home, compared to 27 percent across Melbourne. The waves of immigrants formed a complex pattern across the region, with many choosing the area as their first location in their new country.

There were interesting nuances to Ross's discoveries. For example, information on aged services was needed more by Italians, Greeks, Poles, Croatians, Serbians, and Macedonians, whereas information on children's services was needed more by Vietnamese, Central American, and North African groups. This probably reflected the period of migration and age demographics for these respective groups. Ross drilled down to specific advice for translating information, suggesting that it be brief, in plain language, and used only accredited translators. He concluded with lists of ethnic radio stations, newspapers, neighborhood houses, and other centers where information could easily be disseminated. Today, the website of the Maribyrnong Council, into which Footscray was incorporated, is accessible in forty-six languages.

He also addressed the need for council staff to be more welcoming and customer-service oriented. There was a huge demand for bilingual staff and for prioritizing face-to-face meetings with each ethnic group. Undoubtedly, the experience, information, and networks that Ross gained in this job were invaluable as he looked further afield than his own community.

Ross gave a presentation in 1991 called "The Westgate Pilgrimage" to a church in Templestowe where he talked about his favorite topics: community, local mission, and good news to the poor. He also published an article based on a presentation called "Mission Tailored for Melbourne's Western Suburbs," given in 1992.[2] Although it includes the Westgate story, the canvas is wider, the strokes broader, and the framework of his text more theological and sociological. Starting with Karl Barth's famous quote about doing theology with the Bible in one hand and the newspaper in the other, he commenced with what he read in the Footscray local paper that week: long-term unemployment, homelessness, environmental dangers,[3] migrants, housing prices, and the Westgate Bridge.[4] He made a case for Footscray being the

2. Langmead, "Mission Tailored for the Western Suburbs."

3. A few months prior to this there was a big fire at Coode Island in the west where dangerous chemicals were stored.

4. The Westgate Bridge is a huge, elegant bridge in Melbourne which dominates the view from Footscray, and years before cost the lives of thirty-five workers when a span of it collapsed during construction.

heart of Melbourne's working-class west, and that the church needed to see what the gospel said about all these issues.

He used the Westgate story as a springboard for a wider discussion on urban mission that takes place in a frontier situation with great social problems, and few Christian resources. The theology he developed was:

> obviously contextual, growing out of the urban situation and grappling with it. It is "pilgrim theology" rather than dogmatic theology, more likely to be a theology of the cross than a theology of success or personal peace. It may be evangelical or liberal, charismatic or even liturgical in approach.
>
> Its politics are usually left-of-centre and focus on justice, peace and the environment. Christians in urban mission who analyse society soon find themselves campaigning for public policies which put health, education, housing, and community participation high on the list, and which protect the poor from the rich and powerful. (RL, Mission Tailored for the Western Suburbs, 1992)

As Westgate celebrated its tenth anniversary, Ross acknowledged that, like many urban mission initiatives, it was fragile and vulnerable, but "mirroring God's work in the world by surprising us with hope and joy in the face of sometimes overwhelming odds."

In a further effort to raise the profile of urban mission and to create an advocacy position, Ross lobbied the Baptist Union of Victoria to fund a part-time social justice research position, which he hoped he might be able to fill; he was also supportive of the Ecumenical Coalition for Urban Mission and aware that they were looking for a coordinator.

As he settled seriously into his forties, Ross was experiencing the classic "sandwich era": aging parents requiring more care and attention than before, and children reaching their teens, also needing more attention. And, of course, his dear wife, Alison, facing her own decisions and choices while being impacted by Ross's directions. Both Oliver and Jean, now in their seventies, had experienced ill health. Each episode was distressing for the family and the siblings who were nearby tried to share in the extra support needed. Ross also spent intentional time with family members, having lunch and talking about family history and dynamics. This he would continue to do for some years, believing that understanding his family was a key to his own self-awareness.

Ben and Kia were now both at secondary school. Kia had just graduated from primary school, and embraced the new school with her usual gusto; she was a keen gymnast and pianist and had a wide circle of friends.

Ben did not feel at home in his first high school, so made a move to Footscray/Yarraville Secondary College, where he liked the fact that he did not have to wear a uniform. It was not, however, turning out to be easy to assimilate as the only new boy in Year 9. He enjoyed playing keyboard and was wicketkeeper for his cricket team.

Ross was learning to be the dad of young teens and discovered that there was no rulebook. He bought a secondhand bike, light-framed, nonrusting, and strong. He enjoyed riding it immensely and used it to avoid driving a car when possible; it also helped him to exercise to keep his diabetes under control. The added benefit was being able to ride with his son, and they began to train for the Great Victorian Bike Ride held each summer. Five weeks out from the demanding event, he and Ben did a training ride to eastern suburban Box Hill and back to visit Oliver and Jean, a forty-four-kilometer round trip.

Over 5,000 riders embark on the long ride each year, with twenty-one semitrailers behind them carrying all that is needed to set up a small town each night. The weather was perfect and the scenery stunning as father and son rode their daily kilometers and enjoyed the well-organized camping stops. Ben voted it the best experience of his life, while Ross said:

> My private fatherly hopes that it might be a great time of sharing and long talks didn't eventuate, probably because I'm not a man of many words, and he's a boy of even fewer words. But the bond was understood. I saw other parents yelling at their kids and realized that not a cross word had passed between us, and I felt good. (RL, Letter to Grace, February 1992)

Ross was also humbled because his bike wheel collapsed fifteen kilometers from the end, and he had to catch the "Sag Wagon" to the finish, missing out on crossing the Westgate Bridge to ride over the line with the others. He later did the ride again with Kia, finishing successfully.

Every year after Christmas, the Western Suburbs Family Camp was held at Phillip Island. So many Westgaters reminisce about this event, which gave everyone a chance to relax together, but was especially aimed at giving disadvantaged families a rare opportunity for a subsidized holiday. It was held at the St Paul's Discovery Centre, an arm of the Anglican Church's Mission of St James and St John, which was run for many years by good friend Digby Hannah. Of the fifteen families that attended in 1991, twelve of them were on pensions or benefits. There were many single mums, some Lebanese and Aboriginal families, and three mildly disabled young people. The brief story with its Christian message was given simply each day with respect for the Muslims and other non-Christians attending. Everyone received a personalized affirmation certificate at the end.

> It was a campsite geared for families and children from the kinds of socio-economic backgrounds for which holidays at the beach did not feature. These annual camps were sponsored by Scripture Union and were known as the Western Suburbs Phillip Island Camp. In addition to the broader Westgate Community this camp accepted referrals from social workers in Melbourne's west. The program involved adventures in the outdoors, craft activities, storytelling and group decision-making.
>
> And singing. Every morning the participants gathered in the upstairs lounge and these gatherings became the heart and soul of each day's experience. Plenty of songs just for fun as well as songs to match the themes of each day's story. Ross would always bring with him a song he had specially written, meticulously composed with a verse matching each of the stories planned for the week. By the end of the week, the upstairs lounge was resonating with joyful, unrestrained singing, with Ross's new song the undisputed favourite. (Digby Hannah, 2020)

This tradition grew and was continued by other camps and musicians, and a cassette would be recorded each time, duplicated so that everyone could take one home. The camps for disadvantaged families continued for many years.

> Through all these years and beyond, Ross continued to be an inspiration to me. He inspired me musically and theologically. More than anything, Ross inspired me through his practical, long-term commitment to serving his local community and building faith and resilience. (Digby Hannah, 2020)

Many of the benefits were informal: learning new crafts, acquiring parenting skills by watching others, being personally affirmed, and making new friends were all incredibly important for these families. Many families were subsidized, and hundreds of dollars were donated by friends, so that eventually the SU subsidy was not required. The huge effort Ross and Alison poured into these camps every year right after Christmas when everyone else was kicking back, reflected a deep commitment and a practical advocacy for those who attended. Once again, an idea that began at Westgate Baptist Community had grown to include the surrounding region.

As an adjunct or visiting lecturer at Whitley, Ross's theology lectures continued each year, but he became more involved in the life of the College, especially as a member of the Council. One of his favorite themes was captured in the presentation "Metaphor in Theology: is God really a father?" It explored the use of metaphors in Scripture and the challenges of religious language, no doubt drawing on his thesis in Lancaster. He posited that metaphor is the basis of human thought and language, and as seen in the kingdom parables, is open-ended, ordinary, incongruous, skeptical, surprising, transforming, and revolutionary. He suggested that metaphorical theology helps us to be more imaginative, especially in the arts, and frees us from the thought forms of the biblical era, and from being too literal. Most importantly, it encourages us to look for God around us, in the poor, in the suffering, in acts of love, in beauty, and in each other. In summary, he said, metaphorical theology encourages an exploratory approach, aware of how much we do not know, as well as recognizing God's revelation in the clues we do have.

Fay White recalls that Ross taught a unit on metaphors in her course at Whitley called "Creative Possibilities for Worship." As an exercise at the end of the class, he invited people to put their experiences into their own metaphors.

> Peter Sumner was blind and had been since an accident in his youth. His metaphor was powerful: "God is like the swell of the wave underneath me when I am swimming, lifting me and carrying me forward to the shore until I feel solid ground beneath my feet." For Peter Roberts, it was a moment that actually did change his life because it blew away all dead and tired images of God, and opened for him a freedom to understand and express his relationship with the divine spirit in a fresh and authentic way. It was a factor in charging him with a new kind of courage to leave his work as a furniture retailer and pursue a dream to take his music into hospitals and hospices where people were dying, and to assist that mysterious transition with songs and the playing of his beautiful harp.
>
> Ross's lecture, delivered with that same blinding clarity and simplicity that characterised all his work, also affirmed for me the work I was already reaching for in my song-writing. (Fay White, 2021)

Ross also taught "The Church's Mission for Justice" in 1991, as he began to tie together his pastoral and community experience with his theology. Along with his ongoing involvement in the Baptist Social Justice Group, he was beginning to be heard in his constant reminders about the church's reason for being. He was the editor of this group's newsletter, "Greenshoots," which was published eleven times a year from 1987 to 2000, each edition with an editorial from Ross. For example, the February 1992 edition led with a two-page article called "Fundamentalism and Justice." He told his own story of being "reared a fundamentalist" and asserted that he had met very few fundamentalists who were active in justice concern. He then proceeded to evaluate the movement with seven negative characteristics that, in his opinion, worked against a justice stance.

> My black-and-white upbringing didn't prepare me well for the greys of life. Every act of civil disobedience was the breakdown of society. For fundamentalists, to be radical is to be rebellious and disrespectful. Fundamentalism always selects, spiritualises and individualises biblical social teaching. I then agree with Athol Gill that radical Christianity is more evangelical than evangelicalism, because it really is Good News that we proclaim, and we tend to take its more radical aspects more seriously.[5]

Although Ross judged himself to be less strident than some of the radical discipleship leaders, he did not hold back in distancing himself from what he saw as a rigid belief system; he asserted that the further evangelicals move from fundamentalism, the more hope there was for a social vision. It is interesting to note, however, that the very denomination in which he grew up, the Salvation Army, was and still is deeply involved in "Sleeves rolled up Christianity," as acknowledged in his own testimony. He would claim that the social vision was selective, focusing on alcoholism, prostitution, sexual misconduct, gambling, profanity, and Sabbath observance, rather than the set of issues he felt were more important: war, poverty, class oppression, abuse of power, human rights, corruption, indigenous issues, health, education, the law, welfare, workers' rights, and criminal issues.

> Ross was committed to the pursuit of justice in the church and the world, especially for those who were oppressed or marginalised in our society. He had the courage to stand up and speak for what he believed. For him, truth, justice and reconciliation were at the core of Christ's life and he saw it as a task of the church, and his own calling, to represent, encourage and enact these things in the context in which he was placed. Ross often stood up for causes that were not popular in the church (to say nothing of politics at large) with a calm and measured dignity, because he believed that God's truth and justice were at stake within them. I found this characteristic wonderfully encouraging and illuminating, though often challenging and costly. (Graeme Garrett, 2020)

Principal Ken Manley recalls that in preparation for Whitley College's centenary celebrations, he asked Ross to compose a college hymn, based

---

5. Langmead, "Fundamentalism and Justice."

on the motto "Ad Justitiam—To Righteousness." Ken acknowledges that the motto, which came from a relatively obscure verse in Daniel 12:3, was not an obvious choice for a contemporary hymn. "And they that be wise shall shine as the brightness of the firmament; and they that turn many to righteousness as the stars forever and ever." Ross, however, duly came up with a draft, and after a small tweak to include a requested mention of the cross, it was accepted and has been sung in college worship and at ordination services ever since.

> *God of truth and wisdom's source*
> *Enlighten us we pray.*
> *May we love you as we learn*
> *For as the prophets say:*
> *Through the mercy of God,*
> *Those who are wise*
> *Turning others to walk with our God,*
> *To righteousness and justice,*
> *Shall shine with the brightness of the sky,*
> *Bring light like the stars above for ever.*
>
> *Looking back we praise your name*
> *For those who saw and heard.*
> *May we see more light and truth*
> *Break forth, become your Word.*
> *Help us stir up your church,*
> *Sound out the call,*
> *Turning others to walk with our God,*
> *To righteousness and justice,*
> *To follow the Spirit into joy*
> *Exploring the way ahead together.*
>
> *As we share the things we learn*
> *With all who walk the Way,*
> *May the range of truth and love*
> *Become our food each day.*
> *May our message be bold,*
> *Spoken with love,*
> *Turning others to walk with our God*
> *To righteousness and justice,*
> *To take up the cross of Christ our Lord,*
> *To live in the love of God for ever.*

(RL, *Ad Justitiam* [To Righteousness], 1991)

It was a great shock to the college community and beyond when Dr Athol Gill died suddenly in 1992. Ross admired Athol (they were both seen as "loyal opposition" in the Baptist Union) and felt he was a fellow radical disciple who saw the importance of a holistic gospel. Some would say he was one of Australia's most controversial theologians, with the distinction of having been sacked from theological colleges in two states. He was the founder of The House of the Gentle Bunyip which was an ecumenical Christian community that existed from 1975 to 1996 in Clifton Hill, an inner Melbourne suburb, drawing its members from the Baptist and evangelical traditions; he had commenced two similar centers in other states.

Made up mostly of young adults, they saw deficiencies in their churches and wanted to explore some of the radical implications of the Christian faith in a nontraditional setting. The Bunyip was influenced by the worldwide Christian community movement and changes in Australian society in the seventies. It sought to respond to a decline within the institutional church evident from the sixties, and to the Victorian Baptist perceived neglect of Melbourne's inner-city churches.[6] This resonated with Ross.

In the early eighties, Gill was unexpectedly not reappointed by the Assembly to his long-held position as Professor of New Testament at Whitley. Instead of his tenure being renewed for another five years, a secret ballot was held, resulting in him losing his position. It was a devastating shock to many of his colleagues and friends, including Ross. There was much lobbying behind the scenes; Ross was amongst those who felt that not only had an injustice occurred in the process, but that the denomination and the wider church would be the poorer without Athol Gill's contribution as a leading theologian. A specially convened meeting of the Assembly was called, and the decision dramatically reversed by a 90 percent majority; Gill continued to teach at Whitley until his sudden death at the age of fifty-three. Ross felt the loss of his friend deeply; perhaps it was also a reminder to Ross of the fragility of life and the need to get moving with whatever he planned to do.

Thoughts about his long-term future increasingly occupied Ross. He contemplated reducing his time at Westgate so that Alan could have more time, but he felt restless. He was not sure whether he wanted change in his Westgate role, more tangible results, a career, or more teaching. Others affirmed his teaching gifts, and he was aware that he wrote well. But the thought of committing to a DTheol so that he could be a full-time academic did not entirely appeal because he loved grassroots contact.

On the other hand, he still found pastoral work challenging. He fielded some negative feedback from a couple doing it hard, who felt neglected by

---

6. Munro, "House of the Gentle Bunyip."

the community. While Ross knew that Westgate was a "company of walking wounded," he was stung and had to apologize, as well as "letting pain be pain." He sought and felt God's forgiveness, but the accompanying feeling of inadequacy added to his sense that pastoral work was not something that suited him. It was affecting his faith in both God and other people.

> A sermon idea occurred while playing Mastermind the other night. "Could be" for guesses and "Must be" for deductions. Some of my faith is of each type. (RL, Journal, July 1992)

Frank Rees encouraged Ross to consider a career at Whitley, but he was yet to believe it was his first choice. Ross felt he would be stuck in philosophy of religion, detracting from his teaching of justice and environment. He sensed that he was good at two things: music and his ability to translate theology into clear language, with the latter being a clearer call. This moment of self-awareness was probably the watershed.

> Now we're talking. Applied theology, keeping my feet in the paddy fields. There's probably not a career in it, but possibly a job, and a calling. (RL, Journal, June 1991)

Towards the end of 1992, Ross made an important decision. Having explored advocacy and policy as part of his practical mission, and having looked at a few other job options, he then decided it was time to apply for a position that was being created at Whitley: Lecturer in Missiology. He submitted his application in October, saying that his community relations project would be finished and that he was prepared to resign from pastoral ministry at Westgate to commence the following year.

Ross listed the study that had prepared him: education, philosophy, biblical and systematic theology, the study of other religions, sociology, and justice, but recognized that he would need to commence doctoral studies to complete his qualifications, especially to be able to supervise postgraduate students. He gave his reasons for not having applied for an academic position before as:

1. His strong practical bias;
2. Being caught up in mission itself;
3. Waiting for a subject area he felt passionate enough about—mission studies; and
4. His need to develop beliefs and experience before training others.

Now he felt ready to take on missiology.

Chapter 15

Missiology: 1993 to 1997

> Like all good theology, the work on incarnational mission and evangelism should be done modestly, critically and rigorously. But let it also be done joyfully, with the expectation that we will discover more of what the gospel means.
>
> DARRELL GUDER

> Few scholars are able to explore a topic that burns like a fire in the belly, allows them to read across a whole discipline, prods their spiritual growth, and leaves them eager to explore further in practice what they have tried to express in a disciplined, scholarly manner.
>
> ROSS LANGMEAD

Ross may have felt passionate about mission, but his appointment was not without controversy. He would be the first lecturer in mission not to have served in an overseas crosscultural role, despite his claim in his application that he was the "son of missionaries and Salvation Army officers," giving him an imbibed love for the Chinese. In his application he said that his faith upbringing was a strong influence; the second influence was that of articulate and radical Christians who sharpened his focus. These helped him to see that the gospel speaks to all aspects of life, both spiritual and material, personal and corporate. His own call to be a missionary in the broadest sense grew and focused on urban mission, working with the unemployed and poor. This he had demonstrated in an intentional way at Westgate since

1978. For Ross, mission was the sum of activities that bear witness to the transforming love and power of God, regardless of location.

> Missiology is the area of theology about which I feel most passionately, because the role of the church in the world dominates my theological reflection. The study of mission draws on many areas of theology and the social sciences, as well as practical experience. It bristles with pressing issues such as crossing cultural barriers, Christian lifestyle, prophetic engagement, articulating the Gospel, the challenge of other religions, the challenge of the city, and new models of reaching people outside the church. (RL, Job application, 1992)

For Whitley, however, appointing Ross to the role was a commitment to a definition of mission that was wider than the traditional overseas evangelism and church planting that many saw as "missionary work." Some Baptist Union churches were concerned that the college was moving away from evangelism generally, and overseas work in particular. Not surprisingly, there were excellent applicants with a lifetime of missionary service, impressive academic qualifications, and Baptist pedigrees who would have brought great insights to this aspect of missiology.

The selection committee settled on a shortlist of candidates that represented a range of schools of thought in missiology. Their challenge was to decide not so much which one of the candidates was better suited to the job, as all brought academic ability and practical experience; the decision rather would be based on which theological stance and direction the college would take in its missiological teaching and training.

Ultimately, the recommendation was that Ross be appointed, and that the college would pursue avenues to enrich the diversity of missiology teaching. The committee stressed that in appointing Ross they did not want to be seen to be choosing against the direction of improved focus on overseas dimensions of mission; rather, they felt the need to consolidate the existing position as a basis for further development.

This was one of several disclaimers in the appointment. It was also recorded that Ross's degree in theology did not major in missiology, but noted that his Lancaster studies and later publications extended to missiology, and, in addition, that all his qualifications had been obtained with distinction. In summary, the bases for Ross's appointment were:

1. His capacity to make a clear foundational contribution to the missiology program;
2. The need to consolidate present emphases;

3. His capacity to make significant contribution to an Australian theology of mission; and

4. His excellent and varied academic qualifications, and ability to move toward a doctorate in missiology.

Although this appointment seems like a diversion from Ross's plan to advocate and research, it was as if he had a sudden epiphany about where it had all been heading for him. This would be his opportunity to teach and train in the very area that had consumed his life and ministry to this point: mission. There could be no more influential position in the Baptist church than to teach ordinands and others who came through Whitley, and his heart responded to the opportunity.

Ever the humorist, he wrote to his younger sister about his new job with tongue in cheek:

> I'm enjoying my new job as lecturer. It's great to get paid to sit around and read books. I don't intend to teach anything until I know everything, so it should be a while yet. I've got the easy job where there are no denominational politics. Except for the debate about whether mission includes social justice or not. And the relationship between Christianity and other religions. And the hot argument about the church growth movement. And how Whitley can satisfy the demands of the Baptist Missionary Society. And how could I possibly teach mission if I am neither ordained nor a returned missionary. Otherwise, it is all harmony and light. (RL, Letter to Grace, March 1993)

It had been fifteen years since he reported on the western suburbs churches and moved to South Kingsville prior to establishing the Westgate Baptist Community. His deep involvement had weathered the ups and downs, and would continue to do so, but no longer as a paid pastor on the team. Ron Miers and Ross both resigned at the start of 1993, and the community acknowledged that they had been blessed to have two such committed and talented leaders for so long. A new pastor, Paul Turton, was appointed, and he became the first leader who came to the job from outside the community, and would bring a fresh creativity to the ministry.

Ross's role would now widen to go further than the west. It is interesting in hindsight to frame these moves as his personal version of witnessing in Jerusalem (Westgate Baptist Community), then Judea (western region), Samaria (Whitley College and the Baptists of Victoria) and the world (his international ministry).[1] I am confident that Ross himself never saw his

---

1. Jesus' command to his disciples in Acts 1:8.

life in this light, but, perhaps unconsciously, he was now pushing out his sphere of influence.

There was no putting off now the task of embarking on his doctorate. He needed the qualification to teach in a theological college and to supervise students in their further studies, and was strongly encouraged by his principal, Ken Manley, to get started. More than that, he was ready to bring together what would be his major contribution not only to academia, but what he liked to call "praxis", which at its simplest level refers to the practice that results from—or that provides the raw material for—theological reflection, debate, or discourse. Ross was always aware that the church could talk too much.

His lecturing position was for 0.7 percent of full-time, leaving 0.3 for his own study. He knew full well that the first year in a new job would occupy most of his time in preparation, meetings, and adjusting to college life and entering the field. Every part-timer knows the challenges of the overheads that can add to their part-time job. Although he was grateful to gain direct admission into a Doctor of Theology program, he made little progress in his research in that first year. His thoughts were around the theological issues arising from urban mission in the Australian context, although the focus changed as he started work.

He thought long and hard about finding a suitable supervisor, knowing that his topic would break into a new area in academic theology. Father Larry Nemer, SVD, a member of the Divine Word Missionaries was his choice. A colleague observed that Ross must have overcome many assumptions from his teetotalling Salvation Army background to choose a Catholic priest. The relationship would become a lifelong and deep friendship and was part of the bridge building that was a feature in Ross's life.

> Ross came to see me at Dorish Maru College[2] to invite me to become his supervisor for a doctorate in Mission Studies with the Melbourne College of Divinity. We had a long conversation and I was impressed with the rich background studies he had already done in England. I was also intrigued by the topic he wanted to explore: Incarnational Missiology, which was at the cutting edge of missiological thinking at the time. My one concern was whether his Baptist authorities would allow him to be supervised by a Roman Catholic priest. He said that his

---

2. Dorish Maru College is the Divine Word residence for seminarians who are pursuing theological training for ordination and for priests doing post-graduate study. It is under the patronage of St Joseph Freinadametz, one of the first SVD to serve in China. As well as studying, every student is involved in pastoral ministry to the poor, homeless, and marginalized.

authorities and the Melbourne College of Divinity had already approved of his request to approach me. (Larry Nemer, 2020)

And so the thesis was launched, and as planned, took until 1997 to complete. Frank Rees remembers that Ross was so organized that he booked some accommodation half a year ahead as a celebration for finishing his thesis. He managed to complete it down to that very day.

In March he was inducted into the college faculty as Lecturer in Missiology by the Rev. Ron Ham, College President, acknowledging that the position had been made possible through gifts from World Vision and the Victorian Baptist Fund. The college hymn that he wrote, "To Righteousness," was sung at the service, and Ross preached the sermon, basing his message on Luke 14:15–24, the "parable of the missionary church."

> There is a wholeness and joy which is missing from so many of our attempts to bring communities together. There is a real challenge for me as I explore together with the students the nature of mission to discover the wholeness and vibrancy of the Kingdom of God which is like a feast. To develop, alongside and through the discipline of learning and reading and writing, my own experience of God's bounty and blessing and overflow within my own life. To be open to God's extravagant love and creative surprises. (RL, Induction sermon, March 1993)

Ross's new role at Whitley was both all-consuming and stimulating. He felt the privilege of being on the faculty, loved the job, and saw it as a calling. He felt as though he was building on the work of his mentor and friend, Athol Gill, and colleague, John U'Ren. He reckoned that his first DOM101 (Department of Mission) course was a good overview but was challenged by the need to bring order to the colleges offerings in mission studies, which he called "an exciting but disorderly bunch of missiology subjects." He hoped to build bridges with other institutions, like the Bible College of Victoria, the Victorian Baptist Missionary Society Policy Taskforce, the Evangelism Taskforce, and Crossover Australia Evangelism Taskforce.

He worked hard to fill the gaps in the library's missiology holdings and brought his technology expertise to a computer committee that planned to upgrade the college systems for both staff and students. He brought in some wonderful adjunct lecturers to enrich the courses and cover the areas that were not his specialty, like Ros Gooden, Tim Costello, Darrell Guder, Alan Nichols, and Steve Clarke. As part of his professional development for both his teaching and his own thesis, he attended conferences and seminars, connected with international academics, and mission associations.

It was not, of course, all plain sailing. Ross found that the extras of the job were heavy—like coordinating three intensives in the semester breaks in the first year; it meant that he was not free to attend conferences, mark assignments, do his own study, or recover in the holiday periods.

After the first year, Ross had an extensive list of suggestions for improving faculty meetings. He suggested more delegation and preparation before meetings, tighter follow-up of promised actions, prioritizing of agenda items with administrivia at the end, no all-day meetings, secretarial assistance with minutes, and many more ideas, which may or may not have gone down well. It is possible that the implied criticism of how the meetings were run made him unpopular, but he is also remembered as a very efficient meeting leader, who always kept to time constraints and priorities.

Colleague Keith Dyer recalls his "somewhat pedantic concern for detail and getting processes and minutes straight. Although it was a strength, it was occasionally annoying to others" and Principal Geoff Pound says that "he was very orderly (sometimes painfully), a meticulous conference organiser." Frank Rees also records:

> His need for closure meant that he was also somewhat obsessive. When stressed, he would wash up in the faculty kitchen. Everyone could hear as he worked out some of his tension. Or he would go and clean, meticulously clean, all the white boards in the building, even though that was someone else's job. They could not do it to his satisfaction. These were some of the ways he wrestled with the sheer ambiguity of life. But mostly he simply internalised it all and saw that as part of his commitment to others. (Frank Rees, 2020)

Marita Munro, a friend and colleague, elaborates on this aspect of Ross's character. She says that he was a perfectionist, and that he always prepared extremely well for any occasion. She notes that he was an excellent editor, whose grammar and punctuation were unsurpassed; he was also the acknowledged expert on all aspects of the referencing style guide.[3] He did, however, have a stormy relationship with the photocopier, from which the registrar would at times need to rescue him by telling him to "Step away, Ross." Marita also has kitchen-cleaning memories:

> We always knew Ross was under stress or feeling pressure when he would be in the faculty kitchen. There would be banging of crockery and cutlery, the fridge would be emptied and defrosted,

---

3. In researching for this book and reading hundreds of Ross's letters, journals, and presentations, the author found only one spelling mistake, in a letter written on a turbulent plane flight.

anything past its use by date swiftly disposed of and excess cups removed. Noticeboards would be updated. Out of date signage dispensed to the recycle box. Posters and leaflets were pinned in perfectly straight lines. Only right angles permitted. (Marita Munro, 2020)

It is quite a relief to hear these humanizing stories about Ross. Despite questions in the survey for this book that his friends responded to about what his weaknesses might have been, these few stories are about the only hint of his occasionally obsessive behavior, and indications that he sometimes felt stressed. The only other comment, coming from people in various parts of his life, was that he gave too much of himself to others, and in doing that, failed to care enough for himself. There is no real way of measuring that; while his diaries are testament to an extraordinarily full life, Ross was also more reflective and intentional about how he lived life than are most people. He decided, for example, to accept speaking engagements strictly on a "political value" basis, which meant "yes" to churches that didn't normally invite Whitley faculty, and "no" to mates and ecumenical events.

Ross fell into the rhythm of academic life after the first, hectic cycles. He really enjoyed the atmosphere of the college, his work and the team. Delighted with a new computer (he became a dedicated Mac man), he achieved increased efficiency and worked hard to acquire upgraded technology for all staff. By 1997, well ahead of the norm at that time, he envisaged building online delivery and assessment of material, tutoring via email and electronic libraries. He dreamed of creative use of the web page, video conferencing, distance education, and electronic teaching. All this while maintaining a "personally-oriented pedagogy." He felt that he was in touch with the main missiological issues and literature, and that was reflected in excellent library holdings. Most of all, the teacher in him enjoyed relating to students and recognized the critical importance of pastoral care and mentoring.

The missiology faculty delivered units such as "Introduction to Evangelism," "The Mission of the People of God," "Faith and the Environment," "Christianity and Other Faiths," "Salvation and Justice," "Cross Cultural Mission," "Dialogue with Living Faiths," "Recent Trends in Mission Theology" and "Contemporary Issues in Evangelism" in the nineties, and the offerings evolved with the times and student response, which tended to reflect the contemporary hot topics.

His role at college included connecting with local Baptist churches and preaching in addition to his continued involvement at Westgate. Now he added academic presentations as well, like the Trinity College Midyear School of Theology and the Divine Word Annual Missiology Lecture. Attendance at conferences included giving presentations, such as "Doing Missiology in Australia" in Sydney in 1994, the very first Anabaptist Gathering in Sheffield, and the regular Australian and New Zealand Association of Theological Schools (ANZATS) conferences. Ross also was a member of the Victorian Council of Churches Commission on the Gospel and our Cultures, as well as the Victorian Baptist Missionary Department. He sat on the council of the Melbourne College of Divinity, of which Whitley was a member.

Outside Whitley, Ross continued his involvement with the monthly Baptist Social Justice Group, various social justice and activist groups, and the Baptist Union Consultation on Evangelism. His association with Scripture Union was still strong, and he supported their conferences when he could. With weekly music group at Westgate and two-weekly community small group, and justice events like Walk Against Want, there were not many free spaces in Ross's diary.

At Westgate, there were over fifty people attending small groups, and a new plan was adopted based around a simple meal, communion, study, and support for each other. The relationship between Westgate Baptist Community and the community groups was now an informal link between Lanigiro, Westgate Health Cooperative, WCIG, Learning for Life, and the South Kingsville Community Centre as they assumed independence. A support group was formed for the growing number of Karen refugees in the church, and Alan Marr resigned from the pastoral team. He had just returned from working three months in the Karen camp on the Thai-Burma border, and realized that his passion had changed, and it was time to move on. The founding leadership changeover was complete, but Ross, Alison, Alan, and Jenny remained members at Westgate for many years. Ross stayed there until the end of his life.

The demands of family life were high in these years. Alison was finding her own way with employment opportunities and, as a couple, they were negotiating the merry dance of growing together whilst allowing one another to grow. Ben and Kia were well into their teenage years, loving their parents, but beginning to forge their own paths. Undoubtedly, they were shaped by the lifestyle of their family. That meant keeping an open house, caring for the needy, living simply. Kia realized when she later moved out into a share house, that it wasn't the norm for her friends to welcome knocks at the door at all hours. That had been her way of life and it had influenced her. She recalls instances of when she or her brother were in trouble:

> Mum and Dad invited us into Ross's study to "chat," where they heard us out, listened to our side of the story and then invited us to contribute to coming up with a "fair" punishment or consequence for our actions. It is a powerful approach, as once you've suggested a fair consequence, you have far less ground to contest that punishment. There was the time that I said I was staying at a girlfriend's house, but stayed at my boyfriend's house. The time when Benj made a matchbox bomb and it exploded in the study before he got a chance to get it out onto the street and it burnt the carpet in many places. The list could go on. Good parenting does not avoid rebellious teenagers. (Kia Langmead, 2020)

Benjamin recalls that Ross would refuse some of his requests initially, but then listen to Ben's arguments and ultimately change his mind if he felt the case had validity; this he remembers with appreciation. One of the most significant conflicts was when Ben told Ross he wanted to leave school partway through Year 12. He was suffering from depression, had never enjoyed high school, and had reached a critical point when he felt that he had no option but to leave.

> I told Dad. He dutifully gave me the talk about how finishing school was a good idea for various reasons. I think I burst into tears. He came to accept my decision to leave school soon enough. He could see I was in pain. One of the best decisions of my life, by the way. (Benjamin Langmead, 2020)

We can only surmise how agonizing this was for Ross, the academic, allowing his exceptionally talented son to drop out from school so close to the end.

> I could probably tell a story or two about hiking, the great Victorian bike ride, making cubbies, him taking me to a gaming competition and overcoming moral hurdles to buy me a thick shake at McDonalds. (Benjamin Langmead, 2020)

Building relationships with teenagers came at a cost. Ben remembers Ross as a dad who was fair, present, and caring, and who gave him time.

> I like to think I am like Ross in many ways: fair, reasonable, loving, thoughtful, humble (!), open, accepting. I like a neat edge on the grass (a Ross thing), I like using computers, I'm not very materialistic. He liked and valued music, the outdoors and community, as I do too. (Benjamin Langmead, 2020)

Kia also fondly remembers the street Christmas party that her dad organized for some years. For Kia, it was such an exciting event when they prepared chairs, sports equipment, and the carols that she accompanied. They met the neighbors and consolidated friendships that have lasted to the present. Ross would be thrilled to know that Kia and her husband, Thierry, have perpetuated the idea in their own apartment block, having grown up valuing community and friendships. She also reflects now on his faith journey:

> For me, his faith was a lived, experiential journey. His values and faith were front and centre of everything he did and all his decisions. He was a man of integrity, and transparency in his deep questions and beliefs. As his daughter, his faith had a deep impression on me as a person, and who I am in this world. His faith was not a static, inherited set of beliefs. It was a living, breathing evolving thing. He was willing to be challenged and actively sought knowledge, other perspectives and faith structures, opposing beliefs, to encourage him to review his own ideas and beliefs. (Kia Langmead, 2020)

Ben recalls similarly:

> I think Ross embodied his faith. Practised what he preached. I think he journeyed with himself and his faith so deeply that he had a solid working foundation from which to operate. He said he considered himself on the edge of religion, that it wasn't a perfect system or organization, but he'd still prefer to be part of it, than not. He made so much sense on just about everything.

I think his students would agree. I kind of wish I studied his classes. (Benjamin Langmead, 2020)

In November 1994, Ross's father died suddenly at the age of seventy-three while visiting family interstate. The loss was a shock for the whole family, and Ross was grateful that he had reached out to be closer to his dad in recent years. Ross gave the tribute on behalf of the family at Oliver's funeral:

> Although always busy, he was not an absent father. Only on the thinnest of surfaces was he a distant, shy and complicated man. Scratch him a bit and out came enormous heart and commitment and an overwhelming desire for our wellbeing. Although it was fallible, this love had its roots in the love of God.
>
> From the start Dad introduced us to the wealth of life despite living in poverty. We read books, music was a daily part of life; we learned from Chinese culture; we saw buildings through the eyes of an architect; we all did tertiary study and all of us have pursued at least two degrees or professional qualifications. In the words of Paul, Dad was poor and yet making many rich, having nothing yet possessing everything (2 Cor 6:10). He taught us all to budget tightly, that spiritual wealth is far and away the greatest treasure that humans can have. He demonstrated this by putting God first at every point, whatever it cost him in worldly terms.
>
> He also taught us to love the poor, in the spirit of William Booth, and of course the Jesus he followed. We attended Corps where the little people—the lonely, the lost, the odd and the positively crazy—were welcomed, and taken seriously and patiently worked with. Dad took seriously the sort of friends that Jesus had. His love for God was constantly translated into love for the loveless.
>
> We often clashed, or withdrew. Some of us have had to learn as adults that it's OK to fail and be ordinary humans, and that God accepts us in pure grace. It has not been until recent years that most of us have been able, as adults, to relate easily to Dad, to see his vulnerabilities, and to forgive him and to appreciate what depth of love lay so close to the surface of this shy, complicated, capable, demanding and dedicated man. (RL, Tribute from Ross to Oliver, December 1994)

Jean now needed more support, and it was Ross who instigated the roster of home help by the four siblings in Melbourne; each of them took a monthly turn at cleaning Jean's unit, caring for the garden and making sure that she felt supported. Before long she was facing her own issues, with neck and spinal surgery, and the ensuing rehabilitation. Ross's diaries record countless appointments for Jean that he took care of, grateful that his work hours were flexible. He also increasingly looked after her business matters, as Jean, from her traditional perspective, looked to him as her eldest son to take over from Oliver. Perhaps her Chinese cultural upbringing also tended to assume that the eldest son would look after the parents. This at times was a source of friction in the family, but Ross did what his mother asked of him, while offering to hand over the responsibility to anyone else who wanted to help. As her memory declined steadily, Jean moved to an aged care facility and the whole family rallied around to continue the support in her later years.

As Ross's younger sister, Grace, came and went from China in these years while she worked in "tent-making" mission, she sometimes stayed with Ross and Alison on her furloughs. She enjoyed the welcoming open home, and Ross supported her in many ways, administratively, and emotionally. Grace remembers him saying to her that her being the youngest, single, and a female did not mean that the burden of caring for her parents was automatically hers. That was thoughtful and helpful advice for her as Oliver and Jean aged. He also initiated a group loan from the siblings so that she could buy a car, generously putting himself last on the list of repayments of the money.

In May 1994, Ross went to a concert by his musician friend, Fay White. He was overwhelmed with emotion and wept through most of the first half. As he wrote to tell her what the concert meant to him, he sensed a deep longing and response to the music and the words, and a feeling of being locked and wanting release. He suddenly realized that music was the "only worthwhile language to use," and he felt dry and depleted. The next week, for the first time ever, he went to a psychologist to work through some of his feelings and felt like he had jumped out of a plane without a parachute.

David, the psychologist, steered him towards answering some questions: did he want to decide to demand what he wanted? And what did he want as an alternative to "sainthood"? He needed to explore what he wanted to enjoy for himself, and not just choose things that did him good. Ross's assertion was that his "current arrangement with life was unworkable." David proposed that sainthood for Ross meant that he tried hard to do no wrong by anyone, at the cost of not being kind to himself, but Ross felt that he defended his own space fairly intentionally. He could not see how to cast off the nice-guy image without being a bad guy. One of his colleagues, when asked what he would never forget about Ross, interestingly, also reflected on sainthood:

> I think I will say his "saintliness." I put the word in scare quotes because it has a lot of negative connotations in society at large, and perhaps in the church too: do-gooder, holier than thou, other worldly, God-botherer, and so on. None of which applied to Ross. Paul Tillich defined a saint as a person who is "transparent to the divine." That was Ross in my experience. But Tillich's expression needs a bit of explanation. As it is, it is abstract. What do you mean "transparent"? Which divine?
>
> I would try to answer this by saying that Ross was a true disciple (in Bonhoeffer's sense) of Jesus of Nazareth whom, along with the whole Christian tradition, he knew as the Christ of God. Ross embodied and enacted the fundamental qualities of the life of Jesus as depicted in the Gospels in particular and expounded upon in the New Testament in general. Thus he was loving and also just; compassionate and also committed to the truth; forgiving and also responsible; obedient and also wonderfully free, prayerful and also dedicated to specific actions of peace and justice, centred on God and also thoroughly given to the protection of God's earth. In short, a living window onto the reality of God. (Graeme Garrett, 2020)

Ross would have shrunk from this reflection, but it adds to our understanding of sainthood as others saw him, in contrast to his own inward struggles to cast off the image. The effort to do the right thing by everyone else but himself may have been a sacrificial, desirable, New Testament characteristic, but for Ross, the cost was high.

There may have always been a remnant of the Salvationist upbringing, according to Frank Rees: "well trained in the traditions of the Holiness Movement, and privately assured that he had in fact followed many of the dicta[4] he had set himself." Frank, on the other hand, also recalls fondly that after he and his wife were seriously injured in a tsunami in Samoa in 2010, Ross and Alison were the first college friends to arrive at their home with a pot of tasty soup, "the soup only surpassed by the love it demonstrated," and a loving act he would never forget. This book has tried, despite the many glowing contributions like this, to avoid becoming a hagiography.

Always one to intellectualize and overthink, Ross envied Alison's ability to be more spontaneous and in touch with creativity and relationships yet felt unsure of how to make changes. David encouraged him to take time for himself without feeling that he needed to justify that. Ross logged in his journal that he had decided to resign as worship group convener at

---

4. "Dictum" used here in the sense of an observation intended or regarded as authoritative.

Westgate, and from the school council, and noted that these were big decisions for him that marked the end of eras.

He was trying hard to disrupt his pattern of being driven to continual action for everyone but himself. When asked by David how he really wanted to be, Ross said:

> I said I wanted to be interesting, a character, able to live with conflict, pugnacious, funny at times, deeply enjoying life. I didn't want to be always cautious, bland, saying nothing rather than offend, giving in, working super-hard to keep up. I am deeply sceptical of anyone's ability to help me (a revealing comment) and I sensed that this is when the hard work of change would begin. I am aware of the "black box" of my racing mind between my feelings and my words. I could give him lots of theories; I could manipulate the process by recalling this event or that; I could talk on and on or be terse; I could deny or acknowledge and build on the clues that he throws out. How much will the "self-who-will-not-change" assert itself in these and other subtle ways to subvert the process? Will understanding myself lead to unblocking the barriers to change? I'm a tough case. I resent being so helpless and wonder whether I should be taking more control (after all, who's paying $2 a minute here.) (RL, Journal, June 1994)

While Ross chafed at spending $100 each week to see a psychologist, he persevered. The third visit would turn out to be pivotal. David had summed him up and blew his mind with his analysis. He said that Ross had survived two parents who defined a narrow reality with the order of God, others, and then Ross. He, then, had chosen to respond as a quiet revolutionary: creatively, carefully, deliberately trying to be independent without creating waves, changing things without confrontation. Having survived a somewhat dysfunctional family, Ross had managed to succeed in work, marriage, and balance, but he had absorbed the anger, avoided conflict, and lost some passion for life.

His deal with life was that he could give to others as long as he had a small space for himself with a reward or comfort. Diabetes had now taken away many little pleasures, putting his life at ransom. Ross was stunned but enlightened by this analysis. David's challenge was that Ross should spend more on himself, whatever that looked like. He trembled for some time after at the immediacy and depth of the revelation. David had cracked the tough nut.

At the same time, he had four Trinity College lectures, exam marking, faculty conference, computer committee, farewells for friends, prayer meetings, leading Christmas in June (which he found depressing), Alison away for the weekend, preparation for upcoming courses, and School of Ministry demanding his attention.

> I'm snowed under. (RL, Journal, June 1994)

He began to make more assertive decisions about canceling involvements, choosing to miss important events for more significant needs, delegating, spending time with Alison and the kids, declining invitations, shopping for clothes (exceedingly rare), and not responding to late-night calls from needy friends unless it was an emergency. He and Alison planned a two-week holiday away on their own, which was the first for twenty years.

By October, Ross was ready to sign off with David, partly for financial reasons, but also because he felt he was ready to implement some changes in key areas. One issue that would never go away would be his diabetes with its day-by-day pressure to control the disease, and he knew that the ability to master it every day required good mental health. Every diabetic knows the depressing thought that nothing will change or cure the disease, and that even with optimum management, there is progressive deterioration with the threat of side effects. Ross found it a constant challenge to eat healthily, and to avoid foods that sent his blood sugar up. Contrary to popular perception, sugar is not the only, nor the worst problem; simple foods with high carbohydrates like pasta and rice and other staples impact blood sugar hugely, and every diabetic must become a detailed observer of the effects of different foods. He commented in 1995 in his report to the college that:

> I enjoyed generally good health and my diabetes control has been quite reasonable. Being honest, I feel pretty ordinary for a substantial minority of the time due to both low and high blood sugars, but I have not lost consciousness or had to be hospitalised so far, and I am always able to put in a good week's work. (RL, Review of 1995)

He had explored with David the emotional triggers associated with eating, and knew that depression and overbusyness were not his friends when his eating regime was so important. His blood readings were steady at this stage and mostly within the guidelines, but he was always anxious about the quarterly pathology results. His closer colleagues were increasingly aware of his illness, and many make comment on how it affected him. Geoff Pound reflects that Ross's pedantic concern for detail was a strength that kept him super-organized to keep him on top of his diabetes.

> Teachers and students ate countless meals with Ross in the College dining room. After getting his meal he would routinely begin his meal with a discreet injection of insulin. This was always a reminder to us of the health challenges Ross faced with diabetes.
>
> He surprised us on one occasion when the Whitley teaching team was dining in a Lygon Street café. When after lunch Ross called the waiter and told him to replace his lukewarm, flat white coffee with a coffee that was hot, the usually congenial Ross said to us, "I have lived half of my life and I am no longer going to accept inferior quality and service." (Geoff Pound, 2020)

Part of Ross's block in 1994 was the difficulty he was facing in getting started on his thesis. He felt stymied as he sought for direction. Having spent six solid weeks on it in the summer of 1994–95, he finally tied down his topic: "An analysis of incarnational models of mission." He noted that he had spent a couple of years "fossicking in the foothills" and now was finally "tackling the mountain." Excited, he planned to explore in detail the implications of a form of discipleship championed by the Anabaptists and radical evangelicals and had written 20,000 words as a start. He believed he would be the first to gain a DTheol from the Melbourne College of Divinity clearly in the discipline of missiology. It was the fire in his belly and had many practical implications for local and global Christian mission.

The Anabaptist movement had a profound influence on Ross's theology, and now he wanted to weave it into his missiology.

> I owe my awareness of the Anabaptist tradition to studying under Athol Gill. It was not that he kept referring to the Anabaptists but that his passion was for the Gospel accounts of Jesus

and what they mean for discipleship, community and mission today; this passion led him to own the Anabaptist strands in Baptist history and to re-appropriate them in the cause of discipleship. In considering Anabaptist distinctives in mission it becomes clear how much they have influenced the radical evangelical movement of the last quarter of the twentieth century, in which Athol Gill played such a significant role.[5]

The Anabaptists of the sixteenth century were early proponents of the radical discipleship movement who were persecuted in that era. They gained their name because they believed strongly that those to be baptized should be adult, and capable of professing their faith: thus their name means "one who baptizes again," bestowed on them by those who believed that infant baptism was sufficient on its own. They have historical connections to the Mennonites and the Amish, amongst others.

Ross was one of the founding members of the Anabaptist Association of Australia and New Zealand. While never on the executive committee, he was always supportive behind the scenes, playing guitar and leading singing at gatherings, hosting conferences and meetings at Whitley. His presence on the Australian Association of Mission Studies was seen as a voice for Anabaptists in an ecumenical landscape. Their journal's title reflected one of his songs—"On the Road"—and he wrote special songs for their gatherings.

> At the National Home Church Enrichment Weekend held in Canberra in 1995 we attended a session led by Ross where he asked the participants to list what they liked about being in a home church. He took the answers from the group, went away for an hour or two and came back with a song he taught us. It was called "When Two or Three Can Get Together" and we still teach and sing it today. Writing and teaching that song illustrated what Ross was so good at and what many will remember him for. In his quiet, humble way he listened to the group, used his musical gifts to create a song, and then stepped back and released it as a gift for others to use. I can still see him smiling as we sang. (Mark Hurst, 2013)

Larry Nemer recalls that once he had agreed to be his supervisor, he realized that he had an ideal doctoral candidate. Larry enjoyed the interactions in their meetings, finding that they resonated in the key areas of commitment to God, Christ, church, and mission.

---

5. Langmead, "Anabaptist Perspectives for Mission."

Frank Rees, who was involved as a co-supervisor, had some questions about whether what he saw as the philosophical nature of his topic was really suited to Ross's personality and gifts as a mathematically trained academic.

> He did not like ambiguity. And no matter how hard I tried, I could not convince him to accept there is profound ambiguity in his favourite concept of incarnation. To "become" flesh presupposes that at some time or in some sense Christ was not or had not been enfleshed; this concept forces a timeframe on the nature of Christ, and is somehow inconsistent with all else Christian doctrine affirms about the nature of Christ. In the end, Ross's thesis did not want to go there. (Frank Rees, 2020)

Ross set out to explore the contours of an adequate incarnational approach to mission, set as a comparison to the approaches of a range of Christian traditions.

If Jesus, who was God, became flesh in human form, how does this follow through to apply to Christians today? Ross says that the springboard for the final direction of his thesis was a comment made by Raymond Fung.[6] In a lecture he gave in 1993, Fung observed that incarnational mission has a certain pride about it in saying, "Look at us and you will see Jesus." Having forged his theology from his background of conservative evangelicalism, the holiness movement and the radical discipleship movement, Ross set out to answer some questions:

1. What exactly do Christians mean by mission being "incarnational"?
2. How are Christians meant to attain this ideal, while avoiding perfectionism and legalism?
3. Is incarnational theology a celebration of Christmas without Easter?
4. How does incarnational mission avoid being too human-centered, and embrace the whole creation?

He made no assumptions that this missiological stance was defensible but set out to examine a widely used construct, and see where his critique would lead him. He concluded, in fact, that it could be defended, and settled for three groups of meanings: following Jesus as a pattern for mission, participating in Christ's risen presence as the power for mission and joining God's cosmic mission, evident from creation.

In his critical survey, he examined the Anabaptist tradition, radical evangelicalism, liberation theology, Jürgen Moltmann's missiology, Roman

---

6. Formerly the Secretary for Evangelism in the Commission for World Mission and Evangelism of the World Council of Churches.

Catholic expressions, the ecumenical movement, and Eastern Orthodoxy. These groups were chosen to represent the various dimensions of incarnational mission across the spectrum.

After examining them all, Ross drew together his conclusions:

> The central argument of the study is that God's embodiment in creation, pre-eminently in Jesus Christ, is the ultimate framework of Christian mission and also the central shaping and empowering factor. Christianity is "incarnational"; this adjective refers both to the reality of God's saving action and its manner. Christian mission, similarly, is incarnational in both senses: bodily experiencing a new reality in Christ and sharing it through embodiment as Jesus did.[7]

This led to emphases like self-emptying, integration of words and deeds, the practice of Christ or "christopraxis," good news to the poor, a theology of the cross, the church as the body of Christ, the presence of Christ, the affirmation of creation, and the importance of cultural expression of the gospel. He brought it to a conclusion with an exploration on why the model is particularly apt in Australia, which is a skeptical, post-Christian, and postmodern society.

It was done. In June 1997, he sent his completed manuscript to Larry Nemer, from where it took its course for final submission. In November, he received his result. His thesis was accepted. To celebrate, he and Alison enjoyed a weekend of walking with the family at Wilson's Promontory, savoring at last the new freedom from study deadlines. It had been thirty years of study and research.

He would spend some time converting it to book form for publication; it was finally published in 2004. He called it *The Word Made Flesh: Towards an Incarnational Missiology*. It has been hailed in the years that followed as groundbreaking and the first comprehensive study of this aspect of missiology. It was Ross's magnum opus, and all that he wrote after it came out of this, and built and expanded on the foundation of his study. These are a few of the reflections and reviews:

> His thesis is a huge gift to the church. His thesis is a very well thought out challenge to mediocre evangelism. It's a call for authentic word and deed and Christ-centred evangelism and the imperative of recognising that authentic evangelism includes social transformation. It's very much the mind, heart and soul of dear Ross. (John U'Ren, 2020)

---

7. Langmead, *Word Made Flesh*.

Langmead has done a great service to the missional church in this careful and thorough study. It is easy to read and follow his arguments through with an extensive bibliography and a helpful index. As an Australian it was gratifying for me to see academic reference made to practical missiologists such as Australian John Smith and New Zealander Viv Grigg, as well as the sociological tie of incarnational mission to contemporary Australian society.[8]

Ross continued to recognize the importance of music in his expression. John U'Ren notes that Ross's passion was to teach, preach, and sing the message of social justice and radical discipleship. He also observes that Ross was probably the only lecturer who sang to his students in addition to leading chapel worship. In this period, he wrote seven songs, nearly all of them occasion songs, written specially for events. This one was written for World Aids Day in 1993:

> *See God's face once more*
> *In tending sick and cold and poor;*
> *Without advice or judgement, take the towel, the towel,*
> *See God, partner in our death,*
> *Closer than our struggling breath.*
> *May God's deep new life be ours.*

(RL, "Prayer and Action Meet," 1993)

"Kathie's Song" was written for the funeral of a beloved community member the same year. In 1995 he wrote the song for the Anabaptist Association and composed one for the Christian Medical and Dental Fellowship of Australia National Biennial Conference in Geelong. The third verse goes:

> *Sustaining God, Spirit arising,*
> *Heal your wounded healers as well,*
> *As with new strength in a body made whole.*
> *How you move, who can tell?*
> *Come refresh us with love.*

(RL, "Refresh Us with Your Love," 1995)

---

8. Gallagher, Review of *The Word Made Flesh*.

The following year, he was commissioned to write a theme song for the Victorian Uniting Church Synod. The song is a powerful anthem to the creator. It pleads with the renewing Spirit to:

> *Sustain your faltering church*
> *With word and deed in mission*
> *Tell a new story in this place.*

(RL, "Transform Us," 1996)

Whatever Ross argued in his academic thesis, this song expresses his prayer for the church. Ken Manley tells us about the last song written in this period:

> As I try to record some personal memories of my friend, I find myself inevitably turning to his music. Not only his wonderful repertoire of songs that have challenged faith and enriched the worship of so many, but of occasions in which I had personal involvement. I had been appointed President of the Baptist Union of Victoria for 1996–97 and had selected the theme of "Future Church."
>
> I hoped to challenge the Baptist churches to face the future with faith and an openness to innovative ministries. To accompany the presidential year, I asked the Whitley faculty and others

to prepare papers which were the basis of discussion and were published as "Future Church. A Baptist Discussion." I also asked Ross to write an appropriate song that might be sung at various events and in different churches during my year as president. Once again, he delivered with a song called "Future Church" which beautifully captured my theme and became quite popular in that year. (Ken Manley, 2020)

The song captures the essence of Ross's missiology, catching up in one stanza all his main themes: change, disturbance, marketplace, struggle, and always, the Spirit.

> *Hear the voice of God-the-future-calling,*
> *We can walk the path of change.*
> *With Jesus as our guide, move on;*
> *Though we long for safety, God disturbs us*
> *Out into the marketplace,*
> *In the Spirit, struggling pilgrims*
> *Can be the future Church.*

(RL, "Future Church," 1996)

As Ross was approaching the last stage of his thesis writing, Alison's mother, Joy, passed away in January 1997, a deep sadness for the whole family. They were able to gather and spend precious family time celebrating her life, and Ross continued to look after his own mother through a year when she continued to have many medical appointments and needs.

Benjamin and Kia were reaching milestones, with Ben gaining his driving P plates and Kia her L plates on the same day, just a few days after their joint birthday. Ross still rode long distances on his bike, built in regular family holidays, attended public justice protests and walks, watched test cricket every summer, and mowed the lawns at church, his mum's, his sister's, and others in the community. He attended diabetes seminars, celebrated family and community birthdays and weddings, worked on his car, and, on 27 December 1996, recorded a noteworthy and seemingly unique event in his diary: "Did nothing."

Ross's doctoral graduation was an exciting event. It had been a family effort to reach the goal:

> The sense of relief and joy we experienced as Ross went forward gowned in purple to receive his doctorate was palpable. I am glad for him that much of the reading and research time forged out of his full life will be valuable long into the future. (Alison Langmead, Annual family letter, January 1998)

Through it all, he maintained the cheerfulness often noted by his friends and worked hard at staying simple. The final song from this era sums up that philosophy and has been a popular one in the community and in churches, written about simplicity as he embarked on the most complex academic challenge of his life.

> *Living joyfully, living justly, living simply, taking care of the earth,*
> *In the giving, in receiving, grace-full living comes to birth.*
>
> *Like the widow who fed Elijah*
> *Like the widow in the temple giving all,*
> *May we learn, in simply sharing, of the overflow of this call:*
>
> *On a journey from all that chokes us,*
> *From the cares of having much and wanting more,*
> *Seeking first the way of Jesus,*
> *In God's Commonwealth, what's in store?*
>
> *Yes, it's costly: we need each other.*
> *Living simply may be complicated too.*
> *But in faith, and with the Spirit,*
> *We can venture forth, and pursue . . .*
> *Living joyfully . . .*
>
> (RL, "Simply sharing," 1993)

Chapter 16

Ecomissiology: 1998 to 2002

A Christian who doesn't safeguard creation, who doesn't make it flourish, is a Christian who isn't concerned with God's work, that work born of God's love for us.

POPE FRANCIS

Ecomissiology involves both a worldview and a "God-view." There is a dash of imagination and poetry in it. It has a sensibility which colours our whole approach. Its governing metaphor is relationship.

ROSS LANGMEAD

Ross was reappointed at the end of 1997 for another five years at Whitley, this time as Professor of Missiology, in recognition that he was now the leading expert in his field in the college. He acknowledged in his reflections at the end of the previous five years that he had a passion for education, for missiological research, for the practice of mission, for mono-cultural and crosscultural mission, and for bridge-building

> Of all these, my calling to be a teacher is the strongest, seen in terms of being a co-adventurer, midwife, asker of questions, pointer towards resources, translator of the abstruse, and reflective practitioner. Whitley College is a great place for fostering such ideals, and I feel very much at home. (RL, Reflections, November 1997)

He had resolved his main uncertainties, having now gained the essential doctorate and the self-education it had generated, being able to combine theory and practice of mission, and "be myself." He had made the transition to teaching adults, organized the faculty subject offerings, networked widely, built the library, contributed musically, and helped the college to move forward technologically.

With study leave coming up later in 1998, Ross planned to visit significant centers of missiology and develop a five-year plan for the faculty, which would then add incrementally to the foundational units. He especially hoped to explore the missiological implications of postmodernism on evangelism, and Australian culture that he had hinted at in the conclusion of his thesis. He would now be able to supervise post-graduate students alongside publishing regularly to establish himself in the scholarly world.

Ross recognized that many appreciated his musical ministry, both as part of college worship and in churches as he visited, and wanted to continue to write songs. When his colleague, Geoff Pound, was elected in 1998 as the President of the Baptist Union of Victoria, he, like others before him, requested that Ross write a special congregational song for the year. Ross asked him for some ideas, words, and phrases, and then went off with his guitar to spend the weekend at one of his favorite places, Wye River on the coast. He returned with a song called "Taking Shape," an anthemic sounding trinitarian hymn about God's incarnational dynamic and our response. It captured "God's beauty that shines" in places such as Victoria's Great Ocean Road and how this takes shape in creation, human compassion, word, and deed through the love of God, the freedom of Jesus, and the gentle power of the Spirit. It also captured an emerging theme for Ross: God and us in creation.

> *Taking shape in your creation, Loving God, your beauty shines,*
> *In the waves that sweep the shore, the mountains soaring high,*
> *The creatures of the earth, the colours of the sky,*
> *So fragile in their power—exploited.*
> *And yet you live.*
> *Help us take the shape of holy beauty: our future's in your love.*
>
> *Taking shape as human person, Saving God, you show the way.*
> *In his body grace and truth, compassion setting free,*
> *Incarnate Word of God, he opens eyes to see,*
> *Though evil, so it seems, destroys him,*
> *And yet you live.*
> *Help us follow Jesus into freedom: our future's in your love.*

Taking shape through gentle Spirit, Risen God, we need your power.
Make our worship come alive, give strength when we are tired,
In every part of life, our word and deed inspired,
In unity—Oh God, we fail you.
And yet you live.
Help us be transformed into your likeness: our future's in your love.

(RL, "Taking Shape," 1998)

In his thesis on incarnational mission, Ross focused on three aspects; the third one was "joining God's cosmic mission of enfleshment in which God's self-embodying dynamic is evident from the beginning of creation." For Ross, recognizing the creator always had implications for those in creation: caring for the environment, recognizing the importance of the earth, seeing the kingdom of Jesus displayed on the earth, sharing resources by living simply and justly. These principles were self-evident to him, and he had, from an early age, tried to live by them.

His wider family recall Ross being the instigator of simpler Christmases and of downsizing the present-giving traditions in a growing family. They agreed to share only handmade or recycled gifts for the families, with small presents for the children while they were young. His siblings were accustomed to receiving gifts of note pads made from recycled paper, and Christmas meals were kept simple and shared. His younger sister, Grace, remembers that she always received birthday gifts that were not "objects to clutter, decay or damage the planet, but a get-together for a movie and a chat afterwards," which she appreciated.

In the early days of the community, there were discussions about environmental issues that led to action—recycling before it was fashionable or legislated, and sharing of appliances and tools. They committed to maintaining equipment instead of buying something new, to sharing simple food, and using public transport. Ross's blue trailer was one of the most shared possessions in the community, and mostly came with some human assistance. Jenny Hunter, the wife of colleague Colin, recalls attending his seminars at Whitley and having to turn around her defeatist attitude to saving the planet:

> Not only to pick up rubbish from streets and beaches, and compost green waste and food scraps, as I had been doing for years, but actively seek not to contribute to the enormous piles of garbage we all seemed to be throwing out each week. I learned about bringing a robust mug in a little cotton bag to seminars or conferences for tea or coffee, the cup to be reused throughout

> the day. I heard how Ross never took home supermarket plastic bags, instead keeping cartons in his car boot to be filled from his trolley. All simple and achievable hints that could inspire anyone to think carefully about all the lazy shopping habits that have ultimately contributed to the degradation of our rivers and oceans. (Jenny Hunter, 2020)

Jenny was deeply influenced by these ideas and continued to implement them and teach others, to make cloth shopping bags, collect unbreakable mugs from op shops, and buy from a co-op with her own containers. Much of this was ahead of its time.

> As we sing his songs, I see him up the front as he so often was, leading us through them strumming his guitar, inspiring us all to move forward, empowered by the Spirit within us to make this world a better place for all of creation. (Jenny Hunter, 2020)

When Ross explored the relationship between justice and the environment, he referred to an older perspective, when the two were seen as being opposed: for example, working against famine in Africa or protesting against losing wilderness. He then argued that in nearly every case, justice and environment went together. The interconnectedness of everything meant to him that the renewal of the earth is part of God's salvation, and part of the vision for the gospel must be a life in harmony with the earth. In his words, "Evangelism goes with justice goes with peace goes with green peace."

Presenting to a seminar in 1995, he added to the back of his handout page a list of forty-four ideas for being green. They ranged from using public transport, growing fresh food, reducing waste, repairing things, using green cleaners, to conserving energy, and reporting pollution. Many of his suggestions were prescient for that time.

At the policy level, Westgate Baptist made a submission to a One World Week public inquiry called "Caring for Creation at the Grassroots," which was sponsored by the Australian Council of Churches and Australian Catholic Relief in 1989. On behalf of the community, Ross set out what they believed as Christians and then told the Westgate story, mentioning their long list of sustainability projects and actions. His plea was that grassroots responses be recognized and emulated, so that together, people could make a difference.

His colleagues were well aware of the lengths Ross would go to in his mission to care for the environment. Apart from carrying his coffee cup everywhere, he also rode his bike to the college, about twelve kilometers from his home. Every one of Ross's yearly appointment diaries has the train timetable pasted into the front for ready reference and representing a reflection of his commitment to use public transport. One of Ross's philosophy of education students in the 1980s, who also knew him later, remembers riding trains with Ross:

> Ross, committed to sustainable living, would often take public transport instead of driving to meetings. In those chats on the train, we'd talk about our passions and current movements within the BUV and issues it was negotiating through. I still recall to this day, riding home after one of the chats with my heart moved, feeling a mixture of inspiration, encouragement and always challenged regarding the manner I was living out my faith. (Ex-student, 2020)

He also remembers a classic quote by Ross: "I've never heard a sermon on the environment that wasn't preached by me." A rare moment of pride, or maybe despair.

Ner Dah, a student whom Ross helped to supervise from Nagaland, later became a lecturer; Ross also helped to find financial sponsorship to enable his studies:

> Ross was a person who cared for the environment and the world. One remarkable thing I learned from Ross was in order to reduce carbon emission, he sold one of his family cars. He rode his bike to Whitley and other places. He even turned off lights at night to save the planet from energy and carbon consumption. (Ner Dah, 2020)

In 2002, Ross wrote a definitive article for World Vision, summarizing the broadening of the vision of Christian mission, and arguing that transformation is multi-dimensional.[1] He proposed that our holism needs to grow beyond justice for the poor to include care for creation:

> Activism is not where it starts for me. My Christian environmentalism starts with gratitude for creation. It is first and foremost an opening of my heart to the gifts God gives us in oceans, mountains, gardens, wildernesses and a sense of home. Sometimes on a Sunday morning, the most powerful way in which God speaks to me is through the exquisite warble of the magpie that sits on our church roof and gently adds to our quiet prayer times. All effective Christian action springs from the work of the Spirit in us, and we do well to begin by listening, or stopping, or appreciating the creation we want to save.[2]

1. Langmead, "Faith and the Environment," 1–2.
2. Langmead, "Faith and the Environment," 2.

This was the year that Ross was due for study leave, and so for three months of his break, he would hit the road once again, trying to minimize his carbon footprint as he traveled around the world to connect with mission and missiologists. This time he would go to the United States and the United Kingdom, after which Alison would join him for an epic joint venture through India, Bangladesh, and Thailand.

After a careful dry run of packing his gear the week before, he flew to Los Angeles in April, and caught up once again with his friend Ken Luscombe. Amongst many other visits, he called in on Fuller Seminary, writing in his diary that "the mantle of evangelicalism weighs heavily on Fuller" and noting that there were four hundred Korean students enrolled in the DMin program, apparently all wearing suits. The breathtaking highlight of this American trip was hiking and camping in the Grand Canyon, which left Ross awestruck, and punctuated by a gastric reaction to a hot dog with chili beans that he regretted eating.

> This canyon has a powerful, mystical feel to it. It is so quiet, with only the occasional eagle or raven, though we saw a tiny hummingbird on a scraggy tree. The native American connection is strong. I can't describe how I feel, except that I am on holy ground; that humanity almost pales into insignificance; that God loves painting ever-changing pastel hues on a grand scale; that nothing else in America could ever excite me like this does. It has been an incredible privilege. I have never hiked before where I keep gasping and exclaiming. (RL, Trip diary, 1998)

When he phoned Alison to try to describe the wonders he had experienced, emotion overcame him, and he could hardly speak. He was missing his wife and found it hard to share his feelings by long-distance phone. Heat, cold, snow, and wind did not deter his sore legs and uneasy tummy, and he met many people, some "gentle" and some "ugly." His solo status as he traveled forced Ross out of his self-contained, introvert default, and he reflected that some people he met were fascinating, while others were shallow and loud.

The transition from the canyon in the Mohave Desert to a hotel in Chicago was a shock; he was returning to the same Consortium that he had attended in 1990, noting that the hotel was even more luxurious. The coffee machine and a fridge for his insulin were very welcome, but he was again daunted by the tipping etiquette and not being able to find simple needs with no shops within walking distance. He also had an infected toe, which is dangerous for a diabetic, and paid a small fortune for medical treatment to stave off serious infection. That night, Ross put aside his misgivings about luxury and fell gratefully into his king-size bed to sleep before the commencement of the conference.

Ross was, in turn, stimulated or not so engaged by the conference offerings, but the issues that were addressed raised many questions for him. He fitted in church visits, sightseeing, a baseball game, bookshops, and seminary visits, all of which helped him to put faces to people and institutions and gradually to feel more of a member of the international theologians' club. It was the ensuing reflective process that gives us insights into Ross's thinking:

> My time away confirms my feelings that I don't really fit the normal stereotype of an academic. I'm encouraged that you can be a bit eccentric and still stay in the system. I have proven to myself that you can set practical tasks for students and still get courses accredited. I have also been thinking a lot about my fears of writing and publishing. I see people who write naturally, but I also see lots who write without having anything to say. I've skimmed many books in the bookshops that aren't much chop. So I will discipline myself when I get back. I'd like to write some articles and work towards a book of some sort. Perhaps on discipleship, perhaps on theology of mission.
>
> Basically, seeing all sorts of people "being themselves" both intimidates me and encourages me to be myself too. It's interesting that I boldly beaver away at seeing the world but still hear little voices telling me that I have nothing new to say and little to contribute to the world. (RL, Trip diary, April 1998)

He was deeply impacted by meeting Darrell Guder at Columbia Theological Seminary in Atlanta and bowled over by his gracious, open, and welcoming style. Darrell was involved in a project called Missional Transform in local churches, which was right up Ross's alley:

> What impressed me was his vision to change things; his ability to get big grants which result in research and books and conferences; and his enthusiasm, optimism and good organization. (RL, Trip diary, April 1998)

Ross resolved to work on his reticence for self-promotion and sense of inadequacy, and perhaps to team up when he returned with someone who would help him strategize his own development. He would later quote Darrell at the start of his major book and in his articles.

After a swing through Washington, a meeting with Jim Wallis, a visit to the Sojourners' office, and a great deal of bike riding, Ross arrived in New York. His visit coincided with the centennial of the amalgamation of forty cities and towns into New York City; one of the celebrations was Bike New York, which led 30,000 cyclists on a tour through the whole city. Ross had booked an eighteen-gear rental bike and reveled in being able to see so much of New York with the streets cleared of traffic. They rode on freeways and bridges, fancy and derelict suburbs with great views; it was a dream come true. He experienced again the afterglow of a physical feat, feeling tired but exhilarated, and rated the ride to be up there with the Grand Canyon experience.

As he departed on the plane for the United Kingdom, he reflected on the American trip, somewhat wryly:

> I have struggled somewhat with the privilege of my travel. My world for four weeks has been one of buying meals, taking planes, taking in sights, riding bikes in kingly freedom, being served, being introduced as a professor on sabbatical, and being a moneyed-white-male amongst many others who are disadvantaged. Beggars have approached me. They are powerless, usually homeless, and penniless. My inability to act consistently has bothered me. How will I cope when I see abject poverty in India? (RL, Trip Diary, May 1998)

Ross did, however, firm up his resolve to write more, realizing that it was a matter of priorities and discipline. He saw himself as a "reflective practitioner" rather than as an academic, but he felt himself being nudged to a new perspective:

> How I teach well, write, compose, develop missiology at Whitley, particularly field-based mission education, work less than

in 1995–7, look after my health better; take on the Whitley and MCD administration that a full professor must when not hiding behind doctoral studies—all in one merely mortal allotment of time and energy. World travel expands life; it doesn't focus it or help it come down to size. My feeling is that staying healthy, balanced, happily married, a contributing member at Westgate and a positive, coping faculty member at Whitley would be plenty to aim at. Above all, I don't want to collapse on any of those fronts. (RL, Trip diary, May 1998)

This puzzle of trying to fit all the pieces together in balance would occupy Ross's thinking for some years to come and never be resolved entirely. He was talented in multiple directions, yet unable to give up some to focus on a few; he simply did not have time in his life to be excellent in many things at once.

He arrived in the United Kingdom exhausted, but felt culturally relieved and more at home. He spent the next week or two in London and Oxford meeting missiologists and Mennonites, pastors and professors, theologians and thesis writers, Catholics and charismatics, Anabaptists and Anglicans. He discovered that the term "radical evangelicalism" was now passé in the United Kingdom, and those on the cutting edge preferred "holistic mission," "incarnational mission" (yes!), and "open mission." He enjoyed riding around Oxford on a rattly one-gear bicycle with his books in the basket and felt oddly like a professor on sabbatical should.

At Baptist House in Oxford he was thrilled to be able to find and join a house-church meeting. When each member said to the next, "Ross, we welcome you to this table in the name of Christ the Bread of Life," he replied, "Amen. It is good to be here." Ross's tears overflowed as he felt homesick for Kernot Street, the community and his family. He wept again as he recorded this in his diary, relating how "at-home but away-from-home" he felt.

The next part of his trip, however, would be the most uncomfortable and challenging, fortunately to be beautifully mitigated and refreshed by the imminent arrival of his Alison. He could not remember a more highly anticipated reunion as they both flew at the same time to meet each other on the sub-continent of India. The real challenges still lay ahead of them.

He arrived safely in Delhi and began to prepare for Alison's arrival. Within hours of arriving, Ross had battled century heat while batting off pestering hawkers and rip-off taxis. He had been lost several times, survived terrifying traffic and stinking pollution, and engaged in the daily battle of finding safe food and reliable information.

The reunion at Delhi airport was sweet and Ross's heart melted as Alison appeared, fresh and excited, and "impressively lightly packed." They immediately headed two days' north of Delhi to Manali in the foothills of the mountains to relax in an air-conditioned hotel with views of the snow-capped Himalayas. Ross's blood sugars were all over the place as he adjusted to new food with unknown sugar and carb traps; lots of sweet, starchy bananas and irregular mealtimes were a challenge. He had to accept the fact that while they wanted to travel lightly and simply, there was no escaping that they were middle-aged Western tourists on the move, requiring at least a fridge in their accommodation for his insulin.

For comfort and convenience, they hired a van with an intrepid driver, Satu, who displayed all the Indian driving skills of speeding, horn blaring, and weaving through the traffic. Ross would have preferred a little more of a margin for error if he were to enjoy the scenery. Two days' travel to the north gave them a kaleidoscopic view of India and they were overwhelmed with the milling millions and how hard people worked. What looked like chaos to them somehow was orderly life with its own unwritten rules. They gazed at such profound poverty, juxtaposed with a high-tech society, and had a sense that the whole infrastructure was groaning in the heavily polluted air. Yet amid all this was color and beauty, equanimity, and many smiles. After a few days, their culture shock, which has been defined as an excess of novelty, was subsiding a little.

Satu drove them back down to Delhi in the stiflingly hot and polluted plains, via an overnight stop in Chandigarh. The first leg took twice the optimistic time estimated by Satu, and the second leg was a hair-raising drive on the busiest trunk road in India. Each day, Ross would ask him to slow down, lay off the horn, to avoid passing on blind corners, and skidding around curves. After all, they were paying for the ride. The conclusion was that "our Satu was on the more aggressive end of the spectrum"; fortunately, he also seemed trustworthy and helpful, and was happy to translate and to bargain for them. Alison had been battling a tummy bug for several days and Ross was suffering in the heat. On 24 May 1998, Delhi experienced its hottest day that summer, with a temperature of 113 degrees Fahrenheit and more to come. It was oppressive.

Next came a flight to Chennai and a trip on the classic Shatabdi Express, enjoying the welcome air-conditioning. Then a small plane to Tiruchappalli, the location of Saccidanandam Christian Ashram, set up by Father Bede Griffins. Welcomed by a two-meter cobra sliding by, the first of many, the couple relaxed into the peaceful atmosphere and rhythm of the monastic oasis of contemplation. Apart from not being able to eat easily with his right hand, as a leftie, or sit cross-legged at the low bench table, Ross felt relaxed, and Alison started to recover from her gastric bug. They appreciated the blend of Christian with Indian values and rituals, and were happy to fit in with the roster of shared duties.

For Ross, the heat was almost unbearable without fans. He was sweltering all the time, pouring sweat, and barely able to stay hydrated; it was his turn now to have traveler's upset tummy and he just had to rest. They were doing it hard in the beautiful surroundings and decided that they could not stay as long as they would have liked at the ashram.

> I've appreciated the setting and atmosphere; the experiment in contextualisation; the Christ-centred but cosmically oriented approach; the respect for Hinduism (e.g., reading from its classics at prayers sometimes); the quality of life of the members here; the gracious hospitality given to us; the rhythm of the monastic day (could take it for a while); the simple life pursued here; the freedom to be ourselves; and the sweet, milky tea at morning and afternoon tea. (RL, Trip diary, May 1998)

He felt, however, that there was little space given to community time, and struggled with the exclusion of women. But the ashram was holistic in its program, running old people's homes, encouraging small businesses and a clinic; Ross resolved to raise money for a sewing machine when he got home.

By this time, Ross had developed serious heat rash over most of his body and was suffering from a terrible itch. The meals were spicy, served with hot drinks, while he was dehydrated and craving ice-cold drinks and salad. He began to fantasize about the return on an air-conditioned train and retreating to a cool hotel.

Oh, I forgot, I'm really dedicated to this simple life of prayer and meditation . . .

Next stop was Puri on the coast to connect at the beach with friends Dipti and Pratap, who were graduates and friends from Whitley recently returned to their home. They then traveled on together by train to visit their respective families in Cuttack and Calcutta. Ross's prickly heat was escalating, causing extreme discomfort, with him feeling "beside myself, ragingly itchy all over." Dipti and Pratap cared for the weary couple and used their influence to have Ross seen quickly by a doctor. He needed an antibiotic for his infected sweat glands.

He was given medication for his rash and advised to stay inside in the worst heat hours, which were most of the day. India was the hottest place in the world that day. He needed to look after himself, even if it meant paying for accommodation with air-con if he were going to complete this trip and stay well. It was a great provision that they had friends to care for them when Ross was at his lowest point. He may not have been a long-term cross-cultural missionary overseas, but he was experiencing all the challenges in one short trip.

The ministry part of the trip was still to come. Ross and Alison flew with Pratap and Dipti from Calcutta to the Eastern Theological College in Jorhat, in Nagaland, close to the border with Myanmar. ETC is one of seven colleges run by the Council of Baptist Churches in North East India, which comprises 5,050 churches with 750,000 members. The tribal makeup of this region is complex and turbulent, and they were advised against traveling by train because it was too dangerous. The Nagas are mainly Christian, but the nuances of tribal interactions and lobbying to the Indian government make life difficult.

Ross was exhausted by the time they arrived but had to rise to the occasion as their visit was highly anticipated. He experienced what many Western missionaries have before him: he came bringing greetings, encouragement, good teaching, and the desire to build relationships, but realized that the actual expectation was that he would be a source of finances and scholarships for their very needy institution. He did not feel comfortable being seen that way, but understood the reality of the perspective.

They were, however, able to minister as a couple, with Alison leading chapel "beautifully, setting just the right tone," leading into Ross giving three presentations at a retreat day. And so it continued, with great appreciation for Ross's music. He led master's seminars on contextualisation, discussions about Australian Baptist life, and Westgate and singing sessions. All the while he was being wooed with gifts and being lobbied for the next, highly-prized Whitley scholarship.

With basic and fragile infrastructure, the college in Nagaland is set in a valley that floods to the roof line at times. With cubicles for bedrooms and no showers, life is simple. On the other hand, they have computers and a VCR and a stream of international teachers coming through, like Ross. In these conditions they work faithfully to equip young Karen to serve their own people.

Ross fell into a round of lectures, seminars, and devotions, usually with little time to prepare. Alison did not escape and was asked one morning to give an impromptu word of encouragement to the women. She said she prepared her next sentence while the last one was being translated. Ross sensed that the Karen liked their singing more than their lecturing and teaching, so he wrote a simple song to be sung as a round, "containing slightly adventurous, but to me, defensible theology":

> *In Jesus God was a refugee*
> *The pain of God has set us free*
> *In God we'll find our home.*

(RL, "Refugee Song," 1998)

Ross flicked through the guest book and saw the names of Westgaters who had visited over the previous four years, ten in all. In the list of names, he also saw Desmond Tutu's signature. Ross now understood his mate, Alan Marr's love for the people. It was an exhausting but powerful experience.

It was the climax of their four-year friendship with Pratap and Dipti and felt very precious to be part of their home context in India. After a tearful parting with Dipti, Pratap accompanied Ross and Alison on the eight-hour bus trip north to protect and assist them, as travel to Assam was vulnerable to extremist action such as kidnapping. He saw them safely onto their flight in Guwahati as they returned to Calcutta for the next, even more challenging stage of the trip.

Traveling via Dhaka in Bangladesh, they made brief connections with the Christian College of Theology in Bangladesh and other Baptist organizations in the area, before flying to Chiang Mai in Thailand, where they teamed up with Jason Goroncy, another Whitley graduate, for the final leg of the trip. Jason took Ross to visit the village of a small hill tribe of Lahu people, delivering some gifts and aid, and a car full of Samaritan's Purse boxes for the children. Apart from the missiological subtext in Ross's head that featured words like "rice-Christians," he was pleasantly surprised at the appropriateness of the shoebox gifts, and Jason's short talk which explained that the generosity of Australians was a response to God's love for all.

Pushing on towards the Thai border with Myanmar, a bus took the three of them to Mae Sariang from where four-wheel drive finished the trip into the refugee camp near Mae Kong Kha. Six thousand Karen people lived there and are still in conflict with the Burmese army, together with other refugee camps in the area. The Karen would call their country "Kawthoolei" if they ever gained independence, which is very unlikely. Technically, foreigners like Ross and Alison were not permitted to be there and the area is known for smuggling of drugs, gems, and guns.

Jason had been teaching there for quite a few months but had been very unwell, somewhat unsupported, and given no time for language study. He told Ross that he had been counting the days to his visit. Jason had studied at the University of Melbourne, Ridley College, and then at Whitley; he had been an outgoing young man and enjoyed robust discussion with lecturers. Ross supported and mentored him and was delighted to see him at work in his context. Jason recalls Ross's deep commitment to local community and saw him as a courageous theologian and an extraordinary encourager.[3] Jason is now a senior lecturer in theology at Whitley, living in the inner west of Melbourne with his wife and family, and is part of the Westgate community.

Ross and Alison were deeply impressed by the Christians in the camps, exhibiting the fruit of the Spirit in such a gracious way in adversity. Ross's experiences would enrich his teaching in the years to come and, despite the challenges, bring him back three more times in the future.

Still pouring sweat, battling swollen feet and experiencing both high and low blood sugars, he was ready to go home. Ross and Alison had sensory overload but were overflowing with gratitude for the people they met. Ross could not have imagined doing it on his own and knew that it was unthinkable to have gone alone. They dubbed their adventure their twenty-fifth wedding anniversary celebration, wryly noting its lack of romance but the richness in their mutual support and the sweetness of the shared experience even when it was tough.

Picking up life in the second semester, Ross returned to lecturing, preaching, running, cycling, song-writing, writing articles, turning his thesis into a book, justice issues, and his treasured family. There were family milestones: Alison would celebrate her fiftieth that year and Ross some months later, and Llew, who was still part of their extended household, turned eighty-five. He had had a new library named after him at Carey Grammar and received the annual Carey medal for outstanding service to the wider community.

---

3. Jason recently won a Silver Award from the 2020 Australasian Religious Press Association for the Best Theological Article: "On the Gifts of Street Art."

Kia had turned eighteen, commenced at Melbourne Univeristy studying psychology and anthropology and gained her driver's license. Ben had reached his twenties and was working with disadvantaged kids and exploring festivals and the bush. Ross and Alison were now effectively empty-nesters. Alison's workplace had merged to become Wombat Lanigiro Housing and Support Services, with increased services and staff to address homelessness and life crisis. She had also commenced her training with Wellspring to become a spiritual director and was a deacon at Westgate. In the first half of the year, Ross had reached his goal of losing five kilograms, but he was, however, beginning to notice some complications from diabetes, experiencing numbness and slower healing of injuries.

One of Ross's significant articles was published in 1999: "Ecojustice Principles: Challenges for the Evangelical Perspective."[4] He posited that evangelicals and the environment are an awkward partnership and that evangelical beliefs have undervalued ecological perspectives more than Christian theology as a whole has done. He defined "ecojustice" as "respect and fairness toward all creation, human and non-human" along with a holistic view of creation. In his opinion, evangelicalism had held a high view of salvation and a personal relationship with Christ, emphasizing evangelism, personal conversion, and adhering to a set of doctrines. He believed this had resulted in seeing God's transcendence over creation and therefore his distinctness from it. The separation of the redeemer and creator roles of

---

4.. Langmead, "Ecojustice Principles," 162–72.

Jesus had meant under-emphasis on him as cosmic creator, a general dualism that has separated the spiritual from the physical, and an activism that militates against contemplation. He concluded that we all need a healthy sense of wonder and grace for a livelier relationship with creation.

The following year, Ross traveled to New Zealand to attend the Ecotheology conference held by ANZATS in Christchurch. The major event at this conference would be the launching of the Earth Bible: writers from around the world read the Bible from the perspective of justice for earth. Ecojustice principles were utilized to enquire of the text a series of questions, including: "Does a given text value or devalue the earth?" This was apt for Ross's focus at this stage.

There were other major papers around ecotheology, and Ross found it all stimulating. Trying to come to terms with both an unexpected upgrade to business class on the flight over, and a welcome upgrade to his hire car, he spent time exploring Christchurch, Dunedin, and the Catlins to the south before the conference, and Mount Cook and Wellington on his way home. He responded deeply to the magnificence of the actual creation that he was studying.

His notebooks are full of meeting agendas and notes from events attended, with a noticeable focus on indigenous affairs and the ongoing development of various courses and qualifications at Whitley and for MCD. Ross was always keen to include practical ministry as part of the academic courses. There are lists of books on crosscultural leadership, Christian mission and dialogue, discussion with BUV about what they were looking for in pastors, and notes about the direction of the School of World Mission, which had been established at Whitley. All this is interspersed with worship group meetings, sermon notes, kids' talks, and research notes on computers.

In March 1999, Ross, dedicated to the self-examined life, felt that he needed some wisdom from people close to him who would help him clarify his directions. He prepared a paper for the group of close friends and family he called together:

> Since completing my doctorate I have felt overwhelmed by the number of things I could do with my time. Although some of the choices are to do with my work, what I am seeking is an overall sense of what I want to focus on. Together, my choices are a big step towards who I want to be over the next few years.
>
> My ongoing commitments are fairly stable: I'm going through an interesting and enjoyable phase as a husband and father and I want to be available to my mother as her health problems continue. I'm committed to Westgate, mainly through the Kernot Street group, the worship group and music whenever I can.

Small group celebrating.

> I'm secretary of the Hearing the Cry conference next January, a big job. My job as a missiologist at Whitley is demanding but manageable and enjoyable.
>
> My health is reasonable, but in order to manage my diabetes better I need to reduce my overall workload. I feel unwell much of the time due to the ups and downs and am beginning to suffer from diabetic complications. I have also suffered signs of high stress recently, such as perspiring heavily when preaching,

teaching or singing. (RL, Discernment Meeting paper, March 1999)

He then listed and explained ten areas of involvement: teaching and preaching, scholarly writing, popular writing, taking on Director of the School of World Mission, composing hymns, publishing and recording his music, local mission, promoting justice issues in the BUV, developing overseas links, and recreation. He asked his inner circle to read, pray, and respond and he valued their input. It is true to say that the "struggle to juggle" so many areas would remain with him—some would say it wore him down—but the answers were not simple.

He wanted to enjoy a hobby, but it always came last and there was no time left. His overseas trip had created hundreds of new contacts and multiple invitations to visit and speak and play, but he knew the cost of international travel, which was not just financial. He also knew that John U'Ren's retirement as director of the School of World Mission was imminent, and that he was being considered for the role, but it felt like a cost-saving move that would give him a second job; several things would have to drop from the list for him to take it on. His own prayers and those of friends and family were supportive but could not spell out the details for him of how to make decisions. Ross understood that discerning God's will did not come with a detailed instruction manual.

Westgate Baptist Community, which was still Ross's home church, had been through difficult times in the late nineties, with several people leaving or taking extended breaks as the church approached its twentieth anniversary. Westgate was served by interim pastoral appointments until a new pastor was called; Geoff Wraight commenced his ministry in April 1999. This was the era when community members visited the Myanmar/Thai refugee camps, and Karen and Chin families were arriving in Australia. Many found a welcoming spiritual home in the following years at Westgate, and a Karen Support Group was formed. Ross had always embraced the importance of multi-cultural inclusion, both in his work and in his scholarly writing. In an article written in 1997 around the crosscultural nature of Footscray, his home turf, he had summed it up this way:

> The overall challenge is common to all cultures: to be a sign of the kingdom of God (or perhaps the commonwealth of God), signalling open community, the justice and mercy of God, shared joy, shared resources, and a welcome for all, but especially the outsiders and the poor.[5]

---

5. Langmead, "Gospel and the Cultures of Footscray," 113–24.

Ross always maintained that the community was based on a mix of liberation theology, theology of the cross, and creation spirituality. The last aspect was expanding to involve not only environmental commitment, but acknowledgement of the whole creation in its cultures, and especially valuing the place of the land in indigenous culture. He had long practiced these beliefs in the community at home, but now was writing for a wider, global arena. He introduced a new unit at Whitley called "The Multicultural Church" and resourced the Multicultural Network, attending their breakfasts regularly.

In 2000, Ross had published an article called "The Multicultural Vision in Christian Mission" which pulled together the strands of his beliefs in a compelling and comprehensive manner.[6] He argued that multiculturalism is a justice issue, as the dominant culture needs to realize that it is not the only one, which is a relevant observation in Australia even today. After an overview of the Scriptures on this subject, he explored the theology of multiculturalism, observing that the gospel stands in a "critically affirmative relationship to culture," and that hospitality to the stranger is a strong metaphor in the Bible. There is a tension between unity and diversity which plays out in the arguments for homogenous congregations and the richness of mixed culture churches; indigenous culture has a special claim to being unique:

> One of the central issues in Christian mission in Australia is whether the church will lead the way, on theological grounds, towards a healthy multicultural reality both in the church and in society, or whether the church will change ever so slowly, well after society has changed, dragging its feet because security and comfort is what counts in weekly worship rather than the call to leave our comfort zones and be enriched by the other, in whom we may well discover the presence of Christ.[7]

This article was Ross's shot across the bows on a topic that he would continue to pursue, as part of his growing understanding of the spirituality of creation. An article by the ABC Religion Department in 2016 recognizes that Ross was one of the few who spoke out on this issue:

> Desire for greater interaction between traditional culture and biblical perspectives was included within a statement released by evangelical members of the WCC at that time. But, with the notable exception of the late missiologist Ross Langmead's contribution and a few similar individuals, many white Australian Christians have made little effort towards interfaith dialogue.[8]

6. Langmead, "Multicultural Vision," 1–6.
7. Langmead, "Multicultural Vision," 1–6.
8. Riches, "Redeeming Australia Day."

In January 2000, Arohn (a pastor/teacher) and Esther Kuung, along with some other Chin refugee friends, attended a Westgate service and stayed for morning tea. What happened afterwards was to forge a long and warm friendship that changed the Kuungs' lives:

> To my surprise, Ross approached me and Esther, kneeling down with a smile and welcoming attitude. Later I was told he was Dr Ross, the professor of missiology at Whitley, and my mind was blown. In Myanmar, I have not seen a person who is a PhD and professor who would kneel before an ordinary person like me and greet me. (Arohn Kuung, 2021)

In what the Kuungs experienced as an extraordinary friendship, Ross continued to support them as a family. Arohn was astounded, and even embarrassed, when Ross turned up with the famous blue trailer and helped them to move house on a rainy Saturday morning. Ross and Alison supported the couple in the births of their babies, and often cared for the children, giving Esther and Arohn breaks to have time as a couple. When three-year-old Glorious was very ill, it was Ross who took the worried family twice in one night to the emergency department for assistance. He taught Arohn to drive and was proud when he passed his driving test on his first attempt.

Esther will always be grateful that Ross was able to track down her mother in Myanmar, and to reassure her that the young family were well and settled. He recorded a message from her elderly mother and carried precious mementoes back to Australia for Esther: "Dr Ross actually brought healing to Esther's parents as well as to Esther and me in Australia." Ross's vision for a multicultural and welcoming church was grounded in a very practical expression of going outside one's comfort zone. In his own words, "Any sense of being at home is a gift from God and is to be shared with others."

Some changes and restructuring took place at Whitley. Ross was a full time Professor of Missiology in 1999, and, as he expected, when John U'Ren retired from heading up the School of World Mission, he was asked to take on that role as well. To make that possible, he dropped back to two-thirds professor, and gave the other third of his time to the SWM leadership. He gradually restructured the board and sifted the responsibilities for a new era.

Traditionally the SWM had run alongside the mission faculty and drew students from across Melbourne who were interested in focused mission studies and integrated ministry training. Ross felt very stretched to include the particular needs of the SWM into an already full job, which was exacerbated by financial pressures on the college and increased workloads. The SWM, nevertheless, had a mission statement that really resonated with Ross: "Down the street and around the world." That reflected his theology, lifestyle, and ministry, according to John U'Ren, who was delighted to hand over the reins to Ross.

For all his scholarly research, Ross was taken by colleague Keith Dyer's message in chapel, summarized in his trusty notebook as:

> Four types of missionaries: those who go troppo (go local), go solo (keeping in their own world), go Rambo (on mission for God, confident) and go dumbo (uncritically going with the flow).

This apparently appealed to Ross's love for plain language and communication.

Ken Manley retired in 2000, and the college's new principal was Geoff Pound. Networking was always a top priority in his job, and Ross was pleased to start and convene the Mission Studies Network, to restart and edit Mission Horizons and to bring in quality guest lecturers from overseas, such as Tom Sine, Paul Dekar, and Stuart Murray Williams.

> In my recent travels to North America I have been encouraged to find that Whitley's approach to missiology is still on the cutting edge. Our blend of evangelical passion for the Good News and a holistic vision of the Kingdom of God is leading us to explore many themes that the church is grappling with worldwide. (RL, Review of five-year appointment, October 2002)

An important goal for Ross was to be published in the prestigious and international journal, *Missiology*, of the American Society of Missiology. It was even more significant that when he achieved this, it was to break new ground with the very first article in the discipline of ecomissiology.[9] He writes about the missiological implications of ecotheology, spawning a whole new vocabulary: ecojustice, ecopraxis, and ecospirituality heading the list:

> What would it mean for missiology to be suffused with an ecological perspective? Ecomissiology is an approach to mission that sees the mission of God in terms of reconciliation at all levels, in a reality characterised by relationship and interdependence throughout. When applied to the practice of mission itself, it could be called missionary earthkeeping, mission work with a goal of "wholeness, integrity and renewal of people and Creation and their relationships with each other and the Creator, that is reconciliation of all things (1 Corinthians 15:20–22; Colossians 1:15–20; Romans 5)." (RL, Ecomissiology, 2002)

Encompassing a trinitarian overview of holistic ecotheology, Ross went on to list the missiological implications and methodological keys. He saw the importance of creativity, and championed a view of continuous creation and redemption. Reconciliation was to be at the heart of mission, believing that "wherever we go, God is there already." All of this was to be celebrated in anticipation of the "great feast" as God's people seek ecojustice on their journey. Ross called for seminaries and churches to explore missionary earthkeeping to proclaim a holistic and integrated message.

It is a powerful climax to Ross's journey, which began with reusing coffee cups, refusing plastic bags, and welcoming strangers into his home. He will be remembered not only as a leading missiologist, but also as an articulate and passionate pioneer greenie in the discipline of ecomissiology.

His last song in this period was written for the opening of the Urban Neighbours of Hope center in Springvale, headed up by Ashley and Anji Barker, who would become an important part of Ross's life. UNOH has continued to meet people at the margins; to discover Jesus in their midst. As Ross sang this song in a repurposed Buddhist temple that would proclaim God's kingdom in the now, people wept.

> *Come to me if you are weary*
> *With heavy burdens: I'll give you rest.*
> *Walk in harness with me, for I am gentle,*
> *My yoke is easy, my burden light.*
>
> *We hear the rumour God is here with us*
> *We feel the love that Jesus brings,*
> *We sense the call to walk into this love.*

9. Langmead, "Ecomissiology," 505–18.

But every day? In every way?
An overwhelming call.

We feel the broken dreams, the pain of life.
We stand beside our friends and weep.
We often celebrate the joys of life.
Sometimes inspired, but often tired,
In giving it our all.

We're called to go outside our comfort zone.
We dare to dream a different world,
As neighbours bearing hope in daily life.
Such energy. What is the key?
What if we faint or fall?

(RL, "Come to Me," 2001)

Another creative punctuation mark, and a Spirit-filled emotional valve that kept him centered and being true to Ross.

Chapter 17

Mentoring: 2003 to 2007

Pass on what you heard from me—the whole congregation saying Amen!—to reliable leaders who are competent to teach others.

2 Timothy 2:2

A mentor is someone who allows you to see the hope inside yourself.

Oprah Winfrey

One of the greatest values of mentors is the ability to see ahead what others cannot see and to help them navigate a course to their destination.

John Maxwell

The Langmead siblings were aware that their mum was becoming more than a little forgetful. Jean had proactively booked herself into a specialist center for an assessment and the family gathered for a discussion about the test outcomes. It was official: she was suffering from early dementia. Although her cognitive function was still only mildly impaired, she was struggling in several areas and would continue to decline. The future was confronting, especially for Jean. Ross and his siblings took notes at the meeting, listing issues such as increased support, trial medications, and power of attorney. This next period would require more involvement from the family located near her in Melbourne; even harder was the realization that it would be a slow farewell to the mother they knew.

Ross decided to capture Jean's life history while she could still remember it, and instigated a series of recorded interviews about the eras in his mum's interesting life. These formed a book that he called *Jean's Story* that was published and shared with the family for her eightieth birthday. Although her deterioration was relatively slow, the story was captured just in time. The final chapters of Jean's life would play out without being written down, as her world contracted to her single room at the aged care facility. Ross and his siblings continued to visit her long after she could remember the names of her children, twelve grandchildren, and eight great-grandchildren.

Ross had ended the year before with more travel—a conference in Chicago and sightseeing in New England, followed immediately by a second trip to Myanmar to teach in seminaries in Yangon. It was hectic and he became ill on arrival at home, no doubt from fatigue and post-adrenalin low defenses; his blood pressure was still persistently high. After starting the new year at the Anabaptist conference, he acknowledged that he was tired:

> I'm still hopeful about working less, and have tried to take on less this year. I have to be realistic, however, and admit that I keep lots of balls in the air, so that if responsibilities collide a bit I can't help being a bit flat out at times.
>
> One issue I have been discussing for some time with my spiritual director is my inability to really enjoy things. In daily life I can take or leave so many things that are part of my life— church, socialising, watching a video at home. I seem indifferent to them. Meanwhile my mind goes ninety to the dozen and struggles to forget work.
>
> I can also see a pattern of mild depression in me. Often I don't care what I do. Often I just want to stay home and do nothing. My introversion is sometimes extreme. I can easily come home and recount all the bad things in a day instead of noting the good things. I can be a real wet blanket. I tend to know my feelings fairly well, but I've noticed that my creative feelings haven't been exercised as much recently, nor my tear-flowing grieving for the world, nor my romantic feelings as expressed in notes or flowers. (RL, Journal, March 2003)

With his doctorate complete, Ross had taken on supervision of masters and doctoral students. While his passion was still to be involved in mission on the ground and in the churches, he was now able to channel what energy he had into training others more intentionally. Clearly, it was strategic for him to nurture a generation of postgraduate students. Between 1998 and

2008, he supervised seven doctorates and five masters; some of these people emerged to play important roles in mission over the years that followed. The supervisory relationship lasted up to seven years with some becoming strong mentoring friendships as well.

Ashley Barker was one of these students.[1] He met Ross in the late nineties and looked up to him as an elder of the radical discipleship movement. He chatted with him at a conference and hung out at the School of World Mission before he studied at Whitley, just to have time with Ross. He heard Ross speak, and had read his doctoral thesis, and Ash's heart leapt. The connection was to turn into a long friendship and mentoring relationship.

Ash founded Urban Neighbours of Hope in the Melbourne suburb of Springvale in 1993, a missional order with a vision to immerse themselves long-term in the life of neighborhoods facing urban poverty, working for transformation.[2] This expression of mission obviously resonated with Ross, and he saw in Ash's work a wonderfully practical expression of incarnational mission. As UNOH grew and became established, Ash, along with his wife Anji, felt called to plant a new center in the slums of Bangkok. They left Springvale UNOH in good hands, with its new headquarters in the transformed Buddhist temple, and put their roots down in Klong Toey, Bangkok in 2002.

Life wasn't easy in the slums, especially with a toddler and a newborn. Ash and Anji were often ill with dengue fever and dysentery, and lived in relatively primitive conditions in the stifling humidity. It was their way of immersing themselves in the urban slums and identifying with the people with whom they wanted to share the good news of Jesus. In 2003, Ash attended the Lausanne conference on "Roadblocks to Evangelism" and found, to his surprise, that only three people were interested in focusing on slums. So, he wrote a paper to contribute to the discussion, and that started him on the journey of articulating his understanding of incarnational missiology in urban slums, reaching the most marginalized and the poor.

It was in these conditions that Ash was encouraged to start in Thailand on a DTheol with Ross as his supervisor. Ash readily admits that he was not an obvious candidate for academia: dyslexic, way too busy, and spending most of his time in Thailand. He saw himself as an activist rather than as an academic. His previous qualifications were not from rigorous institutions,

---

1. Rev. Dr. Ashley Barker is Founding Director of Newbigin House in Birmingham, UK. He leads the School for Urban Leadership and works as a chaplain at Winson Green prison.

2. UNOH is affiliated with the Churches of Christ in Australia and Thailand and the Baptist Union in New Zealand.

and he had felt discriminated against on that score. Ross, however, saw the heart of Ash and the fruit of his ministry, and patiently encouraged him to work towards commencing his thesis. The only time that Ash could carve out in his crazy, unstructured lifestyle was to rise early and read at 6 a.m. on his Kindle each morning, and then spend every Monday writing. His conferences with Ross were mainly by Skype or meetings in Kernot Street straight from the airport when he came to Melbourne. He called his thesis, "What Is a Christian Response to Slums?"

For a fiercely accurate speller and writer, Ross had to exercise great patience to guide Ash to persevere and complete the thesis seven long years later. Ash says that it was as if Ross could immediately see the whole essay laid out ahead, and he just had to read, write, and catch up. He was not even able to be in Melbourne for his own graduation in 2012 but can see now that the degree has opened doors worldwide for him. UNOH today has seventy full-time workers and nine teams in three cities and Ash has published several books. He and Anji have relocated to Birmingham in the United Kingdom, where they have once again settled in a poor district and established holistic, multicultural, ecumenical, and incarnational ministry and are focusing on developing leaders with the latest project, called "Seedbeds."

> Ross was the best missiologist Australia ever produced. It is hard not to hear Ross's voice and seek his advice. I want to do for others what Ross did for me. (Ash Barker, 2020)

Darren Cronshaw was another of those students. Today he is Head of Research and Professor of Missional Leadership with the Australian College of Ministries, a support chaplain for the Australian Army Reserve, and is on the pastoral team at Ashburton Baptist Church in Melbourne. He first met Ross when he was a student at the Bible College of Victoria in the mid-nineties and was supervised by Ross for his MTheol. When he began tutoring while doing further study, Ross became his advocate and mentor, and eventually the supervisor for Darren's DTheol from 2005–08.

Darren recalls Ross talking about supervision as "coaching" rather than teaching and making it clear that their relationship was the most important thing. Ross was "gentle yet bold." Darren saw Ross as a reflective practitioner who was also a fine missiologist and worship leader. Darren often invited him to speak and sing at churches and felt that denominational staff had high regard for Ross, even though his environmental theology was sometimes seen as a sign of liberalism.

In later years, Darren worked with Ross as a key player in the early years of the Australian Association for Mission Studies and, typically, Ross would take a tram rather than drive to visit Darren in Hawthorn when they worked on conference planning together. When Darren wrote an obituary for Ross in 2013, he called him "a distinguished Australian missiologist and activist."

Allan Demond, senior pastor at New Hope Baptist Church in Melbourne, also remembers Ross as his thesis supervisor:

> He was a fine academic, a brilliant mentor and facilitator of my learning. An encourager. Ross helped me achieve my academic pursuits. He believed in his students and went the extra mile to enable others to flourish. I often repeat his sensible wisdom that it takes a tribe to achieve a PhD (i.e., a family and support structures) and if you want to write a thesis, you begin by writing one page every day. I will not forget his attendance at my graduation and obvious joy at the achievement. (Allan Demond, 2020)

Ross was a pedant in the best sense of the word, and he used his passion for detail and accuracy to help his students.

> In the University of Divinity, he was the "go to" advisor for research students on how to use Endnote[3] for their bibliographies—and I saw him spend hours helping students from other colleges (not just Whitley) on how to sort out their thesis references. Ross had the office just across the corridor from me—so I saw this first-hand. (Keith Dyer, 2020)

> Ross was a magnificent teacher and communicator. He had the ability to distil complex thought into accessible pathways for students without the material becoming simplistic. (Andrew Woff, 2020)

Marita Munro notes that Ross's eye for detail made him an excellent editor. His use of grammar and punctuation was unsurpassed and meant that his mastery of the style guide referencing systems for research students and faculty was legendary. Marita feels that too many people leaned on him because of that reliability and desire to help, and that it probably took an internal toll. Apparently, Ross's own doctoral thesis did not need even one correction, which set the bar high.

His pedantic passion extended into the outside world: one day he noticed that the mission statement on a passing truck was grammatically incorrect. He and his friends dropped into the office of the organization and Ross explained what was wrong with their slogan and how they could fix it—no doubt to their great surprise.

Ross especially liked to encourage promising students from the developing world. Ross met Ner Dah in Myanmar, sourced a scholarship for him to study in Australia, co-supervised his New Testament theology thesis, and visited his home in Myanmar. By 2003, Ner Dah was ministering to the Karen community at Westgate, which comprises most of the congregation and is now spilling out of the building.

---

3. "Endnote" is a commercial reference management software package, used to manage bibliographies and references when writing essays, articles, and theses.

Ner Dah and family at his graduation, with Ross and Keith Dyer.

Others from abroad were Xaoli Yang from Hong Kong and Inotoli Zhimoni from Nagaland. Ross's appointment diaries are full of frequent and regular appointments with all his students; when the preparation time is added to these commitments, they clearly took a large slice of his time. He obviously enjoyed the mentoring role and felt great satisfaction as his students completed their studies and found their place in the world.

Lectures in missiology continued, and Ross was able to launch new postgraduate units in this period called "Contemporary Mission Theology," "The Multicultural Church," and "New Missional Communities: Mission in Postmodernity."

The School of World Mission had commenced back in 1983. Ross was always enthusiastic about the aims of this institution, which centered around serving the training needs of frontier mission workers in less academic and more practical ways. It effectively reached younger people who were interested in mission and had numerous partnerships with denominations and para-church groups.

Although World Vision was a major sponsor, they struggled for sustainable finances, perhaps because the support base was so broad. Ross worked to integrate his mission faculty with the SWM, combining where possible, sharing lecturers and resources. Many overseas missiologists and other theologians were invited to be guest lecturers, like Thorwald Lorenzen, whom Ross had first met in Switzerland at Rüschlikon International Baptist Seminary in 1976. Thorwald describes Ross now as a "breath of fresh air, an outstanding church leader, an inspirational theologian and a disciple of Jesus."

A new unit in educational chaplaincy was established. Multicultural networks and workshops were supported, and a local Mission Studies Network convened. On the national scene, Ross helped to found the Australian Association for Mission Studies and launched the new Australian Journal of Mission Studies; both were major goals on his list of hopes and dreams.

The SWM had wider connections with other training organizations and mission agencies, but Ross's notes of board meetings frequently questioned the distinctive. He saw that it catered to a wide demographic, from youth volunteers to early retirees, and perhaps would always be a taster course, an introduction to something further. There was much discussion of pathways and reciprocation and collaboration between educational institutions and mission organizations. Many people in Melbourne with an interest in mission did a unit or more in the SWM at some stage. By June 2006, nevertheless, it had closed, to both the director's relief and regret:

> partly because its funding was small, its structures had become redundant and it was taking unnecessary energy to maintain its identity and its advisory board. I have been glad since 2006 to be working in a simpler structure, and believe that there has been no lessening of Whitley's visible commitment to mission, mission education and encouraging collaboration in mission training. (RL, Review of appointment period)

This networking both locally and nationally in missiology was part of Ross's mentoring and he worked hard at it. Larry Nemer, who was his thesis supervisor in the nineties, returned from London in 2005, and he and Ross collaborated in many ways to develop the further study of missions. They hosted book discussions and ecumenical lunches, with Ross providing the leadership and Larry as the genial host. When they commenced the AAMS, Ross became and continued to be the secretary, working with Larry and subsequent presidents. They had a long and warm working relationship, each respecting the other's gifts. They agreed on many things, including that the association would be ecumenical, and that there would be gender equality.

Heather Weedon, a Franciscan nun, was the founding treasurer of the new mission group, reflecting both ecumenical and gender inclusion in the early days. She worked closely with Ross as the group established itself.

> Ross had an extraordinary ability to organise—he was instrumental in setting up the website, in organising the international conferences every two years, and liaising with other organizations in Australia and overseas for speakers at our conferences. His singing and guitar playing was always welcome, for his warm, incarnational theology came through his presentation. He was tireless in promoting AAMS and gave it his all. (Heather Weedon, 2020)

Another founding member of the AAMS was Ross Mackinnon, who joined Ross on the editorial board of the AJMS in 2007. He had a strong interest in mission, having completed his MTheol in missiology. He enjoyed the ecumenical experience with Baptists, Catholics, Anglicans, and Uniting Churchers. It was confusing having two Rosses at meetings, so Ross M. suggested that Ross L. be Ross the Great, and he could be Ross the Less—predictably rejected by Ross. After that, they were Ross Mack and Langers.

> Ross was always very fair when assessing articles submitted to the Journal for publication. More than once he would say, "I don't agree with the writer's theology, but he has researched the topic well and has argued the case well. We should therefore publish the article."
>
> I recall going into the city for an Association meeting at Whitley. I was in the tram going up Elizabeth Street. I happened to look out the window and saw a cyclist in the far lane and the shape seemed familiar. Then the penny dropped—it was Ross en route to the meeting and doing his bit to save the planet. When Ross accepted an invitation to preach at my local Uniting Church in Glen Waverley, sure enough, he came by train. Ironically, we gave him some "petrol" money. I reckon Ross helped the earth to smile in many different ways. (Ross Mackinnon, 2020)

Within the Baptist Union in Victoria, there were various perspectives on Ross, and especially his theology, in the light of his ecumenism, interfaith connections, and association with the left end of the spectrum that makes up any denomination. He faithfully attended the assembly every year and put motions, and every year someone would stand up and question his theological credentials for the position he held within the church.

Colin Hunter, a colleague at Whitley, joined Ross and others in presenting a case to the BUV Assembly that the union should join the Victorian Council of Churches. Colin recalls that Ross presented a compelling, well-considered Biblical and theological case that the historical isolationism of the Baptists was contrary to the spirit and teaching of Jesus. Several others spoke for the motion, which was, nevertheless, defeated, leaving the Baptists as outliers in the action for Christian unity. Undeterred, Ross continued to advocate for interchurch and interfaith dialogue and action in his local congregation. Many remember his "prophetic voice" at BUV Assembly meetings.

> Ross initiated a motion that the BUV should re-enter the Victorian Council of Churches. I was inspired by how articulately, clearly and passionately he spoke, but with no denigration of the views of others. There was much conservative politicking and the vote was lost. Ross never wavered from his gracious bearing. I was pastor in my first church at that time; Ross had modelled for me a compelling vision of what a leader modelled on Jesus was like. I went home with a new light in my life: "I want to be like that." (Andrew Woff, 2020)

Over the years, he presented proposals on many of his favorite themes: health, education, ecumenism, poverty, indigenous affairs, economic sharing. He and Alan Marr once together opposed the plan to build a "blue collar Carey Grammar" in the western suburbs; in the discussion about the Victorian Council of Churches, Ross, however, spoke in opposition to his mate, Alan. Whereas Alan doubted the benefit of joining the VCC, Ross, always passionate about ecumenism, felt that it was symbolically important to belong. The vote was 166 to 164 in the end, which was a sad defeat for the motion, according to Tony Cupit. People were bemused when those two good friends opposed each other in a debate on the floor of the assembly, but they drove home together in good spirits. Their relationship remained strong, and Alan comments that just when he saw Ross as an austere, uncompromising, prophetic leader, they shared a whacky sense of humor. Somehow Ross could be a radical without alienating others.

> I felt that Ross was a creative thinker, unafraid to think "outside the box" in terms of faith and the church. He was also able to be alternative and innovative in ways that were not flagrantly aggressive or divisive. Sometimes I'm sure he faced opposition and criticism for his different ways of seeing things, but he himself seemed always open and warm and a reconciling rather than a polarising person. (Jill Manton, 2020)

> Ross was always courteous, never critical, and, with Alan Marr, very balanced. He was fair and supportive and lived his message with grace and gentility. (Tony Cupit, 2020)

Tony is the associate pastor at Ashburton Baptist Church in Melbourne, where they still sing many of Ross's songs today.[4]

Ross wrote several significant articles in this period. One that stands out is a version of a lecture he gave at the Mission Day of the Yarra Theological Union and Dorish Maru College (Divine Word Missionaries).[5] He set out to explore the relationship between the incarnation and Christian mission, as he had done in his thesis.

He opened with his personal background, as he often did: Salvationist, missionary family, practical and evangelical, pietistic, holiness tradition, radical evangelicalism, Anabaptists, community. Ross found over the years that his own story threw light on his theology and kept it practical. He then raised the question of how to be incarnational without being the Messiah and explained the three aspects of his thesis and how they can be worked out with the poor, in other cultures and in Australia, which was perhaps the hardest challenge.

> I believe that the only approach to mission that will cut ice with Australians, particularly young Australians, is a vigorous embodiment of our core beliefs, that is, an incarnational approach to mission. Australians respect faith with its sleeves rolled up. As people come across Christians who live out what they believe and embody the vulnerable love of God, I am confident that the message will be heard that God takes shape amongst us still. (RL, Taking Shape, 2004)

Ross liked to explore one of his favorite words—praxis—as he looked at the practical end of the theological spectrum. He told the story of his elderly cousin, Margaret the potato farmer. She laughed at Ross's job, dismissing theology, let alone reflection on theology, as a waste of time. She believed in practical Christianity, hospitality and kindness to others; Ross wished that she could have closed the gap between her formal and operational theology. Theology, he concluded, must indeed be practical. Often he illustrated this with his serial cartoon figure, Bruce, through whom he gently made fun of some of the current trends in urban mission.

---

4. Rev. Dr. Tony Cupit was a former missionary, Director of Global Interaction Australia, and Director of Baptist World Alliance, with a lifetime of ministry and teaching.

5. Langmead, "Taking Shape: Incarnational Mission," 173–86.

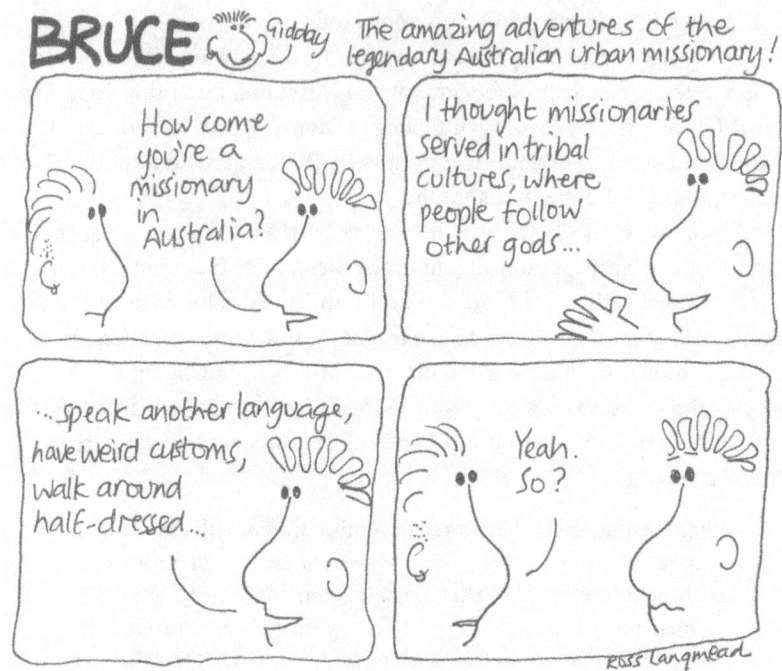

Ross pursued the multi-faith theme in an article in the first edition of the new missions journal that he edited. The article was titled: "Conviction and Openness: Christian Witness in a Multifaith World."[6] He knew how to stir things up and opened by quoting Paul Knitter, who wrote:

> The goal of missionary work is being achieved when announcing the gospel to people makes the Christian a better Christian and the Buddhist a better Buddhist.[7]

That always started a robust discussion. He then made his argument for mission being essentially a dialogue or respectful conversation, while at the same time the Christian church must proclaim what it believes is good news for all—God's revelation in Jesus Christ. For Ross, the tension of this juxtaposition was not as great as for some. He pleaded for humility and eagerness to learn as part of interfaith dialogue. Discussing a diverse range of theologians, from Tom Wright to John Stott, Leslie Newbigin to Thorwald Lorenzen, and referencing Pope John Paul II and Ghandi, Ross concluded with the phrase "bold humility"; he believed that his critical

---

6. Langmead, "Conviction and Openness," 41–50.
7. Knitter, *No Other Name?*, 22.

realist view of truth allowed for both conviction as well as openness. And that is how he lived his life. He encapsulated this belief in a verse of one of his best-known songs.

> Lord, let me learn, learn more and more,
> Learn that what I know is just a speck of what there is to know,
> Learn from listening to my neighbour when I'd rather speak and go.

(RL, "Lord Let Me See," 1981)

Ross's second and last book was published in 2007. He edited a collection of papers called *Reimagining God and Mission: Perspectives from Australia*,[8] which included a who's who of missiologists and theologians[9] who presented papers at the first AAMS conference in Australia. It canvassed the whole spectrum of perspectives, from Anabaptist issues to the intersection of missionary Christianity and Islam with Australian society. The book was a plea for contextualized mission that would be suitable for the Australian scene, and adapted to the spiritual temperature in Western culture. Not surprisingly, the authors reimagined an incarnational mission that would be crosscultural, multi-pronged, ecumenical, and credible, and that would engage the culture.

8. Langmead, *Reimagining*.
9. The fifteen authors were chosen from forty-five contributors to the first Australian Missiology Conference in Melbourne in 2005.

In these incredibly productive years, very few of Ross's friends and colleagues were fully aware of his internal struggles. He shared them with his spiritual director and recorded those discussions in his journals. So often his favorite retreat spot in Wye River was conducive to honesty and reflection for him, and in April 2007 he recorded that he was again anxious, flat, and experiencing symptoms of depression. It was suggested to him that in spiritual direction language, he was suffering from *accidie*, "an ancient term used by church fathers for being knocked off your horse at high noon or being derailed spiritually and emotionally at the peak of activity." It results often in apathy.

Ross's response was to acknowledge that he was maintaining a faster pace than his body was allowing. In fact, he was still increasing responsibility when it was time to be letting go. He admitted that he was facing real losses in his health and grieving deeply. He experienced the progressive pain of arthritis in his neck and arm, he had had four laser treatments for his right eye, neuropathy in his hands and feet with impairment to his mobility, and pain at night. His numbing fingers even made it difficult to play his guitar well. These latter symptoms are part of the progressive effects of diabetes, no matter how well-managed, and he certainly tried with varying degrees of success.

The family dynamics had changed. Llew, their resident wise elder, had died in 2006 and was deeply missed. Ben was married the same year in a glorious celebration in the hills that lasted a whole weekend, and Kia moved interstate with her work. It was a period for renegotiating adult relationships with his children. Kia had been feisty and vocal in her teenage years, perhaps enabling communication and honesty even if it took arguments to do so.

With Ben, however, Ross felt more distant and reflected that he had not found it easy to share his own vulnerabilities with his son. He put that down to his introverted tendency which meant that he didn't speak to others about his feelings unless invited, despite his own rich inner life. When Ben invited Alison and Ross to attend a therapy session, Ross was keen to learn.

> Benjamin opened up the topic of communication, feeling there were gaps. We talked a lot about his depression during high school and its link to his request for home schooling. Our actions "receded" as time went on. I apologised for not hearing the depth of his feelings. I said I wanted to be more open with him but might need some guidance. I was surprised at the depth of Ben's feelings even today.
>
> I was also surprised when he said that he didn't understand why we were Christians and didn't understand what it means to us, or how I relate to the universe. I immediately felt that we can

talk about those things easily if we make the time. I wondered why he didn't ask. I wondered if he remembered my teaching when he was 12 to 14 in the RAD group at Westgate—presumably not. I felt hopeful and positive about the process we began tonight, and honoured that Ben cares enough to want to get to know us better. (RL, Journal, September 2007)

Benjamin's reflections today on growing up with Ross as a dad are like a subtext to Ross's thoughts. He never had any doubt that he was loved by his father, who cared for him and had time for him. Despite the demands on their family life, Ben felt that Ross was fair, and a good listener.

I'm reminded of my struggles growing up. They weren't because of Ross or Ali necessarily; it was just my journey. Some tough things came out of that time. I think their approach was to love, accept and move on. As I learn more about communication, even lately, I am slightly sad about missed opportunities for greater dialogue and processing. I think I developed a pattern of shutting my parents out. Partially to gain my independence as a teen. Partially because I knew I was getting up to things they wouldn't approve of.

I like to think I'm like Ross in many ways. Mainly, he had a lot of love. I feel like I do too. He modelled great parental love, as well as spousal love. Also he lived a life of love as much as possible and in line with his admiration of Jesus, and I always admire the way he humbly served the world in the best ways he knew how. I'm still working on that one. I think he nailed it more than me, but I inherited the sentiment.

Ross and Ali allowed me great freedom to explore who I was and discover my own spirituality, and to express that. There were times I thought there was almost too much freedom, in that I remember getting to my late teens and being extremely unclear about the premise of Christianity. In being so allowing of my own journey, and quite deliberately trying not to indoctrinate me or force me to be part of a religion, like he had been, it meant that I didn't learn much at home of that religion, apart from the ways he lived his life, which is probably the essence of it anyway. I do, however, value this deeply, and think it was one of the greatest gifts I received in my life. (Benjamin Langmead, 2020)

As this five-year appointment time at Whitley came to the last year, Ross was due for another period of study leave. It began in July with a trip to Canberra for the annual ANZATS conference, continued with supervision of postgraduate students, included painting the whole house (which Alison and he had just bought after renting it for thirty years), giving support to Alan, his father-in-law, to self-publish and launch his book, and ending with a road trip around New South Wales. His notebooks are filled with information about cars, notes about working with his friend Jenny Marr who was arranging songs, MCD supervisor's notes, research on a commode for his mother, service notes for Westgate, notes of confirmation panels, minutes of meetings, notes on saving the whales, wood-chipping and animal liberation, multicultural forums and fair trade, and lots of information about train timetables. Ross was right about the need to let go of some commitments, but which ones and how would it happen?

Chapter 18

Leadership: 2008 to 2012

Deans have commented, not entirely in jest, that the job requires the intellectual breadth of Leonardo, the communication skill of Dale Carnegie, and the fortitude of Attila the Hun. Rare is the person who takes on an academic leadership position fully prepared. Theological school deans are learning principally on the job.

JEANNE P. MCLEAN

Whitley College was experiencing an unsettling period of change combined with declining student numbers and the associated financial challenges. Ross's previous five-year term was extended by one year in 2008 along with other staff to allow the college to conduct a review of its directions. With the School of World Mission closed, Ross found the simpler structure for him was working well with what he thought was no lessening of Whitley's visible commitment to mission.

Ross followed his passion for theological training in Myanmar with another visit in the summer before the college started up and lectured at the Myanmar Institute of Theology and at the Karen Baptist Theological Seminary where his connections were now strong. He returned enthused and went to the annual Candidates' Retreat at scenic Wilson's Promontory. Journaling after the first faculty meeting for the year, however, he wrote about his unsettled feelings. The principal, Frank Rees, had outlined the new directions for the college, which involved focus on formation for ministry, discipleship, on-the-job training, and generally less emphasis on the academic and on research.

This felt like a reaction to a perceived over-academic focus and a response to the new generation's educational desires; the bottom line financially was also a driver. Ross believed that some of these changes would be good but was concerned that they would be abandoning their signature rigorous standards and postgraduate focus. At the core of Ross's concerns, however, was the feeling that the faculty size could not be maintained, and that older faculty members, of which he was one, needed to make way for younger teachers. With one-year appointments on the cards into the future, the pressure was on to turn around the drop in student numbers to raise the income, or to go part-time. Ross was adamant that he did not feel called to take on a part-time pastorate over the summer to earn his keep. He began to wonder if he was standing in the way of the new vision. Of more concern was that it seemed that mission was actually part of the problem.

> Although we think mission is a strength at Whitley, mission is a problem at Whitley (even "the problem"). That is, churches don't think we care about the sort of mission they care about: local evangelism, church growth and global mission. To some extent we've always known that our vision is broader than that of the evangelical churches, but it seems that until we fix the approach to mission at Whitley, we won't enjoy the support of the churches.
>
> Putting the most positive spin on it, I could help to implement the new directions, go down to part-time for a while, then move aside gracefully, assisting as an adjunct. But I know what I now feel like doing. I feel like looking around for something else. I found myself dreaming of what I'd do. The main options that came to mind (none of them ideal) were World Vision, an ecumenical body, a church welfare agency, pastoral work, starting a new missional church and teaching in an overseas seminary, probably in that order.
>
> I immediately found myself feeling a strong sense of loss about my vocation possibly being undermined. I trained for years for this and would be changing careers at 59 years of age. I have discovered that where mission and teaching intersect, I have found my identity and calling. By nature, there are few opportunities to carry this out: I'm Baptist, liberal and Australian—where else does one teach? (RL, Journal, February 2008)

This was a crisis of confidence for Ross. The tension between his theology and praxis of mission and the more traditional views of some others would always be there, no matter how much he worked to keep the balance in the mission department offerings. He called himself liberal, yet, unlike many liberals, was deeply involved in mission in a practical way, both at home and crossculturally. Overseas mission and local evangelism were both important to him, but he saw them as subsets of the larger set of the incarnational model of mission in all its manifestations. Perhaps even Ross found it hard to put himself in a theological box. None of the colleagues interviewed for this book have agreed that he should be called a "liberal."

As it turned out, by August of 2008, despite his doubts, things had firmed up, the college vision was becoming clearer, and Ross was still in the picture. He wrote in his review of the year:

> I have a strong sense of call to be involved in mission, particularly as an educator, offering my skills as a teacher and administrator in empowering others in their journey of thoughtful discipleship. In asking myself whether I should move into other work—as I do from time to time—I quickly return to sensing that my calling as a co-explorer with Christian leaders responding to God's call in the church and the world is the one I have passion for and the one I am best equipped for. I believe Whitley is uniquely situated to offer relevant, rigorous and challenging education for mission and ministry, and I am keen to be part of the curriculum review we have begun. (RL, Review, August 2008)

Discussions had commenced with the Principal, Frank Rees, about the possibility of Ross being appointed dean of the college in 2009; he reaffirmed his desire to be involved in shaping the new curriculum, which he hoped would let formation for discipleship set the agenda for the degree units. He saw the vocational potential of theological study and wanted to promote internships and church-based training. Already he was envisioning wider networks, younger mission educators, and was ready to write a book on the theology of reconciliation. It seems that the low point of the start of the year had helped to clarify what was important for him and he now saw that this matched the future direction of the college. Ross was not going to change careers after all.

Student, adjunct lecturer, lecturer, professor, dean: a journey of thirty years; on reflection, the trajectory was clear. The dean was the head of the theological school and represented the college and the BUV within the Melbourne College of Divinity. While still being the Professor of Missiology, Ross would be a member of the leadership team and coordinate the provision of the theological program, being responsible to ensure that the training and educational objectives of the college were fulfilled. The role was wide-ranging, from curriculum to budgets, from professional development to complaints. He had his good friend, Alan Marr, as a member of the college council for support. His colleague, Marita, writes about this period.

Whitley faculty members relaxing together.

> Ross was an excellent colleague from whom I learned so much about what was important in theology and faith; about structuring my lectures and setting assessment tasks. He recommended useful teaching and research resources and provided logical and welcome insights. Being in a meeting he chaired was a good experience. He kept things moving and on target but also injected a note of rationality, sanity and stability when some colleagues would lose the plot or get overly exercised about a particular topic. (Marita Munro, 2020)

Marita also recalls Ross at his desk after an evening lecture asking, "How did it go, Marita?" and that he always had a packet of ginger nut cookies on hand if someone needed a boost. And he would greet Marita's dog, Waifer, when he came into the office—Ross, the academic dean, was a big softie at heart who loved babies and animals. By this stage, he was looking forward to his own grandchildren.

Two more overseas trips rounded out the year—one to Hungary for the International Association of Mission Studies conference, for which he wrote a paper called "Indigenous Reconciliation: What Can the Church Offer and Receive?," and later to Auckland for the New Zealand missions conference, where his contribution was a paper on "Contextual Mission: An Australian Perspective."

Reconciliation was his new focus as a central metaphor: it involved justice that restored rather than punished,[1] that led to international peacemaking, reconciliation between indigenous and non-indigenous, reconciliation with creation, and between Christians (he thought Baptists struggled with this). Ross also organized the AAMS conference in Canberra in October, making sure he was home in time for Alison's sixtieth birthday and the connection of long-awaited solar power at his house that would boost sustainability. He tried to keep his feet on the ground.

Connections with the Burmese Christians were strengthening. As well as returning to Myanmar when possible to offer his services to the colleges there and on the borders, Ross encouraged the thriving Karen and Chin congregations at Westgate. Ross's meticulously kept diaries now had an extra list pasted each year in the front pages, along with train times, passwords, blood glucose records and films he wanted to see. The multicultural families are all listed with their arrival dates, and careful notes of all their children's names. The Chin and Karen congregations seriously outgrew the buildings at Westgate, and in 2008 the Karen church divided, and a group commenced at Werribee, some twenty-three kilometers further into Melbourne's west. There was also a steady trickle of Karen students studying at Whitley, including Ner Dah, whose DTheol was being examined that year.

For a diabetic, life revolves around the trend of the blood glucose average readings. Diabetes, however, never backs away and he was dealing with increasing complications. His diaries record nerve conduction tests for his creeping neuropathy, regular podiatrist visits, and several more eye laser treatments only months apart to repair retinopathies and macular oedema. Ever the researcher, he attended seminars to learn about the latest developments in Type 1 diabetes. He wrote notes between summaries of faculty meetings and missiology speakers on the newest patches, pumps, and continuous glucose monitoring, none of which were on the public health system at that stage, but are more widely available now. The activist in him saw a need to lobby for free access for all as a very personal justice issue.

Thirteen pages of notes from a seminar on diet are evidence of his growing understanding of the glycemic index, and the management of the various carbohydrates to minimize insulin use. His conclusion was that those like him, with retinopathy and hypo-unawareness, should aim at the higher end of blood glucose readings to avoid constant hypos, and he determined to read labels more closely. He even noted down the figures for alcohol, although, as a good Salvationist-Baptist-diabetic he hardly drank a drop in his life.

---

1. Langmead, "Transformed Relationships," 5–20.

Ross quickly found his way into his new role in 2009. Ash Barker was well into his thesis and Ross picked him up at the airport for sessions each time he came to Melbourne. Ner Dah was also close to completing his doctorate, along with others. Ross's lecture subjects on offer that semester were "Multicultural Church" and "Interfaith Dialogue," the latter including excursions to various temples and mosques. After a debilitating bout of flu midyear and yet another eye operation, he was off to Perth for the AAMS conference.

Meanwhile, he was preparing for the big event of the year—a visit to southern Africa to visit crosscultural workers with Global Interaction Australia.[2] He traveled with Keith Jobberns, who was the director at the time. Keith recalls that Ross engaged with the posture of a learner, despite his own extensive mission experience and stature. By the time he had endured long flights, rough drives, and arrived in Mangochi, Malawi, Ross had already been absorbed into the African developing world: the poverty, lack of power and water, a national shortage of petrol, rundown buildings, and dust everywhere in the dry season. GIA had three families, a couple, and a single person working there. Ross's trip diary for this expedition could be published as a book in itself—full of stories, eloquent descriptions, insights, and observations. He did, however, list "missiological questions" from almost the first day, and we can see his mind assembling material for his lectures when he returned home.

Missiological questions related to GIA project in Malawi (Lao people):

1. How the gospel and good sustainable agriculture can be integrally related;

2. How to believe in the uniqueness and divinity of Jesus while not asking Muslims to leave their Muslim community when they become Jesus-followers;

3. Can single women be effective in a patriarchal Muslim society?

4. The issues of employment of local help and how that can distort local perceptions of the wealth of missionaries;

5. Finding missionaries who will allow new Jesus-followers to decide for themselves how they will practice their faith;

6. When and how to partner with other organizations with similar but different ways of operating.

---

2. Global Interaction Australia is the international intercultural sending agency of Australian Baptist churches and facilitates the service of Australian Baptists in global mission.

7. The extent to which mission can be called incarnational in South Africa, given the standard of living provided for missionaries;
8. Could national Christians do it better, given it would be much cheaper?
9. If the first world has most of the resources but the two-thirds world has the vigor and enthusiasm for mission, how can the wealth be shared without creating dependency and the West controlling things in the name of accountability?
10. Is it syncretistic to present Christian beliefs as complementary to Muslim belief, letting them decide for themselves whether it will lead to a break from Islam or not?
11. How long can a Muslim-Christian accord be sustained before there is a dividing of the ways?
12. What is the fine line between people responding because God's love includes concern for their poverty, and people responding because they're hungry (creating rice Christians)?
13. How do those who want to share the way of Jesus with Muslims steer a course between "This is an enrichment of your Muslim way of life based on the truth about Jesus," and "This is an alternative to your Muslim beliefs, though you may choose to remain culturally Muslim" with integrity and truthfulness?
14. Whether the poorest can pull themselves up by themselves, or whether, ultimately, following the way of Jesus, or more broadly reconnecting with the creator, leads to greater transformation.

The Malawi region at the foot of the lake is "David Livingstone, I presume," territory, and in the nineteenth century the British fought and won against the Yao people, who were Muslim slave traders. Mangochi was a strategic battle area because of its location between inland and the coast of Mozambique, where the slaves were put on boats for Northern Africa and America. Rina, a GIA agriculturalist, was proud of her nickname, "Mother Manure" in Yao, hoping that every time she was remembered after she left, they would recall the need to turn the goodness of the soil back into it. She also showed Ross how to deal with Question 4 (employing local help) by gardening alongside her workers. Missionaries have wrestled with this issue for a long time.

Ross was amazed with the growth of Christian faith in this Muslim community and saw that the life groups established by the GIA were remarkably successful:

> Ten years ago, Scott and others built relationships with the villages, and with the permission of village chiefs, began telling parables from the Bible and stories about Jesus ("Isa" to Muslims). They were well received, and weekly Life Groups were formed. As people gradually identified themselves as followers of Jesus, local leaders were appointed by the groups and receive regular training by the missionaries. There are now Life Groups in 180 villages, with up to 60 in each. They can't respond fast enough to requests from other villages. I'm still getting my head around it. (RL, Journal, December 2009)

This amazing growth caused Ross to ponder a great deal, and he recorded the following analysis of why the GIA model of work amongst the Yao people in Malawi was so fruitful:

- It majors on what is held in common between the Qur'an and the Bible;
- It uses culturally sensitive ways of communicating;
- It starts with the missiological assumption that God is here already;
- It begins with parables and stories of biblical passages they've heard of—not doctrinally oriented;
- It uses the Yao language;
- Teaching is accompanied integrally with community development which empowers the Yao without lots of money being poured in;
- While basic teaching is given, the Yao are trusted to respond in their own way—not asked to stop going to the mosque, nor taught hymns. Nor asked to be baptized. No institutions are set up nor buildings built, so no outside money is needed;
- It uses an incarnational approach where the quality of the missionaries' lives shines through;
- It fits into the existing authority structures, only going where invited;
- It takes risks missiologically and isn't afraid to adapt and learn from failure;
- The Yao are a distinctive people, Muslim culturally but not doctrinaire, a proud minority group; and
- The life groups are trained through a classical pyramid shaped leadership structure.

He continued to Johannesburg, feeling challenged by the size and bustle of the South African metropolis, and even more so by his confronting visit to Soweto. It was, however, a pilgrimage that was deeply moving for him. Moving on to Cape Town and traveling by car through the scenic south, he was, of course, headed for Robben Island, and Nelson Mandela's cell. He stood silently with respect before the cairn of stones started by Mandela when the prisoners returned in 1995 for a reunion. He saw the maximum-security section where political prisoners were incarcerated and Mandela's little garden patch, still alive, that kept him sane. When he saw Mandela's cell:

> It reminded me of the saying, "What doesn't destroy you makes you stronger." The remarkable thing about Mandela has been his strong message of reconciliation, non-revenge, forging a nation for all groups in South Africa and hope for the future. His stature has grown to such proportions that I don't know of a world leader who is respected as much. I don't have many heroes among the living but Mandela is my hero. (RL, Journal, December 2009)

Back home again after such a rich and impactful trip, Ross finally resigned from the worship group at Westgate after thirty years of involvement, ending a long era of musical contribution. Significantly, he had written no songs since 2006—probably a combination of over-busyness and his declining ability to play either the guitar or piano because of his numb fingers. He experienced it as a major personal challenge, along with feeling unsteady on his feet and the difficulty of managing his diabetes. He also felt somewhat alienated from Westgate at this time as they were having their own struggles and changes. He decided to pull back and set boundaries for himself to focus on his work and self-care.

And then in February 2010, Zara Joy burst into his life—his first grandchild (in addition to Sage, his step-granddaughter). Zara was born to Benjamin and Pauline after the deep sadness of their previous loss of "Sprouty," an almost full-term baby, and her middle name said it all. Joy was her great-grandmother's name and Alison's middle name, and it was joy that she brought to the whole family. Ross had become a grandfather, and many of those who have entered the world of grandparenting understand the profound feelings of holding the child of one's child. Finally, he had a new baby to cuddle and love, and his perspective on life changed immediately. He wanted space in his life so that he and Alison could fully enjoy the experience. Ross and Zara would develop a close and special relationship.

Four generations.

Ross's friends were all turning sixty, and the year held an array of family and community events. The Melbourne College of Divinity was facing challenges as it celebrated its centenary, planning for the AAMS conference filled his thoughts, the dog died, and the car radiator cracked. Life has a way of interweaving the small happenings with the significant, and sometimes reversing their impact.

Ross was now two years into a three-year position, and he still wrote often about being too busy. In 2010, the word "retirement" first appears in his journal, and he found himself thinking about it and how he would manage the transition to that point. He now began actively to plan to limit his working hours and by the next year, he knew that he had to signal his adjustment to part-time employment.

He still loved the job and could not imagine a better one, and liked Whitley, "its team, what it stands for, its role in the BUV and beyond." He loved teaching itself, the students, and promoting mission. He didn't mind administration because he was good at it. He did not, however, enjoy managing work safety, building issues, and risk assessment—perhaps no one does. He had asked for paid, professional supervision when he took on the role of dean and appreciated the sessions he had with his supervisor. When they discussed these issues, and he was asked what gave him intrinsic pleasure, it was often Zara who was mentioned. In later discussions, he also identified making compost, and sorting his dad's bolts and screws as things that satisfied him.

In Alan Marr's eulogy for Ross in 2013, he said that Ross told him he had been reading Richard Rohr's book about the second half of life:

> One of the major blocks against the second journey is what we call the "collective," the crowd, our society, or our extended family. Some call it the crab bucket syndrome—you try to get out, but the other crabs just keep pulling you back in. What passes for morality or spirituality in a vast majority of people's lives is the way everybody they grew up with thinks. Some would call it conditioning or even imprinting. Without very real inner work, most folks never move beyond it. You might get beyond it in a negative sense by rebelling against it, but it is much less common to get out of the crab bucket in a positive way.[3]

Ross had always been intentional about getting out of the crab bucket. Most of us think of the second half of life as largely about getting old, dealing with health issues, and letting go of our physical life, but the whole thesis of Rohr's book is exactly the opposite. What may look like falling can largely be experienced as falling upward and onward, into a broader and deeper world, where the soul has found its fullness, is finally connected to

---

3. Rohr, *Falling Upward*.

the whole, and lives inside the "Big Picture." Ross did, however, reflect wryly to Alan one day over coffee:

> We used to talk about changing the world. Now we talk about changing our medications.

The real issues were bigger than that for Ross. He wondered if, in pulling back at Westgate, letting go of his music, and not intending to teach or write in retirement, he would be "dousing his passions." John, his spiritual director, suggested that he see retiring as "refiring"—life in the future would be expressing the same self, passions, and gifts, but not in the same way. Ross looked into the future and wanted to do less and enjoy it more. Llew, his wise elderly friend, would have asked, "What adventure does God have in store for me?" Not so much loss, rather, change was on the horizon. The French philosopher, Paul Ricoeur, referred to the later part of life as the "second naïveté,"[4] when, particularly in the area of religion, one has moved through critical thinking to a new stage of accepting insights while maintaining faith.

Perhaps the dean of Whitley was a little tired of Endnote and pedantic corrections—his notebooks have entries like "Repeated author doesn't always have the long dash," and "sometimes the comma is missing between the publisher and date," "stray right bracket" or "non-smart quotes." At least these seemingly trivial miscellanea were manageable and had become second nature to him, and were useful to those whom he was supervising.

His real energy in 2011 went into the next AAMS conference in Sydney; he traveled there for a planning meeting and then for the actual event. These conferences and the associated networking were high on his list of most satisfying involvements. He made some notes of possible articles to write soon, listing love and justice, indigenous reconciliation, and reflections on the city as ideas.

Ross still took his turn in leading the Kernot Street small group that met every two weeks in their home, and enjoyed his community. The dynamics in the family changed continually as Kia moved to Sydney with her partner, Thierry. Alison had surgery the day Kia moved and needed extra care and support for some time after that; Ross managed to fit his travels around these needs. His friend, Alan Marr, was finishing his role after ten years as director of ministries in the BUV and was about to move from Westgate to a pastorate at St Kilda. Ross wept as he prepared his farewell speech: they had walked a long road together. Ross was feeling the endings but not finding new beginnings so easy to imagine as he wrestled with the changes:

4. Ricoeur, *Symbolism of Evil*.

> I talked (with my spiritual director) about letting go today. Books date and are worth little to others when I die. I'm trying to clean up the house gradually. I'll have little trouble letting go of work when I retire, though letting go of leadership may be painful. Barriers to letting go include my commitment to simple living (keeping older things in case), being only 62 (I might do things when I retire), living in an old house (we have room). But it's dying to stuff, practising for the Big Letting Go Day (dying), as John put it. I feel it is a spiritual issue both living appropriately to our age and realising that it all is transitory and being gradually freed from the burdens of ownership. (RL, Journal, November 2011)

And so the plan gradually became clear. Ross would relinquish the dean position in May 2012, take his next sabbatical in the second semester, then return to limited involvement in 2013 until he retired mid-2014. Once a decision was reached, the forward momentum seemed irresistible; Ross gradually began imagining himself finishing work. In his dream, there would be more time and space to spend with Alison, travel to explore, projects to complete at home, and the enjoyment of being involved with his family, and especially precious Zara.

In March 2012, Ross accepted an invitation to do something entirely new for him. He would give the opening speech at his brother-in-law's art exhibition. With Peter, an activist for the West Papuan cause, he had shared deep discussions about missiology, especially liberation theology. Peter, an artist,[5] had mounted an exhibition called *Hidden Heroes: West Papuan Women of Resistance*. It featured paintings of the women in West Papua who often bear the brunt of the struggle for self-determination, courageous but feeling despair as they bear children who do not experience freedom. Peter recalls:

> I loved Ross as an adopted brother and over forty-one years. In spite of the distinct possibility that proximity by family relationship could diminish one's perspective, my deep admiration for Ross did not lessen. Despite our different personalities and giftings, my experiences had brought me to a closer perspective on matters of justice. I particularly appreciated meeting with him and discussing where the theme of gospel justice may relate to the church's resistance to a government deemed illegitimate or evil. For this reason, I felt it was appropriate and a privilege to have Ross open the exhibition. (Peter Woods, 2021)

---

5. https://www.peterwoods.com.au.

Ross was deeply moved and resonated with the justice theme, delivering a memorable speech that captured some of his own journey:

> As I view the art works at this powerful exhibition, I have a similar feeling of awe. Others may see women who are poor and downtrodden, often protesting politically in the farthest reaches of Indonesia's sprawling country. Peter, on the other hand, sees the lion—or perhaps the lioness—in them. Through the suffering he sees proud West Papuan women. He sees their life-force and love. He sees their fierce determination never to stop working for freedom and dignity.
>
> I'm pretty sure he didn't invite me to say a few words because of my knowledge of art. My appreciation, as he knows, is that of a complete amateur. I'm still recovering from a fundamentalist upbringing that could see the importance of truth and the good—legs of a three-legged stool, we might say—but not the importance of the third leg, which we could label beauty, art or creative expression.
>
> What I see powerfully represented in this exhibition is this energy and passion—I'm prepared to call it divine in inspiration. It comes, I believe, from the interaction of the three things I just mentioned: truth, the good and beauty. Another way of saying those three things is "Truth-telling, justice-seeking and artistry." To me they are abundantly present in this exhibition. (RL, Opening speech, March 2012)

In May, Ross handed over the role of dean to Bruce Tudball. He felt, with gratitude, that it had been a smooth transition, with a sense of moving from one era to another. He shared with John that he was "strongly feelingful," welling up with pride, relief, tiredness, and celebration. The pressure had eased, and he had just another month of rounding off tasks before his sabbatical. He remarked often that Zara was a great blessing. Somehow, he saw the "first naïveté" in her as he was entering his second, and the connection was strong.

The Langmead siblings met for a family meeting earlier in the year to plan a celebration for their mother's ninetieth birthday. Although Jean's cognitive facility had declined, they felt it was important to mark the occasion, as much for the family as for her. It turned out to be a prescient decision. Because the siblings rarely met all together, they took the opportunity that night to discuss how the family would respond when their mother died, whether sooner or later. Decisions were made and tasks shared around, but the thought was laid aside while they prepared for her party.

It was a wonderful occasion in June as the extended family gathered for the celebration. Jean felt the vibe and knew that her family were there for her—she even attempted a short speech, which mainly featured the words, "Praise the Lord." Her children, grandchildren, great-grandchildren, and extended family had a riotous party, and many photos were taken; no one knew they would be the last and would become very precious mementoes. By the time Jean had been delivered back to her room at the aged care facility, she had forgotten why she had been out.

Six weeks after her milestone birthday, Jean deteriorated very suddenly, and the family gathered around her over a couple of days and spent time with her until she died. Her last words were "Amen," to a prayer, "Thank you," for a sip of water, and "Praise the Lord," as she lay on the edge of eternity, listening to the murmur of her family talking around her bed. Ross had now lost both his parents and the siblings could stand down from the years of care and support they had given their mum; they had now become the oldest living generation.

Arrangements were made for the funeral at Box Hill Salvation Army, and her coffin was brightly painted with Chinese and Australian references by her artist son-in-law, Peter. There were some wry chuckles at the viewing of her body before the service—Jean, who had never worn makeup in her life, had been prepared for her next life wearing red lipstick. Ross felt at peace as he farewelled his mother to her shalom rest, or, as her Salvation Army friends would say, she was promoted to glory.

Somehow Ross was able to fit in around the family events another retinopathy surgery, annual leave, the College School of Ministry, and the

ANZATS conference in Brisbane. By this time, he and Alison were enjoying minding Zara every Thursday and sometimes overnight. Ross noted in his diary that he had built a sandpit as he warmed to his grandfather role.

Just a few days after Jean's funeral and the associated administration of her estate, with amazing timing, he was able to depart for Canada for the IAMS conference in Toronto. As always, he built in some sightseeing, this time going to Ottawa by train and on to Montreal before heading home. He enjoyed exploring new places, even on his own, but always wished he could share the experiences with Alison.

His last trip to Myanmar was a few weeks later in October. It was a familiar trip now, and he met up with old friends, taught, sang, and connected with possible candidates for scholarships to Whitley. This time, Alison joined him again and shared in the richness of the community experience and the refugees who were now firm friends with Ross.

After all his solo trips, it was precious to travel together this time, and they called the venture their fortieth wedding anniversary present to themselves, a little early for the next year. They had no sense of course that this would be their last overseas travel together, nor that the early celebration would be the only one for what would have been their ruby wedding anniversary. His connection from now on with the Karen and Chin communities would be through Westgate, and he began to prepare an article for publication that explored the multicultural congregational model.

The remainder of the sabbatical was filled with reading and writing. An inveterate list-maker, he wrote in his notebooks a long list of books taken out on "Justice and Love": Furnish, *The Love Command in the New Testament*; Neibuhr, *Love and Justice*; and Jackson, *Priority of Love* were a few. By December he was assembling his usual list of films that he wanted to see: *Romulus my Father*, *Australia*, and *Little Fish* were on that list.

As always, there was work to be done to keep up with his diabetes. His records show that the average blood glucose figures were rising, now firmly in the nines, which is above optimum, especially with his raised blood pressure. He faithfully kept his list of readings up to date in the front of each year's diary.

The year finished with Ross, together with his Melbourne siblings, gathering in the Box Hill Cemetery to add Jean's ashes to Oliver's. As they stood around chatting, it was remarked that, obviously, one of the siblings would be the next to go. Everyone laughed a little uneasily, realizing that they had no way of knowing who it would be, nor when.

Chapter 19

Love: 2013

Jesus intervened: "Let the children alone, don't prevent them from coming to me. God's kingdom is made up of people like these."

MATTHEW 19:14

This would be the last working year for Ross. Having cut back his lecturing time to two subjects and signed off on most of his thesis supervision, Ross was feeling more relaxed. He looked at the rest of the year and wrote:

> It's been hard already saying no to prospective postgrads and planning 2014 beyond my time. It's been harder than I thought being a has-been. Some days my To Do list seems very thin, and while I'm not twiddling my thumbs, what I do feels much less "significant" than when I was running the SWM or supervising seven postgrads or being Dean. I know I should be thankful that the pressure has decreased greatly, and mostly I am. (RL, Journal, June 2013)

Ross would not be the first leader with influence to find it hard to step back, and yet he had been preparing himself for some time to make this transition. If his career had followed an upward and mostly intentional trajectory, his transition to the kind of retirement he had in mind was equally purposeful. That did not, however, make it any easier to put into action or to experience the reality of becoming less influential. Like many good leaders, it was influence, not power, that he valued. He did, however, admit to Alison that he felt tired at the prospect of working another year.

His last article was published in May that year: "The Multicultural Congregation as a Welcoming Space." He had already worked with his good Korean friend, Meewon Yang,[1] on a previous article on the same theme, and referenced her work again. In this article, he called the presence of multicultural congregations a "litmus test of the catholicity of the church." After an overview of the Scriptural call to inclusive diversity, he posed the earthy metaphor of minestrone soup as a model: cultural differences can still be celebrated and seen but enrich each other. Drawing on his own Westgate experience of three congregations in one church (English speaking, Karen, and Chin), he explored different examples of how cultures can be celebrated in churches. As always, shared meals, shared stories, and celebrations were his favorite paths to enriching congregations, but these needed to be active and intentional. He believed that

> If a congregation is to grow towards embracing all of God's people, it will also reach out in interfaith dialogue and cross-cultural evangelism. While the two models are a little different, they overlap in the respectful, intentional reaching out across the divides of faith and culture. (RL, "Creating a Welcoming Space")

Ross's main energy was going into the planning for the next triennial conference of the Australian Association for Mission Studies to be held in Adelaide in 2014. The theme would be, "Margins, Mission and Diversity." In the call for papers, it was noted that while mission had reached outwards to the margins in the past, it was now time to consider mission from the margins. Ross was enthusiastic about a theme he had been pursuing for years, so he fully expected to deliver a paper and to be part of this exciting event. The world was coming to Western countries through migration, and Ross knew that hospitality to migrants and refugees was the attracting and inviting element to mission as he saw it.

His annual list of movies to see is in the front of his diary: *Les Misérables*, *The Quartet*, *Life of Pi*, *The Intouchables*, *Silver Linings Playbook*, and *Song for Marion* make up the list of choices. He and Alison often took someone with them for a night out to enjoy a movie and relax with a friend. Because the Langmead Christmas Day gathering had ceased as the family expanded and scattered, an inaugural family picnic was held in January so that everyone could catch up at least once a year. Ross had always loved children and was very fond of his great nieces and nephews; he always managed to get a cuddle with a small child.

---

1. Langmead and Yang, "Multicultural Congregations," 121–32.

Zara loved to sleep over with her grandparents and Ross looked forward immensely to these times. One page in his diary has an outline of Zara's shoe drawn on the page as new shoes for her were apparently on the list. Ross cared for her most Fridays and sometimes she stayed with Alison and Ross for the whole weekend. Beaches, parks, and walks were favorites, and those Fridays were like a reward that motivated Ross to get through each week. The three-year-old enchanted him, entertained him, played with him, and loved him unconditionally. While the pain of the loss of the stillborn older sibling would always be there, Zara had indeed brought the joy of her name. Her grandfather knew very clearly what he wanted in retirement.

In early June, on retreat at Wye River again, Ross wrote another song. His daughter, Kia, was to marry Thierry, her Frenchman, in October and had asked her father to bless the occasion with a new song for them. He labored over this creative challenge: how could he write a song worthy of his daughter's wedding? He began to draft some words:

> *Love surround you,*
> *Love from within and behind and before.*
> *Love be constant like the*
> *Waves breaking upon the shore.*

(RL, Chorus of "Song for Kia and Thierry," 2013)

Ross worked on the verses to go with the chorus, and when back at home, he and Alison made a quick recording of the song for Kia and Thierry to listen to. As he hummed the song, he felt happy with it and the joyful occasion it would celebrate. While at Wye River, he returned to Richard Rohr's *Falling Upward*, this time highlighting some passages. While he prepared his meals, he listened on his iPod to episodes of the ABC podcast "The Spirit of Things" and particularly enjoyed the spiritual diaries of Jo Swinney, Ross Fitzgerald, and Moira Rayner. His thoughts turned to the future, which was looking closer every day. Only a few months to go.

> I've not always found the words to express what retirement means for me, despite coaching myself with John. I know what I would not like to do: teach, supervise, write academic papers and be on standing committees. I have thought of many things I might be interested in doing: justice work, peace work, local mission, creative pursuits, composing music, grand-parenting, support at Westgate. But I don't want pressure or a full list of commitments. I recognise in myself a tiredness and a certain confinement to an image of being a full-time mission theologian.

Rohr would say that this restlessness is a sign of moving into the task of the second half of life, and I'm in the middle of absorbing and clarifying that. Notions of "being present," of mentoring, of serving as an elder, of slowing down, all seem attractive to me. I often feel that I've been giving 100%, even sprinting, since I was a teenager—that's fifty years—and even the question, "What are you going to do?" doesn't fit the way I feel. I feel like saying, "Nothing," but that is a negative way of characterising retirement. I'm looking for a succinct way for me to move into the next phase of life and be less bound to the rhythms of a job and a desk. (RL, Journal, June 2013)

His last journal entry on this retreat, and last entry ever, was about Alison.

A recent TV show on happy couples suggested a six-second kiss each day. I should go back to my notes on Alison's languages of love. (RL, Journal, June 2013)

A couple of weeks later, on 14 June, Kia and Thierry in Sydney suffered a sad loss when Kia miscarried at nearly twelve weeks. The tiny life had been incredibly loved and anticipated by the whole family, and the loss of this baby shattered their world. Kia was informed about the stark statistics of miscarriage in a dark, clinical room by a doctor "who had majored in medicine and minored in empathy"; they had lost their baby. Ross and Alison would not be cuddling this much anticipated grandchild.

Kia spoke with her parents as the day unfolded and they all shed tears. Ross and Alison were on their way to Wye River again, together this time for a relaxed week away that included time with Alison's brother, Murray. When they arrived, Murray had lit a fire to warm the old house and prepared a special meal for them all. It was a lovely welcome; they had no idea that it would be a final time together.

With patchy mobile reception, they had to hike up the hill to talk on the phone and to process the loss together. Murray noted later that Ross seemed out of breath as they climbed the slope several times over the following days to keep in touch with Kia, who was struggling with the reality that they had lost their Christmas baby. It was so hard to relinquish their hopes and dreams. Benjamin was empathetic after the experience of his own loss of his and Pauline's Sprouty, and the suggestion was made that he and Alison could go to Sydney to be with Kia and Thierry. They felt the grief as a family, and this was how they would express their solidarity.

Ben and Alison flew to Sydney on Thursday 20 June and spent a couple of days supporting and comforting Kia and Thierry in their sorrow.

Kia's aunt, Marijke, joined them and they shared a time of ritual in grief and gratitude to acknowledge the little life that had been part of them for three months. Kia received two large, beautiful bouquets of flowers—one given to her at work when she announced her pregnancy, the day before she miscarried. Another was sent the next day to acknowledge their loss. "Bitter sweet," she recalls.

Marijke dropped Alison and Ben at the airport for their return flight to Melbourne while Kia and Thierry ordered takeaway, and began to watch a movie after their emotionally exhausting day. They knew they had to pick up the pieces and get on with their life.

Ross was in grandparent heaven back in Melbourne. He had Zara to himself for the usual Friday time, and with Alison and Benjamin away, he offered to keep her overnight and then take her to meet them at the airport. It was such a special time for Rossy, as the three-year-old called her grandfather. Ross had thought about taking her to the spot he loved so much at Wye River, but after discussion with Alison, decided against it in case he had a health issue while away alone with the three-year-old. He had confided in Alison that he had tripped seven times the day before around the rustic Wye River house. He would stay at home and plan a safe program full of fun.

On Friday, he took Zara to one of her favorite places, a kids' fun park called Monkey Mania, and just basked in Zara's playfulness and childish fun. On Saturday, he Skyped Kia, Thierry, Alison, and Ben with Zara on his lap and shed some tears for their sadness; it was the last time they heard him speak. Then they went with great-grandfather Alan to the swimming pool, to the playground, enjoyed music, made meals together, and just hung out. The sadness of Kia's miscarriage made time with Zara even more precious. He loved to listen to her chatting, was amazed at her curiosity and insights, and relaxed into play mode with her. To-do lists seemed unimportant for once and the day felt like a taste of things to come. The trust in Zara's eyes and her little hand holding his as she skipped along beside him or dozed in the pusher melted his heart.

On Saturday evening, 22 June, Ross bathed Zara, helped her into her pajamas, brushed her hair and packed her bag neatly. She was all ready to hand over to her parents. He was happy to have given Pauline a little break from parenting while Ben was away; one of the privileges of grandparenting. He buckled Zara into her car seat, and they headed onto the freeway to the airport to meet and welcome Alison and Daddy home from Sydney.

Chapter 20

Endnote: 2013

Hour by hour I place my days in your hand.
PSALM 31:15

The Hebrew vision of *shalom* in relationship with God includes peace, well-being and justice; it is the same peace that Jesus promises us. John 14:27 Christian mission is living for *shalom*.
ROSS LANGMEAD, 2004

We're restless till we find our home in you, O Lord,
Find our resting place in you.
A place we're never alone, a place where we are known,
May we find our home in you.
ROSS LANGMEAD, "FINDING OUR HOME," 1982

Benjamin and his mum felt emotionally drained as the Tiger Airways flight hit the runway at Tullamarine airport. They had not talked much on the way home from Sydney as they processed the feelings and emotions of the previous few days, glad that they had been able to be a support to Kia and Thierry at such a hard time. Alison was ready to pick up her commitments at home with Ross and had a busy week ahead of her. Ben had missed his little family and imagined Zara's leap into his arms when he arrived. They retrieved their bags from the overhead storage and disembarked, walking quickly along the walkway to the gate lounge in the terminal, full of anticipation.

An airport is like a hub for pilgrims; everyone is going somewhere or coming home. People are often with their families yet surrounded by strangers. Known but not known. An airport is never the final destination, yet signals the start or the end of many journeys. Ross had come and gone from this airport countless times; with Ross's fondness for metaphors, he had unknowingly arrived at a place where he would welcome his family home in the company of strangers while at the same time be farewelled on another journey.

Scanning those lined up to welcome friends and family for his first sight of Zara, Ben felt a flicker of concern. Where was she? Why hadn't Ross brought her to the gate to meet them? That was when he realized that she was near the seats, tapping Ross on the leg, thinking he was pretending to be asleep, saying, "Wake up Rossy, wake up Rossy."

Ross was sitting in an airport terminal seat with his head on one side. Ben could see his protruding tongue and quickly realized that all was not well, and rushed towards him. The people around him—there were probably three hundred people in the lounge—saw that there was a problem and began to help Ben to get Ross down onto the floor.

Alison took in the scene and immediately recalled a dream she'd had the night before of exactly what she was seeing. While Benjamin went straight towards Ross, she walked directly to the help desk and alerted the staff to the emergency, who made an announcement asking for medical professionals to come and assist. Alison looked on in shock, and then remembered the need to protect Zara from the distressing scene. She had to leave the doctor and intensive care nurse who came to volunteer their skills to help Ross. They began CPR before the ambulance arrived after an interminable twenty minutes, screens were set up and the defibrillator was used. His heart restarted. Benjamin was managing the surreal and incredibly intense scene, yet he too was in shock. Life had changed in an instant.

When her phone went, Kia was surprised to see that her mum was ringing so soon after landing, and then went cold when Alison told her briefly what had happened; that CPR was being performed as they spoke, and help was arriving.

For the second time that week, Kia had been plunged into a place of devastation and disbelief—this time she was a thousand kilometers away from what was unfolding. She and Thierry found a recent photo of Ross, Alison, and themselves and lit a candle. Kneeling in front of it, with Thierry's arm around her, Kia phoned Ross's older sister, Jeanette, asking her to let the siblings know and to pray. She contacted Alison's family as well and the word went out quickly. Kia and Thierry stayed on their knees on the lounge room floor and wept together, again.

In disbelief, Kia remembered a dream that she had had a few weeks prior but had kept to herself. It was vivid, and clear in its detail, not a jumbled, blurred memory of a dream that evaporates on waking:

> I had been in the car with Dad, just the two of us. We were driving down Brunel Street in South Kingsville, past Edwards Reserve, only a couple of blocks from Mum and Dad's house. Dad turned to me and said calmly, "I want to let you know, that Alison and I are parting." (Kia Brusa, "Stories of Dad," 2020)

She had woken from the dream feeling confused and unsettled. As far as she knew, her parents were deeply committed to their marriage and each other. She could not imagine them "parting" and so set the disturbing dream aside. It now came back with force and she felt that she was saying goodbye:

> A sense of profound peace came over me. Time stood still. At some level he had visited me to let me know. He had prepared me, so that in this moment, instead of panic, I could know peace. I held that deep, strange peace in juxtaposition with my imagined versions of the panic of the scene taking place in Melbourne airport at that very moment. And I rocked. I toned and I rocked and held that heart-wrenching juxtaposition in my being, while I waited for the phone to ring. (Kia Brusa, "Stories of Dad," 2020)

Thierry booked the first available flights to Melbourne, and Marijke drove them to the airport at dawn on Sunday 23 June; her second trip there in a few hours.

The paramedics worked on Ross for over thirty minutes, but no one knew how long he had been unconscious before that. He was taken to the Royal Melbourne Hospital and admitted to ICU in an induced coma. The family had to make sense out of the confusion and shock: Alison went with the ambulance and Pauline came to pick up Zara. As Pauline was driving out of the airport with her daughter, Zara asked, "Is he better now?" to which Pauline replied, "We are hoping he can get better, we really are."

A moment later, Zara said, "He's OK now. He has a new skin," and was asleep in minutes. Profound words from the small child who had unknowingly shared Ross's last moments.

Ben was faced with the daunting and weird task of finding Ross's car in the vast parking area, without having any idea where it was. He was immensely grateful for the offer of airport staff, who ran around pressing the remote key button to find the car and then escorted Ben to where it was parked. The practical and mundane complications of an emergency somehow felt more overwhelming than the life and death issue that was unfolding, and his mind was racing as he began to text and email those who needed to know.

At 8:52 p.m., Ben emailed Alan, Ross's father-in-law, and said, "At this stage, Ross has died. They are attempting to revive him. Thank you for praying." At 9:04 p.m., "Ross now has a heartbeat. They are assisting him breathing."

Family and friends began to gather from Melbourne, Sydney, and overseas, and the news spread quickly to Ross's extensive circle of shocked friends, colleagues, and connections. It would be a waiting game.

ICU staff realized very quickly that their latest patient would not be alone. Family and friends were meeting in one of the waiting areas and they all sat together, taking it in turns for two people at a time to be with Ross. Close friends, like Jamie, Paul, Tammy, Jenni, Lyn and others, created a roster to join the family and keep a vigil beside Ross through each night; he was never alone. Sometimes Alison sat in the early hours with her beloved and journaled. People brought food, drinks, thermoses of soup and special treats for the growing crowd that took over the area. They sat quietly, sharing stories, shedding tears, and praying. It was hard not to interrupt other families as they also waited: ICU is always about waiting.

Those who went into Ross's cubicle talked to him, touched and kissed him, and sang and played music to him. The sounds from the keening, gentle music from Murray and Dorothy's lyres, Ross's own songs, and songs of faith from believers mixed and floated. The staff could not believe how many people came and how beautiful the music was.

Ross's niece, Naomi, had new technology for her Type 1 diabetes inserted that week. As she waited with the family, she talked with another family member with Type 1 about diabetes, and they reflected on how Ross would have embraced the insulin pump she had just received. He would not need it now:

> May the loving Spirit be with him, and give us all courage in these hours, days, weeks? So many lives have been touched by the love of this dear man, may the love come back 10-fold in his moment of need. (Kia Brusa, Facebook, 23 June 2013)
>
> Beep. Cycle finished. Whir. Dosage administered. In, out, in, out. The sound of artificial breathing. Alarm. Something wrong? Liquids need replacing. Nurse is onto it. Tubes. Machines. Numbers and figures, only some of which I understand.

> Ross Oliver Langmead. My dear dad. And in amongst it all, the following song comes to mind. "Shower the people you love with love." James Taylor, one of Dad's favourites. Perfect. Small blessings. Big Heart. Life in the ICU. X (Kia Brusa, Facebook, 24 June 2013)

Benjamin stepped up immediately into the role of family spokesperson, sending out emails to the immediate circle to keep everyone in touch. They were informative, articulate, and poignant; he sometimes signed off as Benjamin Ross, as if invoking his middle name from his dad brought strength:

> The doctors are very cautious about suggesting any type of outcome at this stage. It really could go either way. We are feeling very blessed, cared for, loved and held by our family, community, extended community and just heaps of just generally amazing, caring people. Angus has assured us that they are doing all they can for him. He said, "It's out of our hands now." I wonder who's hands it's in. (Benjamin Langmead, Update to family, 23 June 2013)

Ross would have said that he was in God's hands; his life had been lived in that assurance.

The news had gone out, and messages came from near and far. In their shock, those who knew and loved Ross hoped and prayed that he would recover. With an impressive array of equipment and the wonderful nursing care in ICU, he looked healthy and pink-skinned but was deeply unconscious. Doctors began to speak of bringing him out to test for brain activity and it was clear that there were no guarantees. Almost certainly he had gone too long without oxygen. Two attempts were made to bring him out slowly, but both failed and the doctors called meetings with his family.

> We were told that those who do make meaningful recoveries typically wake up sooner. Whilst no outcome is certain, each day leaves us less certain of a full recovery. We know Ross and family are being prayed for, and we are feeling very cared for. Thanks for all your support. It's a difficult time. (Benjamin Langmead, Update to family, 24 June 2013)

> The week itself is a bit of a blur. So many people came through. For me, I was deeply torn between wanting him to live because he's my Dad, and I wanted him around and it seemed like he had so much living yet to do and letting him go. Accepting the dream that I had as a "premonition" of the fact that he was ready

to go. Being grateful that he had lived a quality life right up to the moment of his heart attack, and hopefully had not suffered.

Then there was everyone else's journey happening around me. People who simply couldn't accept that a man "as good as Ross" would die so young, and so suddenly. We/they wanted a miracle. There was a sentiment that if anyone could pull through, Ross could pull through. With all the love and prayers flowing his way, surely, we could pull off a miracle. I questioned who we wanted the miracle for. Dad? Or us? (Kia Brusa, 2020)

Just two weeks previously, Ross and Alison had watched a "Four Corners" television documentary on organ donation and were deeply touched by the moving stories of the recipients. They confirmed their desire to register as donors, never contemplating that the actual situation would arise so soon. For the family, what transpired in the hospital was a mixture of hope and trauma: hope that there might be life-giving gifts to other families, and trauma as they faced the agonizing process of making an enormous decision and its ensuing detail. Whatever, they determined that they would honor Ross's wishes. Tests were carried out and the search began for matching recipients. Any transplant would have to take place within ninety minutes of him stopping breathing, which was expected to occur shortly after removal of life support. The time had come.

On Friday, the family gathered with him and sang many songs in harmony, prayed, and farewelled him. Ross surprisingly then continued to breathe on his own too long for the organ donation to take place, but his tissues were suitable for later donation to the bank. At 1 p.m. on Saturday 29 June, when, for the first time in that long week, there were no friends or family in the room, Ross breathed his last and passed peacefully into eternity to be with his Lord.

He had found it difficult to imagine retirement, and had called 2014 "beyond my time," but would explore it in his resting place—his forever home. The family would never be able to fill the void left by his death but would be always grateful for his well-lived life. As the news spread, there was sadness, disbelief, and gratitude all at once for his extraordinary life of service to Jesus and to countless people. Ross, the pilgrim, had been welcomed home after a life of welcoming others into God's kingdom.

You are homeless and rejected, and you send us into byways,
Calling anyone who will take on what you went through.
Yet you call us to your mansions, to your fireside, to your ballroom,
Will we come and celebrate living with you?

(RL, "Finding Our Home," 1982, v3)

No longer would he need to live by his full diary. Already the appointments of the week of waiting had come and gone without him. The "Endnote" tutorial scheduled for 2 p.m. Tuesday 25 June with Tommy, a student, did not happen—Ross was moving to his own endnote. Other diary appointments—planning meetings, the car service, preaching on "Celebrating with Refugees" for BUV and at the Karen fellowship, the kids' spot at Westgate, and the second semester School of Ministry at Whitley—would all happen without him. He and Alison would not be eating out together on 3 July as they had planned.

Ross had reached the destination that had driven the journey of his entire life: Shalom, the place of peace and rest, the reconciliation of all things, and the cessation of strife. Shalom is multidimensional, complete wellbeing: physical, psychological, social, and spiritual. It flows from all of one's relationships being put right with God, within oneself and with others. It had been Ross's signature signoff for most of his life and now he was experiencing the fullness.

That night, when Ross was supposed to be the speaker at the service for refugees, his passing was acknowledged in the handout order of service:

> For so many years, Ross has been our teacher—helping us to realise that in the Kingdom of God everyone is welcome—especially the poor, the disempowered, the outsiders, asylum seekers and refugees. Ross has offered this gift as a teacher, a pastor, a supervisor, and mentor, a singer/songwriter, a colleague, a friend—a humble human being of exceptional intelligent grace.
>
> Last Saturday, Ross suffered a heart attack and we held our breath and waited. Today he passed into the presence of God. Tonight as we pray, we pray for his family, his colleagues and friends and we pray for the cause of justice and peace for people of all languages and races.
>
> Eternal God,
>
> You embrace all our life: our living and our dying, our celebration and our sorrow. Even through our broken hearts and tears this night, we thank you for the extraordinary gift of Ross's life; for the way we saw the goodness and grace of Jesus reflected in him.
>
> And we affirm afresh our trust in you that death is not the end but a doorway to a new beginning. Ross's journey is fulfilled and we thank you that he finds his home in you.

Ross yearned for the justice and peace of the Good News of Jesus and we would tonight continue his prayer.[1]

Ross's Chin friends, the Kuungs, were shocked by the sudden loss of their dear friend and supporter. Esther felt as though "her arms and legs were broken." As the Chin community prayed for Alison and the family when the news broke, their little girl, Glorious, whom Ross had raced to hospital some years before, had a clear vision of two angels taking Ross to heaven. She told the adults that they did not need to cry any more.

> She asked me to tell Alison too. We no longer see Dr Ross on this earth but we are very excited with great and joyful hope: one day all our family will see him in heaven. Hallelujah, amen! (Arohn Kuung, 2021)

Alison summoned her strength for the immediate task of arranging what would be a big funeral and drew her family together to mourn and be thankful, all at once. It would take place in Collins Street Baptist Church, in the heart of Melbourne's CBD, to accommodate the large number of those who would gather to celebrate Ross's life, and Alison felt very supported by the grieving Whitley community who offered their generous help with the arrangements and catering for the large crowd. Folk were encouraged to use public transport to get to the city, in the spirit of Ross, and to take a single flower rather than send large wreaths. It would be "simple and grounded, as he would have wished." The music would be Ross's own, and children were welcomed and included. "Academics, refugees, and friends will sit side by side." And they did. Over six hundred people crowded into the church and stood outside.

Ross's niece, Nici, organized hundreds of beautiful white ceramic "grace leaves" that hung as pendants and were distributed lovingly to many people; they would be a life-connected memento for those who still wear them. She also painted Ross's handmade coffin and included the words and music of the song he had taught and led so many times: "God is Love."

Ross's guitar, decorated with a single yellow rose, stood at the front of the church while children played around it. A beautifully embroidered textile hanging was displayed behind it, made by Westgate friend Cherry Jackson. People jammed into the seats, the aisles, and then the gallery and the foyer. They may not have known who was next to them, but they all came for Ross.

The sound of Benjamin playing the didgeridoo resonated through the crowded but silent church. and then the strains of the first of Ross's songs began, led by Fay White, Phil Hudson, Digby Hannah, *Daddy's Friends*

---

1. BUV, "Celebrating with Refugees," order of service 29 June 2013.

member Alan Austin, and musicians from Westgate. The crowd joined in like a heavenly choir, harmonies lifting the roof and beyond.

> *We are not alone in suffering,*
> *Jesus goes before us,*
> *We are not alone, he knows our sorrows,*
> *He will turn our tears to joy.*

(RL, "We are Not Alone," 1987)

Simon Holt led the service, which was a moving mix of reflections, memories, prayers, tears, art, flowers, cultural richness. The Chin choir sang their tribute, and the readings from the Bible were from Romans 8, read by Deb Mountjoy and John 1, read by Newton Daddow:

> Neither death nor life, neither angels nor demons, neither the present nor the future, nor any powers, neither height nor depth, not anything else in all creation, will be able to separate us from the love of God that is in Christ Jesus our Lord. (NIV)

Geoff Wraight told the Westgate story and described the importance of the Kernot Street group. He spoke of the place for lament, quoting the song Ross wrote to express his struggle as a pilgrim with the disappointments and challenges of life. Many find this song is the one that speaks to them in their own low times.

> *It's not easy to walk in the rain, and I walk with my eyes to the ground,*
> *And I often ignore the rainbow above, and the coming of the sun.*
>
> *There've been times of heavy weather when I've thought of giving up*
> *And questioned whether anyone else has made it through.*
> *But I stake my life on what I know of Jesus and his love*
> *And see the rainbow as my sign that it is true.*
> *And see the power which comes from sharing all the power we have*
> *And the glimpse of peace and justice on the way*
> *Is enough to make me lift my eyes and take another arm,*
> *Strong enough for one more day.*

(RL, "The Pilgrim Song," 1985, v3)

Kia summed up her thoughts as "Grief and gratitude"; Benjamin spoke of freedom and love, and that Ross's life of love lives on in us all; Ross's sister, Jeanette, told stories of his childhood escapades, and the emerging of his musical gift; Alan Marr reflected on a lifetime of friendship and ministry.

Whitley College staff had prepared a special litany of thankfulness, led by Frank Rees and Roslyn Wright.

Alison drew on her journaling from that long week when she spoke:

> Today, Jesus, I ask your help to be deeply present to each and all, but especially to the transition of our most precious, generous, committed, struggling man, dear Ross as he moves from the constraints of his sick body to the freedom of your presence. He has always desired to live Your way of Love. He has often experienced the anguish of that commitment—the cost in his body, mind and spirit. Your Spirit has enabled him to see the world with different eyes, and to live with love and energy and longing towards a better world.
>
> Please enable our farewell hours, oh God. Be with those of our most vulnerable friends for whom Ross has been a rock. Bring new light and strength to them, and to us all, in the darkness of losing our faithful friend. May Ross's inspiration help us to grow, not reduce, in becoming who we are.
>
> Now, my darling, what can I say to you in your final night? Truly our partnership has been a blessing for both of us. We have so often been so grateful for being "on the road" together, bringing warmth and comfort and teamwork and fun to the stretches of our commitments. We have laughed and played and sung and cried. We have shared our home and explored mission through community. We have camped and travelled. We have walked and talked; parented and grand-parented; filmed and climbed; small-grouped and family-camped; street-partied and neighboured; joked and argued; served and loved; we have been glad in the sharing of life, very glad.
>
> It's so painful to lose you, but you are part of who I am now.
>
> Thank you, my love. Thank you God, and thank you all for surrounding us with your prayerfulness, your love and your practical support, even as you also grieve.
>
> May the "grace leaves" you have been given today remind you of the amazing grace which restored and enabled Ross to live his passion. (Alison Langmead, Eulogy for Ross, July 2013)

Alison felt cushioned in her grief and loss by the incredible waves of love and prayer surrounding her, holding her. The entire crowd moved out of the church, accompanying Ross on his last journey in the busy main street while the rest of the world went by. Traffic roared and trams clanged their bells but the crowds spilling onto the sidewalk were moving with Ross. The procession walked to the final song, a doxology.

Creator of this great land we adore you.
Renewer of your people hear our praise.
Transformer of all life, you often take us by surprise.
Continue to be present in life-giving ways,
Great God.

(RL, "Transform Us," 1996)

People from near and far gathered afterwards over lunch and remembered Ross: family, neighbors, small group members, colleagues, academics, pastors, students, musicians; life would go on for them, touched and inspired in some way by Ross's life.

When Whitley College staff and students began to gather on the following Monday morning for the start of the new semester, they were drawn to the chapel where Ross had led them in worship so often. Someone started to sing his songs. Others joined them as they sang and wept. No more lectures from Ross, but his music continued to fill the chapel.

OBITUARY FOR ROSS, PUBLISHED IN THE AGE, A MELBOURNE NEWSPAPER

LANGMEAD, Ross Oliver

After a sudden heart attack June 22, Ross passed peacefully on June 29 surrounded by family and the love and prayers of friends around the world. Loving husband, father, brother, uncle, grandfather (adoring), colleague, mentor, neighbour and friend, Ross lived an authentic journey into the way of Servant Love shown by Jesus. Ross, our hearts are overflowing with gratitude for your generous commitment to this way, and for the universal chord your song strikes in us.

Shalom our beloved. (30 June 2013)

ONLINE TRIBUTES IN THE DAYS FOLLOWING

I met Ross on numerous occasions many moons ago when my father was the pastor of a neighboring church. News of his passing having reached folks here in Belgium, I fondly recall as a teenager receiving encouragement on how to play guitar from Ross (approx. thirty years ago now.) Deepest sympathy to his family. Greetings from Belgium. (Alan, Antwerp)

Dear Alison, I will never forget all that you and Ross did for me. A terrible loss greatly missed. How fortunate to have had Ross in our lives. (Connie, Williamstown, Victoria)

Thinking of all the Langmead family at this time. So many special memories of Ross as troubadour, friend, faithful person, forty years ago at Melbourne Uni. (Susan, Ann Arbor, MI, USA)

What a wonderful tribute to a man who attracted so many because of his humble expression of incarnational ministry. A man after God's own heart who believed that Jesus became flesh and moved out into the neighborhood. (July 5, 2013)

I, too would like to express my deep appreciation for the life, music and ministry of Dr. Ross Langmead. As a fellow member of the Australian Association of Mission Studies Executive for five years, he was welcoming, encouraging and inspiring to those of us who were practitioners as well as academics. And he appreciated the contribution of women in mission. I and the AAMS will miss him sorely. Our deepest condolences to Alison and his family. (Wendy, Melbourne, Victoria)

Very sad to hear of Ross's untimely death while I have been out of Australia. The best theological teacher I had and an inspirational Christian thinker, practitioner, and musician. (Chris)

You were humble when sharing your vast theological knowledge and you were humble with your great compassion for others—Ross, you are the greatest servant of our great Lord I have met. You were a great healing light on earth, as you will be in heaven—our great Lord utilized your great gifts to maximum effect. You have left this world a richer place, we all have the responsibility of using the time that we spent with you to continue on the great deeds you have in some small way. (Ashley, Newport, Victoria)

We remember Ross from our times at University of Melbourne and a music tape he "knocked up for his friends." "We're restless till we find our home in you." (Rob and Jen)

Loving memories of Ross. He had a significant effect on my worldview at Uni and also in recent years. The world is a richer place because of Ross and much poorer without him. (Sue, Ballarat, Victoria)

As the news of Ross's death spread, tributes, and loving responses came from around the world to the family, to Whitley College and to the church community.

Chapter 21

Inspiration

With all this going for us, my dear, dear friends, stand your ground. And don't hold back. Throw yourselves into the work of the Master, confident that nothing you do for him is a waste of time or effort.

1 CORINTHIANS 15:58

May Ross's inspiration help us to grow, not reduce, in becoming who we are.

ALISON LANGMEAD

The crowd gathered on a headland above the beach at Anglesea, Victoria. The weather was picture perfect on Saturday, 5 October 2013. Family and friends had assembled, dressed in the twenties-themed clothes suggested, ready to celebrate the marriage of Kia and Thierry. Still only three months after Ross's death, there was an unspoken but palpable determination to make the day a happy one for the couple, but they all knew that there would be tears amidst the joy. Thierry waited under the arch of flowers and Alison took her place in the front row and then all heads turned to look back as Kia came down the steps on the arm of her brother. Ross's absence felt like an indefinable ache, but Benjamin smiled with pride as he took on his father's role in supporting his sister. Sage and Zara scattered rose petals and there were embraces all round as the couple met at the front.

The ceremony was conducted bilingually by Alan Marr and recorded for Thierry's family in France, where the celebration would be repeated later. They spoke their vows to each other in both languages and the reading and message were translated into French by a friend. When the formalities were complete, the crowd shuffled and collectively breathed deeply: it was time for Ross's song, written and captured just in time. The group who had learnt and rehearsed the song moved to the front, and with the glorious seascape behind them, began to sing to guitar and flute accompaniment:

> *Love surround you,*
> *Love from within and behind and before.*
> *Love be constant like the*
> *Waves breaking upon the shore.*
>
> *Here by the sea and alive to the world around us*
> *We gather now and with one thing in mind.*
> *Blessings upon you and may you know the joy*
> *Of life free and yet now intertwined,*
> *Enjoying lives fuller when lived combined.*
> *Love surround you*

> *Back in the round of each day when you're tried and tested—*
> *money or tiredness or hours in the day—*
> *May your horizons be lifted to the ocean*
> *swell, keeping you both on the Way,*
> *And now we pledge you our support and pray:*
> *Love surround you.*

(RL, "Love Surround You," 2013)

Suddenly, in the last chorus, there was an imperceptible transition in the voices and a shocked realization that those assembled were listening to Ross's voice. The miracle of technology had made it possible for his draft recording when he wrote the song to be merged seamlessly into the singing of the group. There were few dry eyes as Ross's and Alison's singing blessed the couple with his very last song; it was a benediction for everyone. There was a sense of the Celtic "thin air," the holy space where heaven and earth meet.

In the week after Ross died, a student called Stephen Said had an appointment to phone him so that they could map out the next year and a half when Ross would supervise Stephen's missiology thesis. In a moment of reflection, he realized what a significant role Ross had played in his life. The anticipated mentoring and friendship were not to be, but Stephen decided to write in his blog some of the things that Ross had taught him about mission.

> Anyone who has had any kind of experience with Ross will tell you that the most important thing in his world was whoever was sitting in front of him in the present moment. Ross was one of the most person-centred people I know. When you were with him, you were what mattered. He lived a life very much in the present, and if you were part of that "present," he was fully present to you. You felt valued, important, listened to, supported, encouraged, challenged, pushed and loved. His immediacy is something that I pray will continue to challenge me and make me a better man. (Stephen Said, 2013)

He then continued his list of other important lessons: to love God intelligently and know the truth, to live humbly.

> I remember meeting him for the first time. I was running a workshop on mission as part of a conference being held at Whitley, where he was the Professor of Missiology. His introduction was incredibly generous and gracious, and I was totally intimidated. However, after about five minutes into the workshop, it dawned on me that Ross was there to learn. This fellow

> with a PhD and other degrees wanted to hear what I had to say. (Stephen Said, 2013)

He also wrote about "minding the gap" between theory and practice, living life from the heart, moving into the neighborhood, and seeing mission as something you are, not something you do to other people. These were part of his legacy from Ross.

> I just need to acknowledge that Ross, as a broken man, yielded to the transforming love of Jesus, embraced this broken man and helped him to slowly yield to the same transforming love.[1]

Stephen, the son of Maltese migrants, brought up in a household shaped by family violence that sent him out onto the streets, has taken the baton from Ross as a self-confessed "subtle reformer," radical disciple, and incarnational missiologist. He came to missiology as a mature-age student who did not enjoy school, dipped out of university, and became a Christian as an adolescent. Self-educated in the booming computer world, he studied at several Bible colleges, ending up in justice work with groups like Forge, TEAR, and Urban Seed.

He heard about Ross from several people he respected and was drawn to him, finding him "kind" in a world of cut and thrust where even Christians did not seem to hold back. Ross became a significant influence in his life, a role model who filled the void left by his family life. Ross believed in him.

Stephen did not even know that Ross was the dean of Whitley College, but accepted his challenge to him to upgrade his theology with a GradDip, with a view to starting a master's degree. He was shaken when his first essay scored a "D," thinking he had failed, but was astounded to discover that it meant "Distinction," and he never looked back. He has emerged from a Western suburbs migrant family with an extended circle of forty-five cousins, to be the first tertiary educated teacher.

Having gained the required level to commence his research, he clearly remembers the conversation he had with Ross that gave him confidence to go on. Ross said, perhaps remembering his own double culture dissonance as a child growing up in Hong Kong,

> You have something important to say, Stephen. I have never met anyone so gifted at critical contextualisation as you. You have had to do it to survive. You live between two worlds and belong to neither.

---

1. Said, "What Ross Langmead Taught Me about Mission."

Stephen wept on the phone as he shared with the author this revelatory memory of Ross that affirmed him and has shaped his life, study, and ministry since then. His first formal subject under Ross's teaching was in the first semester of 2013, which was Ross's last. They planned for Ross to be his research supervisor, but the phone call never happened. They had met for coffee down the cobbled laneway in Parkville so many times, but not anymore. Stephen still walks down that lane and thinks of Ross.

At the end of the year, Stephen was awarded the inaugural Ross Langmead Award for Excellence in Missiology. Now he just had to put it all into words and action. He dedicated his first published article to Ross and presented it to a workshop in the very same room where Ross had listened to him. He is making his own unique contribution to missiology in the context of the special needs of migrants. After Ross's death, Bruce Tudball, the dean, asked Stephen to teach a subject at Whitley the next semester. When he hesitated, Bruce said, "Ross would want you to do it." And that was that.

Westgate Baptist Community continues today with a multicultural component to the congregation and a large Karen congregation meeting separately but staying connected. Its links to the community are still broad and the small groups have changed, merged, and been reshaped. They feel Ross's influence in the music ministry and his songs are still sung often. Some unexpected developments have also borne fruit in the churches that were part of his original report.

> As the Western Suburbs Commissioner Ross recommended that Williamstown Baptist was not closed, but given support to see what God would do in future days. This led to us being able to make a decision in 1988 to sell the church buildings, enabling us to explore the new things God said he was doing. We eventually used part of the proceeds to buy a house in which we established Beth Tephilla Ministry Centre, a vital healing prayer ministry staffed by many from all parts of the Body of Christ, and a "third place" for many. It continues today, offering teaching, healing and friendship. Through the years since we have touched the lives of many people who would not have connected with us at Cecil Street. (Diana and Malcolm Dow, 2020)

Paul Mitchell is a more recent member of Westgate, joining in 2008. He remembers Ross as an inspirer and encourager who helped to launch him on his career path as a writer.

> I'm a writer and had a piece published in *The Age*'s "Faith" section about singing Christmas carols on my acoustic guitar. I explained that singing what many would find to be hokey songs

calmed me if I was in despair. The piece also noted that I found it difficult to attend church at those times. To my surprise, Ross got up in church the day the piece was published and praised me for its openness and vulnerability. I was encouraged to know he was moved by it and that he valued what I could bring to others. He made me feel that my writing gift was valuable and that I had something to contribute to church and society. (Paul Mitchell, 2020)

Since then, Paul has become an acclaimed and awarded writer of poems, short stories, plays and a novel.[2]

An important and ongoing part of Ross's legacy is the Australian Journal for Mission Studies. He was part of the founding of this journal which has continued to be the arena for academic discussion of missiology. In 2016, Mick Pope published an article in the AJMS on "The Ecotheology of Ross Langmead." He was introduced to Ross when completing a thesis on ecomissiology and the book of Romans. Ross helped him with papers and material which became influential in shaping his thesis. He wrote this later article to summarize Ross's work and to engage further with it. He called himself "a budding ecotheologian following in his footsteps." The summary says:

> Ross Langmead left us a valuable legacy in the fields of ecotheology, ecomissiology and ecospirituality. In trying to bring evangelical theology to bear on such fields, he was both challenging and generous, seeking to stay within the bounds of what many would consider orthodox, but also stretching both our doctrine and our praxis. Ecomissiology is still a young field and its development is highly important both in terms of the urgency of the state of the planet and the need for the Church to engage more with issues that matter.
>
> As scientists have often stated, progress is only made on the back of giants. It is up to us to continue to build on the back of this giant, who was taken to be with his teacher too early for the rest of us.[3]

Ross's work is also ongoing in his lasting legacy of missiology networks. The Australian Association for Mission Studies, of which Ross was the founding convenor and secretary, came out of the South Pacific association, and has continued to hold triennial conferences since the first one in Melbourne in 2005. He also nurtured the connection between the Australian groups and the peak body of IAMS. Their conference was scheduled to

---

2. Mitchell, *We. Are. Family.*
3. Pope, "Ecotheology of Ross Langmead," 24.

be held in Australia for the first time in 2020, a plan that was disrupted by the COVID-19 pandemic.

In 2013, planning was well under way for the AAMS conference scheduled to be held in Adelaide in 2014. Ross had engaged with Emeritus Professor Anthony Gittins, a colleague in the IAMS, and the planning committee agreed to invite him to be the keynote speaker for the "Margins, Missions and Diversity" conference. Ross's sudden death left a big gap in the preparation for this conference, but all agreed that it would be an opportunity to honor him, his passions, and commitment. A book was born out of the conference, with chapters that reflected Ross's heart and mission: *We Are Pilgrims* was brought together by editors Darren Cronshaw and Rosemary Dewerse. The chapters

> Honour the person who was Ross Langmead. Between them they model, display and discuss diversity, mindful of the margins and of mission. The voices include women and men, older and younger, people from across the theological spectrum and Christian traditions, people with greatly varying personal experience and cultural perspectives, and people based in Australia, New Zealand and Cambodia.
>
> In a 2009 paper, Ross wrote about the changing landscape of mission since the 1910 World Missionary Conference in Edinburgh. He went on to speak of five areas that challenged effective contextual mission in the Australian context in particular: indigenous reconciliation; a multicultural vision; mission in a post-Christian society; engaging the postmodern mind; and the Asian horizon.[4]

These five areas became the framework for the book, with each section "giving Ross the first say," with quotes from his writings or songs. Section B, "A Multicultural Vision"[5] opens with a song from 2006:

> *From around the world, we're a rainbow church,*
> *And our prayer is one for the nations to be healed.*
>
> *Different cultures, different tongues,*
> *But we gather today.*
> *Different dress and different songs*
> *Sung a different way.*
> *We're a sign of the commonwealth of God*
> *Jew and Gentile, women and men*

---

4. Cronshaw and Dewerse, *We Are Pilgrims*, 20.
5. Cronshaw and Dewerse, *We Are Pilgrims*, 171.

> *God's great love through all the world,*
> *Let it grow.*
>
> *Often thinking we're complete,*
> *We just shut out the rest.*
> *God invites us, "Open out –*
> *I'll be there in your guest."*
> *We are a sign of the different in God,*
> *Open table, Jesus is here,*
> *God the stranger, breaking in.*
> *Open out.*
>
> *So much learning. We still fail,*
> *Yet God's Spirit is near.*
> *So much joy. We're so enriched.*
> *There is nothing to fear.*
> *We are a sign of the colours of God,*
> *Breaking barriers, welcoming all,*
> *So diverse yet one in Christ.*
> *Live it out.*

(RL, "From Around the World," 2006)

Alison wrote the foreword to the book and concluded with this paragraph:

> As Athol Gill's death inspired Ross in exploring God's missional journey, may all of us who have benefited from particular aspects of Ross's commitment continue to discover the fire within that will be feet, voice and wings to the work of God's Spirit present among us and ahead of us in the whole creation—even though our feet must so often remain in the mud.[6]

Ash Barker was invited to deliver a public lecture during the 2014 Adelaide AAMS conference at an evening honoring the life and work of Ross. As one of those who shared a vision with Ross, it is appropriate for Ash to have the last word.

> I feel privileged to deliver this lecture in honour of my mentor, friend and hero, Ross Langmead. He had always been supportive of the community we founded, Urban Neighbours of Hope, but he saw the scholar in me in a way I did not see myself.

---

6. Cronshaw and Dewerse, *We Are Pilgrims*, 10.

Ross's premature death shocked me, and I am still in deep grief. I do feel a new kind of responsibility. God's work through Ross's passion for creative mission, justice and shalom is unfinished. In many ways that is why I am going to the United Kingdom to establish the Centre for Urban Life and Mission at Springvale College, Birmingham. After twenty-five years in urban mission, including the last twelve in Klong Tuey slum, Bangkok, a new generation of thoughtful, committed, radical disciples need to be mobilised, formed and equipped for this new urban world. I need to focus my best energies now on offering the same opportunities Ross gave me.

As we have transitioned out from UNOH and into this new role, I have longed to fill Ross in and seek his wisdom. I do sense Ross keeps smiling and enjoying our journey.[7]

Indeed.

7. Cronshaw and Dewerse, *We are Pilgrims*, 225–26.

Contributors

Alison Langmead
Benjamin Langmead
Kia Brusa

Alan Austin
Rev. Dr. Ashley Barker
Rev. Tim Costello, AO
Rev. Dr. Darren Cronshaw
Rev. Dr. Tony Cupit
Rev. Newton Daddow
Rev. Dr. Ner Dah
Rev. Dr. Allan Demond
Diana Dow
Malcolm Dow
Dr. Keith Dyer
Peter Francis
Shirley Frost
Jill Francis
Sue Garner
Rev. Dr. Graeme Garrett
Dr. Kristine Glasby
Rev. Dr. Jason Goroncy
Digby Hannah
Rev. Prof. Dr. Philip Hughes
Rev. Dr. Colin Hunter
Jenny Hunter
Mark Hurst
Cherry Jackson
Bill James
Rev. Keith Jobberns

Laurie Krepp
Lyn Kroker
Rev. Dr. Arohn Kuung
Esther Kuung
Grace Langmead
John Langmead
Leslie Langmead
Pauline Langmead
Roy Langmead
Rev. Prof. Dr. Thorwald Lorenzen
Ross Mackinnon
Rev. Dr. Ken Manley
Rev. Jill Manton
Rev. Alan Marr
Jenny Marr
Dr. Paul Mitchell
Rev. Dr. Marita Munro
Fr. Dr. Larry Nemer, SVD
Leslie-John Newman
Anne Paltridge
Rev. Dr. Geoff Pound
Rev. Dr. Frank Rees
Stephen Said
Rev. Ken Sehested
Jennifer Shields
Rev. John Simpson
Rev. Dr. Bruce Tudball
Rev. John U'Ren
Ernest Vladica
Heather Weedon, FMM
Fay White
Rev. Peter Woods
Rev. Andrew Woff

Bibliography

Barr, James. *Escaping from Fundamentalism*. London: SCM, 1984.
Cronshaw, Darren, and Rosemary Dewerse. *We Are Pilgrims: Mission from, in and with the Margins of our Diverse World*. Melbourne: UNOH, 2015.
Disraeli, Benjamin. *Contarini Fleming*. New York: Routledge, 1832.
Gallagher, Robert. Review of *The Word Made Flesh*, by Ross Langmead. *Missio Nexus*, October 1, 2005. https://missionexus.org/the-word-made-flesh-towards-an-incarnational-missiology.
Goroncy, Jason. "Theology for Ministry." *Jason Goroncy* (blog), May 2015. https://jasongoroncy.com/2015/05/02/theology-for-ministry.
Hilton, Cliff. *George Walker of China: A Biography*. Sydney: Trade Department, 1976.
Knitter, Paul F. *No Other Name?* Maryknoll: Orbis, 1985.
Langmead, Ross. "Anabaptist Perspectives for Mission." In *Prophecy and Passion: Essays in Honour of Athol Gill*, edited by David Neville, 328–45. Adelaide: Australian Theological Forum, 2002.
———. "Conviction and Openness: Christian Witness in a Multifaith World." *AJMS* 1.1 (2007) 41–50.
———. "Ecojustice Principles: Challenges for the Evangelical Perspective." *Ecotheology* 5–6 (1998–99) 162–72.
———. "Ecomissiology." *Missiology: An International Review* 30.4 (2002) 505–18.
———. "The Epistemological Status of Religious Belief and Its Implications for Education." MEd diss., University of Melbourne, 1975.
———. *Evaluation Report February–June 1980 Inner Northern EPUY*. 1980.
———. "Faith and the Environment." *Grid* 2 (2002) 12.
———. "Fundamentalism and Justice." *Greenshoots* (1992) 1–2.
———. "The Gospel and the Cultures of Footscray." In *The Gospel and Cultures: Initial Explorations in the Australian Context*, edited by Randall Prior, 113–21. Melbourne: Victorian Council of Churches, 1997.
———. "Mission Tailored for the Western Suburbs." *SPJMS* 9–10 (1993) 32–35.
———. "The Multicultural Vision in Christian Mission." *SPJMS* 23 (2000) 1–6.
———. "On the Road." Original track, 1987.
———, ed. *Reimagining God and Mission: Perspectives from Australia*. Adelaide, Australia: Australian Theological Forum, 2007.
———. *Report on the Footscray Community Relations Project*. City of Footscray, 1992.
———. "Taking Shape: Incarnational Mission." *Verbum SVD* 45 (2004) 173–86.

———. "Transformed Relationships: Reconciliation as the Central Model for Mission." *MS* 25 (2008) 5–20.

———. *The Western Suburbs Conference Report*. Melbourne: Baptist Union of Victoria, 1978.

———. *The Word Made Flesh: Towards and Incarnational Missiology*. Lanham, MD: University Press of America, 2004.

Langmead, Ross, and Meewon Yang. "Multicultural Congregations: A Victorian Baptist Perspective." In *Crossing Borders: Shaping Faith, Ministry and Identity in Multicultural Australia*, edited by Helen Richmond and Myong Duk Yang, 121–32. Sydney: Uniting Church in Australia, 2006.

Mitchell, Paul. *We. Are. Family.* Adelaide: MidnightSun, 2016.

Munro, Marita. "A History of the House of the Gentle Bunyip (1975–90): A Contribution to Australian Church Life." PhD diss., University of Melbourne, 2002.

Pope, Mick. "The Ecotheology of Ross Langmead." *AJMS* (December, 2016) 19–25.

Riches, Tanya. "Redeeming Australia Day: How Aboriginal Christians are Challenging Australian Spiritually." *ABC Religion & Ethics*, January 2016.

Ricoeur, Paul. *The Symbolism of Evil*, Translated by Emerson Buchanan. 1969. Boston: Beacon, 1969.

Rohr, Richard. *Falling Upward: A Spirituality for the Two Halves of Life*. London: SPCK, 2011.

Romsey, Avril. "Submission Supporting the Provision of General Religious Education in Victorian Schools." *Avril at Romsey* (blog), May 1, 2001. https://avrilatromsey.wordpress.com/2012/05/01/submission-supporting-the-provision-of-general-religious-education-in-victorian-schools.

Said, Stephen. "What Ross Langmead Taught Me about Mission." *Neurotribe.Net*, July 5, 2013. https://blog.neurotribe.net/post/54658929920.

Smart, Ninian. *Secular Education and the Logic of Religion*. London: Faber, 1968.

Together in Song: Australian Hymn Book 2. Melbourne: HarperCollins, 1999.

Twain, Mark. *Autobiography*. New York: Harper, 1924.

www.ingramcontent.com/pod-product-compliance
Lightning Source LLC
Chambersburg PA
CBHW050839230426
43667CB00012B/2061